Stewart Baird

SAMS
Teach Yourself

Extreme
Programming

in 24 Hours

Sams Teach Yourself Extreme Programming in 24 Hours

Copyright © 2003 by Sams Publishing

International Standard Book Number: 0-672-32441-5

Library of Congress Catalog Card Number: 2002107091

Printed in the United States of America

First Printing: October, 2002

05 04 03 02   4 3 2 1

Trademarks

All terms mentioned in this book that are known to be trademarks or service marks have been appropriately capitalized. Sams Publishing cannot attest to the accuracy of this information. Use of a term in this book should not be regarded as affecting the validity of any trademark or service mark.

Warning and Disclaimer

Every effort has been made to make this book as complete and as accurate as possible, but no warranty or fitness is implied. The information provided is on an "as is" basis.

EXECUTIVE EDITOR
Michael Stephens

ACQUISITIONS EDITOR
Michelle Newcomb

DEVELOPMENT EDITOR
Songlin Qiu

MANAGING EDITOR
Charlotte Clapp

PROJECT EDITOR
George E. Nedeff

COPY EDITOR
Chip Gardner

INDEXER
Erika Millen

PROOFREADER
Suzanne Thomas

TECHNICAL EDITOR
Genevieve Burt
Rob Hawthorne

TEAM COORDINATOR
Lynne Williams

MULTIMEDIA DEVELOPER
Dan Scherf

INTERIOR DESIGNER
Gary Adair

COVER DESIGNER
Alan Clements

PAGE LAYOUT
Rebecca Harmon

Contents at a Glance

Contents

Foreword

When I first heard about this book my first reaction was "Do we really need yet another book on Extreme Programming (XP)?" and my initial answer was "not really." Then I read it. Now I believe that, yes, we really do need this book. Hear me out.

One of the criticisms of XP is that it will only work for you if you have a guru or two on staff. As a software process expert, I've been asked to review the work of several software development teams that successfully build systems by following the XP methodology. All of these teams were successful, yet none of them had the benefit of the involvement of a guru such as Kent Beck, Ron Jeffries, Martin Fowler, or Don Wells. A primary strength of this book is that it reflects the experiences of real-world developers, people who had to struggle to figure XP out for themselves, and then apply it effectively. These people are very likely a lot like you.

How do project teams succeed with XP? First, they need responsible, motivated people that truly desire to create a working system that they can be proud of. This includes both software developers and project stakeholders. As you read this book think about this concept: Everyone needs to focus on the activities that directly influence the success of your project and avoid activities that are little more than busy work. Sounds like a naïve ideal? Perhaps, but then again you might want to reflect on the "success" of previous projects that didn't follow this naïve approach.

Second, XP teams succeed because of their people focus. XP practices of *on-site customer*, *collective ownership,* and *Pair Programming* promote active collaboration. At first these ideas seem wacky: Letting your project stakeholders see how software is really built? Allowing anyone on the team to work on any code, model, or document that they need to? Having two people working together at one workstation instead of at separate workstations? The truth is that these are wacky ideas. When you actually try them you'll quickly discover that they do in fact work incredibly well. This book explores these sorts of issues and shows you how to make XP's practices work in your real-world environment.

Third, XP teams succeed because they're willing to rethink the way that they work. The wacky ideas that I listed above are just the tip of the iceberg. XP tells you to write your testing code before you write your business code to ensure that you always have working, tested code. XP takes an emergent approach to design, modeling just enough to get you started, and then advising you to refactor your code to keep it loosely coupled and highly cohesive as your system evolves. These ideas sound strange, and even risky, but when you try them you'll discover that they work.

I truly believe that this book will show you how to succeed with XP and make it work on your project. It's easy to say, "that's fine for other people, but my organization is different and XP simply won't work here." It's very difficult to choose to overcome the difficulties within your company, to have the courage to try a new technique. It's very easy to choose to give up, but it's very difficult to choose to succeed. People who want to succeed at the software development game should read this book.

XP is real, it works, and it's here to stay.

Scott W. Ambler, August 2002
President, Ronin International, Inc.
www.ronin-intl.com
Author, Agile Modeling, www.agilemodeling.com

About the Author

Stewart Baird is an independent consultant who splits his time between software development, leading, and writing. Prior to starting his own company, he worked for KPMG Consulting, New Zealand, where he was a leading evangelist in their Extreme Programming (XP) implementation. He's presented and taught on XP in both the United States and New Zealand. Nowadays he's kept busy by helping clients develop their solutions using XP and other Agile techniques.

Though spending most of his recent career working with Microsoft tools, he's a strong advocate of open source development. Initially, he started his working life in the avionics and embedded systems fields. Sometime in the late 80s he met and fell in love with the C programming language. Before long he was writing applications in IBM's OS/2 operating system; he never looked back and has been "doing software" ever since. That fact that he's lived and worked in the United States, England, New Zealand, Australia, and Germany might help to explain his outrageous accent. Currently, he and his family make their home just outside Wellington, New Zealand. He can be contacted through his company GDS at `www.greendoorservices.com`.

Dedication

I would like to dedicate this book to my lovely wife, Laurel, who put up with the lonely nights without me; you make it all possible baby! I'd also like to dedicate this book to my sweet children, Henry, Victoria, and Noah who never quite knew why Daddy was taking so long on "that book." Let's go out and play!

Acknowledgments

I always knew that books were collaborations, but now I really know! So many patient and talented people were involved in bringing this book to you; I only know of a few. My thanks go to Michelle Newcomb for guiding, pushing, and for answering all of my silly questions. Thanks to Songlin Qiu, my development editor, who managed to have just the right balance of straight talk and encouragement. You took a pretty rough diamond and polished it up! It was treat to work again with Genevieve Burt, this time as my technical editor. Your eye for detail, insight and "wacks on the head" (when required) helped me immeasurably, thanks! Thanks go to Rob Hawthorne, my old teammate at KPMG Consulting for stepping in at the last minute to do some technical editing when we really needed it. Cheers, mate; I owe you yet another latté.

Special thanks to Scott Ambler for the technical review on the Agile Modeling chapter and offering to write the forward. Scott, I appreciate both your help and commitment to excellence in our field. Keep writing those great books!

That genesis for this book began years ago when I was working for Levi, Ray & Shoup, Inc. in Kansas City. Randy Schrock was my manager at the time and steered me into a whole new line of collaborative thinking. But perhaps more importantly, he introduced me to Kansas City BBQ, and for this I will always be grateful. We had good and bad times, but the good far outweighed the bad. Thanks to the whole team at that time; Bob ("Bobio") Conner, David Breslin, Dan Young, Mark "Shark" Abousharkh, John ("I've got a bad feeling about this") Ouverson, Jamie Smith, and Don Huff.

Lastly, my thanks go to my first boss Alan "Mac" McAulay both a true gentlemen and leader. Mac you taught me that the customer is always right, how to think positive, and that people are more important than profits. It was an honor to know and work for you. Thanks!

We Want to Hear from You!

As the reader of this book, *you* are our most important critic and commentator. We value your opinion and want to know what we're doing right, what we could do better, what areas you'd like to see us publish in, and any other words of wisdom you're willing to pass our way.

As an executive editor for Sams Publishing, I welcome your comments. You can email or write me directly to let me know what you did or didn't like about this book—as well as what we can do to make our books better.

Please note that I cannot help you with technical problems related to the *topic* of this book. We do have a User Services group, however, where I will forward specific technical questions related to the book.

When you write, please be sure to include this book's title and author as well as your name, email address, and phone number. I will carefully review your comments and share them with the author and editors who worked on the book.

Email: feedback@samspublishing.com

Mail: Michael Stephens
           Executive Editor
           Sams Publishing
           201 West 103rd Street
           Indianapolis, IN 46290 USA

For more information about this book or another Sams Publishing title, visit our Web site at www.samspublishing.com. Type the ISBN (excluding hyphens) or the title of a book in the Search field to find the page you're looking for.

Introduction

Extreme Programming (XP) is the most popular of a whole new breed of simple, fast, and easy-to-use software development approaches. You're holding in your hand a book that can give real, practical advice on what XP is and how to use it. Why do we need a fresh way of building software? What was wrong with the old, rigid methodologies of the past? Over the next few hours I'll explain how the rapid pace of business, fueled by the Internet, exposed the weakness in these methodologies.

XP has a rock-solid, software engineering base where integrating tests, real-time code review, and quick release cycles all ensure quality of code. The good news is that most of the software development tools used in XP are free! You'll discover how to use these tools to both test and build your applications.

XP can be used across development languages and platforms. You'll learn how XP works equally well on both Java and .NET platforms. Common approaches and tools mean that developers can switch easily between either platform—that is, as long as you know the development language!

It's time to put the fun back into programming!

How This Book Is Organized

Sams Teach Yourself Extreme Programming in 24 Hours is divided into six parts. Each part builds on your knowledge and understanding of Extreme Programming. The parts are as follows:

- Part 1, "Learning the XP Basics," introduces you to XP and explains how it overcomes today's software development problems.

- Part 2, "Understanding XP in Action," introduces the lifecycle of an XP project along with the roles involved and the practices used.

- Part 3, "Running Your XP Project," explains what you need to know to lead and manage your XP team. You'll learn how to plan your project, gather user requirements, and write program code.

- Part 4, "Using the XP Tools," describes how to use the common software development tools used in XP. It leads you through tutorials that outline how to write tests and create automated build scripts.

- Part 5, "Rolling Out XP in Your Organization," takes a close look at how you can implement XP in your organization or environment. You'll also learn how to sell the XP approach to management, developers, and customers.

- Part 6, "Extending the Use of XP and Other Advanced Topics," builds on your knowledge by explaining how you stretch the use of XP to large software development projects. In this part, you will be introduced to the concept of using Agile Modeling and learn about the other Agile methodologies.

- Part 7, "Appendixes," contains additional references.

Who Is This Book's Intended Audience

If you're a project manager you'll be interested to gain some insight into this innovative, lightweight way of running software development projects. The simplicity that XP is famous for can be seen in the way XP projects are guided by the use of simple, paper-based tools, and how they focus on people rather than process.

Developers will learn how they can adapt their existing modeling techniques to this documentation-light approach. XP is about building great software in a fast-paced, uncertain world.

How to Use This Book

Use this book as your roadmap and the best place to start your journey into XP. Throughout the text I suggest other books or Web sites for further reading, and you might decide to detour into these from time to time. Just make sure you come back! The reality is that XP is evolving as the user community grows and the boundaries of XP are stretched. Use the Web sites mentioned in the text and listed in Appendix B to discover the latest developments in XP.

One word of caution though, XPers love to throw around ideas and theories; sometimes they are just that! Some of what you'll hear is a personal slant or viewpoint. That's another reason to start with this book as a sure foundation. As you go through the next 24 Hours you'll no-doubt recognize some of the practices and ideas. In fact, they are often best practices, where XP differs is that they are applied together. Following the methodical flow of the book will build on your knowledge, enabling you to gain a balanced view into XP.

A number of the Hours include code samples and examples, these can be downloaded from the book's Web site at www.samspublishing.com.

Will each chapter take one hour? Most likely they will take less time to work through, but you should allow an hour for any extra reading that's suggested in the text. Some developers might get sidetracked after they discover the power of automated testing, and these hours might turn into days! By the end of the book you'll have a balanced view of both the technical and process aspects of XP.

What's on This Book's Web Site

All of the code in this book is available for download on the Sams Publishing Web site at `http://www.samspublishing.com`. Enter this book's ISBN (0672324415) in the Search box and click Search. When the book's title is displayed, click the title to go to a page where you can download the code. You will find code for Hours 14, 15, 16, 17, and 21.

Conventions Used in This Book

The following typographic conventions are used in this book:

- Code lines, commands, statements, variables, and any text you type or see onscreen appears in a `monospace` typeface. **`Bold monospace`** typeface is often used to represent the user's input.

  Note that code lines are numbered when they are referred to in the accompanying body text. These line numbers are not part of the program code and should not be entered.

- Placeholders in syntax descriptions appear in an *`italic monospace`* typeface. Replace the placeholder with the actual filename, parameter, or whatever element it represents.

- *Italics* highlight technical terms when they're being defined.

- The ➡ icon is used before a line of code that is really a continuation of the preceding line. Sometimes a line of code is too long to fit as a single line on the page. If you see ➡ before a line of code, remember that it's part of the line immediately above it.

- The book contains special elements:

> Tips often include shortcuts to help you work more efficiently. You'll benefit from the best practice or advice that Tips will give you.

> Notes often help you spot important or useful information more quickly. You will also find that Notes include references, and they also further elaborate on key concepts contained in the text. Notes will often include useful Web links to aid you in study.

Cautions explain roadblocks you might encounter when using Extreme Programming. They also warn of problems you might encounter. Cautions are an important special element because they offer advice that will save you both time and money.

Part I
Learning the XP Basics

Hour

HOUR 1

Setting the XP Landscape

Extreme Programming (XP) is a new, vibrant way of developing software. But with dozens of software development methodologies in existence—RUP, Waterfall, and RAD, just to name a few—why do we need a new one? To answer that question, we first need to understand a little about what software development is, how it has evolved, and what problems it faces.

In this hour, you will learn the following:

- What software development is
- A brief history of software development
- An overview of the development methodologies
- How XP attacks and resolves the challenges of software development
- How XP compares to other development methodologies

Brief Overview of Software Development

In this hour, we will discover how software development has evolved from its early days in the academic and military fields into a number of distinct methodologies. All methodologies have one underlying characteristic: They are designed to enable developers to solve customer problems. Some of these problems have nothing to do with computers at all and can be traced to other factors such as poor communication or unexpected change.

Software developers realized that closing the gap between themselves and customers would be key to success. The ultimate success is keeping the customer happy! We'll see how the problem of how to obtain flexibility remained even when using techniques such as rapid development. A new breed of highly flexible, customer-focused development methodologies have been emerging over the last decade that are beginning to turn the tide back on project failures. XP is the most popular of these Agile methodologies and combines adaptability with high-quality software results.

Software development is a mix of art and engineering. It can be argued that all knowledge about how to develop software is based on trial and error. It can be said that the only way to truly validate software is through testing. Testing or validating in the sense of listening a little, building a little, checking with the customer, and then repeating the cycle all over again. The hardest challenge facing development teams is ensuring they have received clear requirements from the customer because historically requirements are often unclear and ever changing! The next step, after developers understand users' requirements, is to create software to meet them. Many experts think that the computer industry has spent the last 40 years attempting to solve this puzzle. How do we *create* software that *unites* the ideas and needs users have?

Fundamentally, software development is really just an ongoing conversation between the customer and the developer. Figure 1.1 demonstrates the master conversation that fuels a software development project.

The conversation example contains a number of assumptions, most notably, that the customer and developer understand each other perfectly. This assumption coupled with the uncertainty surrounding the end product (what is the developer doing?) can make or break a software development project. Communication is hard when the ideas are abstract or conceptual.

Over the next few pages you will discover how software development has evolved, and why a new breed of methodology like Extreme Programming is necessary.

FIGURE 1.1

The software development lifecycle as a conversation.

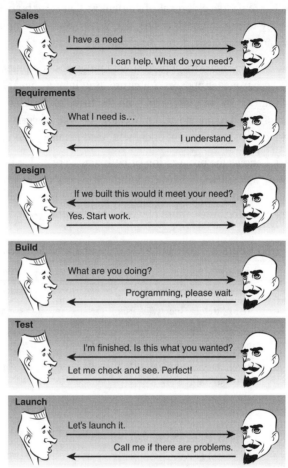

The modern computer was developed during World War II, primarily for military use. Programming these football field–sized colossuses required intricate knowledge of their inner workings, which was the left to scientists and engineers. The difficulty programming these computers limited their versatility and market. Most early computers were made-to-order monsters that literally dimmed the lights when they ran!

The limitations of hardware and the low speed of operation limited the use of computers in business. Performance began to increase around 1948 with the invention of the transistor and the dawning of the age of solid-state computers. During the 1950s, IBM and Sperry developed the first supercomputers for atomic energy research, and as you might expect, their cost was too high for businesses to afford. Business had to wait until the 1960s to see the development of computers that were both affordable and programmable in an easy-to-use language (COBOL). With the introduction of FORTRAN and COBOL a new career was created: the *programmer*.

NEW TERM A *programmer* is a person who programs computers to perform tasks. The terms *programmer* and *developer* are used interchangeably throughout this book. Programmer is the original term with the focus on writing software code. Developer is commonly used today, however, because the role is clearly much more than coding. Developers analyze, design, document, test, manage, and code.

Table 1.1 shows the progression of both hardware and software over the last 50 years. Hardware and software drive each other forward. For example, a more advanced software requirement, such as Apple Macintosh's windowing and mouse interface, in turn generates the need for faster, more powerful processors.

TABLE 1.1   50 Years of Computer Hardware and Software Evolution

Time	Hardware	Software
40s	Expensive, specialized	Binary, machine code
50s	IBM Stretch, Sperry LARC, scientific research	Assembly language
60s	Mainframe, solid-state, IBM 1401	COBOL, FORTRAN, Compilers
70s	Intel, Integrated Circuit (IC), Apple, TRS-80, DEC PDP	C, Smalltalk, BASIC, Pascal, Unix
80s	IBM PC, Apple Macintosh	DOS, dBase, Lotus 1-2-3, Graphic User Interface
90s	Laptop, Palm, PC Servers	Windows, OS/2, Java, C++, Visual Basic, Linux, Web, ASP, Perl
Today	Pocket PC, Mobile devices, Tablet PC	Web services, C#, Microsoft .NET

The Development of Software Engineering

The growth of software development continued to accelerate during the 1960s fueled by both the expansion in the U.S. military and the new generation of computers. Yet, there was no clear direction on how to write software, understand requirements, or complete projects successfully. Systems developed at that time were generally simple and batch-based.

Unfortunately, building systems without constraints and using the "just make it work" philosophy resulted in project failures. At a 1968 NATO conference called to address the software crisis, the term *software engineering* was first used. The resulting solution to increasing project chaos was to apply the tried and tested approaches from mechanical and civil engineering to software development. There are problems with assuming that software development can be compared to other engineering disciplines because the state of software cannot be scientifically verified or derived. There are no first principles in software development; the nearest we have is a set of best practices.

 Best practices are the methods, practices, tools, and processes generally regarded by the industry to be optimal or proven.

The Personal Computer Revolution

Software development remained out of reach for most users until Apple demonstrated their Apple II at a trade show in 1977. Both the Apple II and Randy Shack TRS-80 included a built-in BASIC-language interpreter that enabled owners to create their own programs. The 1980s saw the IBM PC enter the market and with it the computer became both powerful enough and affordable enough for small business to use. Software applications such as Lotus 1-2-3, WordPerfect, and dBase were stimulating the rapid acceptance of the computer.

As software development was taking off, the speed of creating applications and solving problems was in turn creating its own set of new problems. Development in languages such as dBase and BASIC required little, if any, formal training. The upside was that software could be written on-the-fly with results immediately available, but the downside was the fragility of the software. Programmers patched live systems with little if any process and the results could be disastrous. This new generation of programmers was creating applications and tools without restraint or process. The lessons learned during the 60s were forgotten in the scramble to develop applications as fast as possible with these new, easy-to-use development tools.

Building Applications Quickly with Control

Developing applications free from the confines of process and *methodology* seemed to work quite well, as long as each computer was isolated from the other. In cases where customers had multiple, disconnected machines any changes in client software only affected the local PC. If there were any problems or conflicts with new applications they were limited to the user's machine. The relative safety that this isolation brought was short-lived as the 1980s saw the launch of networking software, which enabled computers to be connected together. Running software from central file servers or using databases in a client-server model raised new problems for developers.

NEW TERM *Methodology* is a collection of procedures, techniques, principles, and tools that help developers build computer systems. In this book this term is used interchangeably with software development lifecycle (SDLC), approach, and method. Arguments abound in software engineering circles about the use of methodology versus method. They are unimportant for us as we learn XP.

The challenges of developing software in this distributed environment could not be overcome by the freewheeling development style that had evolved around the PC. Rapid Application Development (RAD) was an attempt to find a solution to the question "how do we build systems quickly, yet have control of the outcome?" Figure 1.2 shows how RAD attempts to increase flexibility by introducing a feedback loop between the customer and developer.

FIGURE 1.2

The typical rapid development cycle.

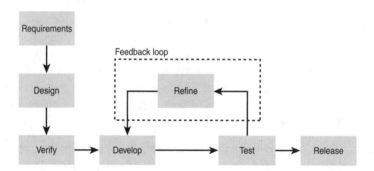

After development has reached a predescribed completion point, the development team demonstrates the software. The customer tests, and then gives feedback to allow the team to adjust its development direction. Feedback in this manner is very difficult if there is no user interface element, or the interface is incomplete. XP improves on the idea of feedback in RAD by increasing its speed and frequency. The time lag between development and demonstrating to the customer is very short with XP.

A number of differing RAD approaches have been invented or allow rapid, reliable development to occur. We will discuss these in a little more detail at the end of this hour.

Developing Software in Internet Time

Rapid application approaches continued to be tailored for client/server projects. Systems were developed for internal use and, therefore, had a defined user base. External customers were rarely able to access these systems and didn't need to be considered. The Internet changed all this. The rapid increase in global connectivity made it possible for companies to expose, or open, their internal systems to their wider customer base. Literally, overnight an application's demand could grow from hundreds to millions of users. Scalability was the word on every developer's lips.

The Internet fleshed out four main challenges for developers:

- How do we develop systems that can scale quickly?
- How do we develop systems quickly?
- How do we develop systems that can interoperate with other systems?
- How can we quickly react to ongoing change?

In response to the failure of RAD methodologies to solve these problems, a completely new breed of agile approaches began to emerge. At the forefront of this new wave was a methodology called Extreme Programming.

Understanding Software Development Methodologies

Let's take a few minutes to describe some of the common development approaches. Doing this will help frame in your mind where XP sits in the software development world, and how it is different to what has gone before.

The Code–Fix Approach

The Code-Fix approach is not a methodology at all, but it does need to be mentioned because some development continues in this style. Code-Fix revisits the "just make it work" approach. Initially, the customer may supply a specification of what they need, but this will not be substantial. This might take the form of a whiteboard sketch, email, or some other flimsy specification. They might rely on your local or expert knowledge of their business to fill in the cracks. Development then starts with fast cycles of coding followed by fixes. From time to time the developer demonstrates the application to the customer gathers feedback, and then continues development. Figure 1.3 demonstrates how developers spend most of their time coding and fixing.

Code-Fix has some fairly serious negative side effects:

- Quality of the product is low.
- Systems often end up as uncoordinated tangled messes of code that lack adaptability, reuse, and interoperability.
- Systems developed ad hoc are hard to extend and maintain.
- Overly complicated systems that tend to have poor scalability.

FIGURE **1.3**
*The Code-Fix develop-
ment cycle.*

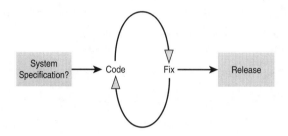

The Waterfall Approach

The Waterfall approach was developed by the U.S. Navy in the 60s to enable development of complex military software. In the Waterfall model, the project follows an
ordered sequence of steps. At the end of each phase the project team completes a review
or sign off. Development does not continue until the customer is happy with the results.
Figure 1.4 shows the project progress in a linear fashion.

FIGURE **1.4**
*The Waterfall method-
ology showing the flow
from stage to stage.*

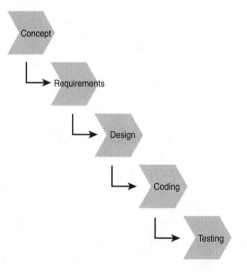

If change is required, retracing the development team's steps in the project is difficult
and cumbersome. The Waterfall is quite formal, as you would expect from a methodology whose roots were in the military. It can be said that the Waterfall is document-
driven, and it certainly has a large number of *deliverables* or outputs that are simply that:
documents. Another characteristic of this model is the high value placed on planning. This
up-front planning reduces the need for continuous planning as the project progresses.

NEW TERM A *deliverable* is any tangible output, often documents, from the software development process. The most important deliverable from the customer's view is the finished software product.

The Waterfall works best when user requirements are rigid or can be known early. The guidance system for the Space Shuttle, for example, would be a good candidate for the Waterfall approach. However, the reliance on documents to describe what customers and users want can lead to problems. More often than not, communication problems arise that result in poor-quality software. The documents produced by the process of development might be perfect, but the actual product is flawed, broken, or unusable.

In some ways most other development methodologies are variations on the Waterfall— the difference being speed, type of deliverables, and increased flexibility.

Let's take a look at Table 1.2, which highlights the benefits and drawbacks of the Waterfall methodology:

TABLE 1.2 The Benefits and Drawbacks of the Waterfall Methodology

Benefit	Drawback
Output is defined up-front	Phases are disjointed
Strict control	Amount of documentation required
Can work well with technically weak or inexperienced staff	No real output until the end
Works well when the quality of requirements is high	Reliance on documentation
	Change is difficult
	Difficult to fully specify at the start of the project

In summary, the Waterfall approach can work well for tightly controlled and rigorous environments (for example the military), but has serious shortcomings in a business scenario. There are cases where the software-development contractor benefits from the audit trail imposed by Waterfall methods. These would include projects that have high-risk components such as medical or public safety engagements.

The Evolutionary Prototyping Approach

Evolutionary Prototyping is a RAD approach that sees system concepts develop as the project moves along. This model hinges on the use of a visual prototyping or mock-up of the final system. These mock-ups might take the form of simple whiteboard sketches, graphic images, all the way to full HTML copies of the expected system. The customer gains more certainty of the end result using this visual approach. Figure 1.5 illustrates how this works.

FIGURE 1.5

The Evolutionary
Prototyping method.

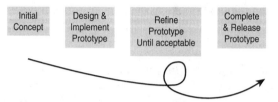

Real development doesn't start until the prototype is signed off. The EP approach is quite flexible with changing requirements, up to a point; however, it still requires sign off and control. The downside is that effective planning can be difficult and projects can be reduced to the Code-Fix cycle after development begins. The planning aspect of development can be a challenge because the team is not really sure how long the work will take. This is partly because the model is interface driven, so component or back-end interdependencies are specifically addressed. The customers have an idea of how they want to use their new system and are leaning on the prototype as a guide. The value of the prototype should not be overstated; after all it's not working software! There are risks associated with planning because of the iterative nature of development, but those are lessened somewhat by prototyping and smaller release cycles. After development begins the project manager or lead developer must ensure that programmers don't adopt Code-Fix. With an approach that relies heavily on interface modeling, the component-level modeling might fall by the wayside when the customer fires the starting gun. Reverting to Code-Fix is perhaps more a reflection on bad management than an inherent weakness of prototyping. If developers slip into Code-Fix the result will be that quality can be hard to maintain. XP tackles the problems with planning and prototyping, by shortening cycles even further while focusing on developing working software.

The Staged Delivery Approach

The Staged Delivery method is another modified Waterfall approach. There is a definite flow from start to finish, and sign offs occur after each stage. The main difference is that the customer's complete business requirements are broken down into large components, and those components are then delivered in discrete stages. An example of this is an online bookseller that must be able to sell books in stage 1, while postponing personalization features until later. Figure 1.6 demonstrates this kind of approach.

Using Staged Delivery where the emphasis is on themes or feature sets enables the customer to get the most important requirements developed first. The customer gets a working system faster. This kind of Staged Delivery does require careful planning and is still not friendly to change. Developers need to understand any interdependencies between components and functions that must be considered for stage planning. Development teams that use staged delivery have reduced risk by building in bite-sized chunks, but change must still be controlled and monitored.

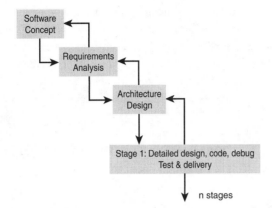

FIGURE 1.6
The Staged Delivery method.

The Rational Unified Process Approach

The Rational Unified Process (RUP) is a process that provides a disciplined approach to development using a standard set of tools, templates, and deliverables. RUP differs from the other methodologies we have looked at in that it is owned by a vendor, Rational Software (http://www.rational.com/). The standardized approach can be attractive to large organizations that require a common language and tools usage across the company. RUP uses the Unified Modeling Language (UML) to communicate requirements, architectures, and designs. UML was originally created by Rational Software, and is now maintained by the standards organization Object Management Group (OMG http://www.omg.org/).

The Rational Unified Process is another iterative development methodology with a focus on reducing project risk. Figure 1.7 illustrates the typical project flow.

FIGURE 1.7
RUP flow.

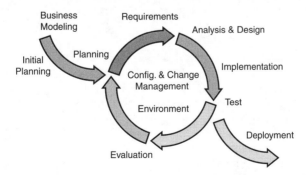

RUP does add real value to an organization that needs to maintain standards for both external communication and communication within the development team. The downside is the increased documentation requirements, customers need some understanding of UML, and the methodology is tied to a software vendor. Increasingly, developers are mixing RUP with XP, where there is a requirement to develop within existing guidelines, yet XP clearly has advantages over RUP in the speed of development and build processes.

The Microsoft Solutions Framework Approach

The Microsoft Solutions Framework (MSF) uses models to explain the development process and, therefore, is not a methodology, strictly speaking. The idea behind MSF is that each development team that uses it will modify it to fit their local needs. There is a series of templates available for key deliverables (Vision/Scope and so forth), and these are freely downloadable from `http://www.microsoft.com/business/services/ mcsmsf.asp`. Unlike RUP, MSF can't be presented to your organization out of the box because it doesn't describe how to do the real work of development. This flexibility can be a positive aspect of using MSF because your implementation can be molded to fit your existing development style. On the other hand, it can leave users of the framework struggling to visualize how the core development work will be managed. Figure 1.8 shows the cyclical nature of MSF.

FIGURE 1.8
MSF application development model.

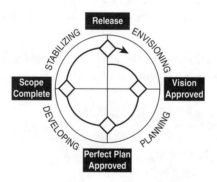

The application development model is of most interest to us in understanding MSF. Table 1.3 explains the four phases of the development model and the relevant milestone.

TABLE 1.3   The Four Phases of the MSF Application Development Model

Phase	Description	Milestone
Envisioning	Working with the customer to understand the high-level requirements for the solution	Vision Approved
Planning	Creating a project plan that describes the tasks, dependencies, and resources required to complete the solution	Project Plan Approved
Developing	Development, coding, and testing of the application	Scope Complete
Stabilizing	Final acceptance testing and release to the customer.	Release

MSF is really just another form of rapid development that still requires sign off and change control. The lack of definition to what MSF actually *is* maybe the greatest drawback to its use. It does offer some interesting observations around team structure and risk management. These can be adapted to fit most other development approaches. Some software developers are combining MSF with XP to produce a hybrid. This hybrid leans on MSF for the up-front, high-level requirements (vision), uses a small number of key milestones, and then uses XP as the core development, or build, approach.

Solving the Software Development Paradox with Agile Methodologies

We can now see how software development has evolved over the past 50 years, from its early research beginnings, through the military and rapid development approaches. Still the paradox remained—how to develop systems quickly, while staying open to change, maintaining quality, and controlling costs. In response to these questions, new, lightweight development methodologies began to emerge during the 90s. Collectively these lightweight approaches are now known as *Agile* methodologies. Table 1.4 lists the current Agile methodologies (we cover these in more depth in Hour 24, "Other Agile Development Methodologies").

NEW TERM   *Agile development methodologies* are light in documentation requirements, adaptable to change, and customer focused. Visit `http://agilemanifesto.org` for a list of Agile methodologies.

TABLE 1.4   The Agile Methodologies

Agile Approach	Web Link
Extreme Programming (XP)	http://www.xprogramming.com
	http://www.c2.com/cgi/wiki?ExtremeProgrammingRoadmap
Feature Driven Development (FDD)	http://www.togethercommunity.com/
Scrum	http://www.controlchaos.com/
Crystal Light	http://crystalmethodologies.org/
Adaptive Software Development (ASD)	http://www.adaptivesd.com/
Dynamic Systems Development Methodology (DSDM)	http://www.dsdm.org/

Although each approach differs in execution, they do hold key principles, or beliefs, in common. Most namely that development should be customer directed and that documentation requirements be light. The focus is on delivering working software.

Learning How XP Delivers Quality Software

During 2001, the Cutter Consortium surveyed the use of Agile methodologies and found that more respondents (38%) used XP than any other approach. Clearly, XP is the most popular of the Agile approaches and is particularly suited to the dynamic world of Internet development. It differs from the more traditional Waterfall, or so-called RAD methodologies, in that it accepts change as a fact of life. Small- to medium-sized teams (6–20 people) work closely with customers, foregoing detailed, up-front planning in favor of rapid iterations that provide direct, real results to the customer.

The full text of this article "The Decision Is In: Agile Versus Heavy Methodologies" can be found at
http://www.cutter.com/freestuff/epmu0119.html.

Most developers, programmers, and software engineers are taught that change is fundamentally bad—to be avoided, controlled, and managed. The Waterfall methodology works entirely from this premise. It is good to desire to control change as early as possible in the development cycle because costs tend to rise rapidly as the product is implemented. XP uses techniques and practices to effectively flatten the cost of change; it remains the same throughout the project. In Hour 3, "Overcoming Software Development Problems with XP," I will explain how this works in reality, but for now we can accept that XP has integrated ways of keeping costs low.

XP delivers quality software by working at both ends of the quality spectrum: accuracy of requirements and robustness of product. Rather than rely on a single "silver bullet" method, XP brings together 12 key practices, such as pair programming, collective ownership, and continuous integration, under the guidance of a handful of focused values. We'll introduce these practices in the next hour, and they will be covered in detail during Hour 6, "XP Practices in Action." The synergy of these components is what empowers XPers to quickly and accurately develop quality software for their customers.

Comparing the Methodologies

By now you have a good understanding of the software development landscape. We've covered the classic Waterfall approach, RAD methods, and the Code-Fix cycle. Variations of RAD have been very popular over the past 10 years as developers and customers struggle to find a good balance between cost, quality, risk, and control. Look at Figure 1.9 and you'll see how each methodology compares.

FIGURE 1.9

Comparing development methodologies.

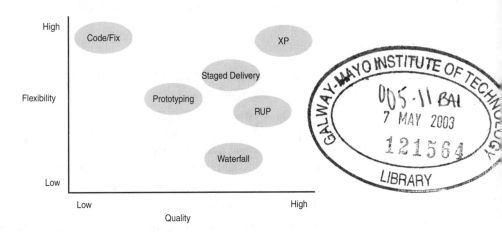

In Figure 1.9 we're comparing the flexibility and quality of each approach. By flexibility, we mean how well the approach accepts change; quality refers to both defects and accuracy of product. If we use the Waterfall method as the benchmark, we can see that high-quality products can be delivered, but the customer must sacrifice freedom. Extreme Programming allows for change in the project lifecycle and improves quality by resolving defects early and provides constant feedback on the product.

The capability to combine both aspects of quality (meeting customer expectations and lowering defect counts) is where XP really shines. In the past, new methodologies have sought to tackle shortcomings in other approaches by increasing rigor and adding over-head; control was seen as the answer. XP turns this on its head, reversing the cycle of growing complexity. XP proves that thinking simple works in the real world!

Summary

In this hour, you've learned how software development grew out of the desire to deliver high-quality software products to customers. Most of these methodologies attempted to control the outcome of software development by adding restrictions and tightly monitor-ing change.

Control-based methodologies work well where change is either slow or manageable. You've learned that the fast pace of business, and change in general, has exposed the tired old approaches, such as Waterfall. Agile methodologies have emerged from this pressure to deliver value and results quickly. The foremost of these Agile methodologies is Extreme Programming.

XP is leading the pack in terms of both acceptance and adaptability. In the next hour you'll learn where XP comes from and how it works.

Q&A

Q XP seems a lot like the Code-Fix approach where developers just code without control. Is this true?

A No. XP builds in testing throughout development; in fact, with XP tests are written before the code. These tests are executed routinely to give real, verifiable feedback to the development team. Aspects of XP such as code reviews, code sharing, and commitment to quality are typically not evident in Code-Fix.

Q What are the core problems with applying a general engineering approach to software development?

A Using engineering as a basis to understand development lessens or deemphasizes the creative design aspects of software development. Unlike building bridges, soft-ware *design* is never really complete until the product is finished. It can be said that everything up to the actual compile or link is design. Even then the evolution of the product may continue. The levels of uncertainty and change are much higher with software development where there are no real first principles, such as the laws of physics. Careful thought needs to be given before applying all the general principles of engineering. Programming is design *not* construction, and the compiler is the only person not designing.

Q How do I select the best methodology?

A It depends on your customer (their culture), the target market (civil, medical, business, and so on), the level of expected change, and your developer's skill sets.

Workshop

This workshop tests whether you understand all the concepts you learned today. It is very helpful to know and understand the answers before starting tomorrow's lesson.

Quiz

1. Why was software engineering created?

2. What new challenges did the Internet bring to software development?

3. Which lifecycle model has the least flexibility?

4. What do all RAD methods have in common?

5. Why was XP developed?

Answers

1. As a reaction to the rising rate of project failures in the 1960s. The idea was to employ general engineering principles to software development.

2. Four main issues: the need to interoperate with other systems, the need to be scalable, the need to accommodate high-speed development, and the need to accommodate quick change.

3. The Waterfall is the most inflexible lifecycle with tight control and sign offs.

4. Increased feedback to the client.

5. To meet the demand for both quality and flexibility.

Activities

1. Compare your company's development methodology to those we have covered. Considering what you now know about the challenges of development, highlight possible areas for improvement by using Agile techniques.

2. Use the Internet as a research tool to discover the major causes of project failure. Good places to start are http://www.cutter.com and http://www.cio.com.

Hour **2**

Discovering What XP Is All About

In this hour you'll gain an understanding of XP's features and the benefits derived from its use. By the end of the hour you will have learned

- Where XP came from, and why it is so different
- The key elements that make up XP
- XP's key features
- How XP compares with other methodologies

The First XP Project

It is impossible to talk about the history of XP without referring to Kent Beck. Beck is generally regarded as the father of XP, and his book *Extreme Programming—Explained* is the foundational XP work. Sometimes known as the "White Book," it isn't a practical guide, but more of a manifesto of this new development approach. It was during the Chrysler Comprehensive

Compensation (C3) project (1996–99) where Beck, Ward Cunningham, Ron Jefferies, and others assembled the essential elements of what we now know as XP.

In 1996, Chrysler called in Kent Beck to help with their struggling C3 project as an external consultant. The C3 project was designed to aggregate a number of disparate payroll systems into a single application. Initially, Chrysler attempted to implement a package solution, but it failed because of the complexities surrounding rules and integration.

From this point of crisis Kent Beck and his team took over, effectively starting the project from scratch. The classic development approach had been tried and had failed, so something drastic was required. In Beck's own words he "just made the whole thing (XP) up in two weeks, marker in hand at the whiteboard." Fundamentally the C3 team focused on the business value the customer wanted and discarded anything that did not work toward that goal. XP was created by developers for developers!

The XP team at Chrysler was able to deliver their first working system within one year, and in 1997 the first 10,000 employees were paid from the new C3 system. Development continued over the next year with new functionality added through smaller releases. Eventually the project was cancelled because the prime contractor changed and the focus of Chrysler shifted away from C3. When the dust settled, the eight-member development team had built a system with 2,000 classes and 30,000 methods. XP had been refined and tested and was now ready for the wider development community.

Defining XP

XP is an Agile methodology for small- to medium-sized teams developing software in the face of rapidly changing requirements.

XP consists of four parts: values, principles, activities, and practices. Figure 2.1 demonstrates how they are built on each other, with activities that run around or throughout the lifecycle.

It's better to say XP has emerged from a series of collaborations, streams, and systems rather than been invented or created. In keeping with this organic view of software development, XP is founded on values and guiding principles. From this core, XP practices and activities stand. In Figure 2.2 we can see how XP is a synergy of four components that were developed from key influences, and the result of this is quality for the customer.

Figure 2.1

XP is based on core values and is supported by activities, practices, and principles.

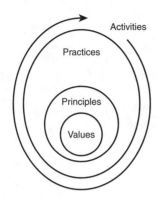

Figure 2.2

XP has evolved from the need to create quality results.

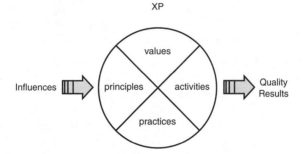

Values

XP is driven by a set of shared values that establish the tone for XP development. Here are the XP values (see Table 2.1).

Table 2.1 The Four Values of XP

Value	Description
Simplicity	Simplicity in XP is defined as "doing the simplest thing that could possibly work" (http://www.c2.com/cgi/wiki?YouArentGonnaNeedIt). We solve today's problems simply and trust that tomorrow's will be solvable, too. Typical development methodologies expect a degree of up-front planning, where the customer attempts to guess or estimate the totality of the system. An implicit understanding exists in this model that change in the future is hard if not impossible. XP reverses this by targeting development at what the customer needs right NOW. There is a saying in XP circles: "You aren't going to need it," or YAGNI. What this means is that with simplicity in mind the development team should only implement what the customer *actually* needs not what they *expect* they might need. Why design in features you might need? Normally, this

TABLE 2.1   continued

Value	Description
	happens because the cost of change will be too high later. Keeping the cost of change constant removes the need for up-front guessing. We will explore this further in Hour 3, "Overcoming Software Development Problems with XP."
	In the final analysis simple systems are easier to communicate about, have less integration points, and scale better.
Communication	All methodologies have built-in communication processes; with XP it is a core value. The focus is on oral communication not documents, reports, and plans. Without constant communication between all team members collaboration will wither and die. XP has practices such as pair programming that require communication to work. In Hour 1, "Setting the XP Landscape," we discussed how *understanding* is one of the greatest challenges faced by software developers. XP recognizes this and seeks to remove barriers between team members. Any documents that are produced facilitate communication between people.
Feedback	The value of feedback is vital to the success of any software project. With XP the nagging questions over the state of the system are answered by constant, concrete feedback. In Hour 1, we discussed how software development is in a continual state of design; the product can only be verified by trial and error. This being true the development team must produce software quickly, and then demonstrate to the customer. Closing the loop by getting customer feedback on progress to date is vital to accuracy and quality.
Courage	Courage is the confidence to work quickly and redevelop if required. Courage in XP should be thought of in the context of the other three values; without these courage leads to chaos. XP courage is a boldness to act based on a strong, automated-test harness and not about reckless endeavors into the unknown. XPers have changed the development mindset of tentative, uncertain coding into development at top-speed with confidence. Simplicity is another key value that supports courage. Team members understand the system and have hard metrics that support source-code refactoring.
	Courage without the other values results in another mess of tangled code, complexity, and poor maintainability for the software.

Principles

Building on the foundation of XP's core values, we have five main principles that guide software development, as described in Table 2.2.

TABLE 2.2 The Guiding Principles of XP

Principle	Description
Rapid Feedback	Rapid feedback means developers use short feedback loops to quickly learn if their to-date product is meeting customer's needs.
Assume Simplicity	Assume Simplicity is treating each problem as if it can be solved simply. Assume Simplicity means you design for only the current iteration; no crystal ball gazing into the future about what you may need.
Incremental Change	Solve problems with a series of small changes. This applies to planning, development, and design. An example of this could be where a customer has an existing static Web site and wants to port to Java Server Pages (JSP). Rather than redevelop the site in one release, the XP team will roll out many small releases as the business dictates.
Embrace Change	Adopt a strategy that preserves options while solving pressing problems.
Quality Work	Quality of work can never be compromised. XP elevates the importance of code and testing with test-first programming.

Activities

With all this talk of values and principles; what do you actually do in XP? A handful of activities run throughout the XP lifecycle (see Table 2.3).

TABLE 2.3 The XP Activities

Activity	Description
Listening	XP is grounded in communication and has practices that require active listening. With less reliance on written formal documentation there needs to be quality verbal communication. Beyond simply saying that developers should listen to customers, XP has practices that direct and guide toward better communication. Without the reliance on documentation, XPers must learn and mature in other forms of verbal communication.
Testing	Testing in XP is not an afterthought to be done before delivery to the customer, but an integral step throughout the process. This is to the extent that developers write tests before they develop code. Not limited to accuracy or defect measurement, XP tests check for performance and conformance. The ability to write tests before the code requires a shift in thinking for developers. The result is code that has quality built-in rather than waiting to catch bugs late in the development cycle where costs are usually higher.
Coding	XP is about programming after all, and writing code is a craft that is refined through practices such as refactoring, pair programming, and code review.

TABLE 2.3 Continued

Activity	Description
	With little written design, XP developers write code that intentionally expresses their meaning. By the mere reading of source code, other team members can understand logic, algorithms, and flow. It must be understood here that we are not talking about comments in code, but the code itself as a form of communication. Remember that the software's source code is as close as we can get to the actual end product, after this we pass our source to compilers, linkers, and other building tools.
Designing	One of XP's radical ideas is that design should evolve and grow through the project. Design is not stationary or assigned to one role, but is both team-based and dynamic. In one sense, software is always in a state of *being* designed. Instead of ignoring this fact by limiting design activities, XP accepts the natural evolution of the system. Those who don't acknowledge that software design is ongoing and fluid pay for their stubbornness with systems that devolve into a complex, stagnate, and bug-ridden mess. The difference between XP and other approaches is the fluid, responsive nature of design.

Practices

So, how do we physically *execute* the XP activities? XP expresses these activities in 12 core practices. These practices are what XP teams use each day to develop systems. Table 2.4 lists these practices with a short description of each.

TABLE 2.4   The 12 XP Practices

Practice	Description
The Planning Game	The role of the Planning Game is to quickly derive a high-level plan for the next release or iteration.
Small Releases	XP cycles consist of frequent releases that deliver business value.
Metaphor	Metaphor is the common vision, terms, and language used to describe the project.
Simple Design	Design must be simple. Simple in an XP sense means that the code does the simplest thing that could work.
Testing	The heart of XP development is the use of automated tests. Tests are developed first and are implemented in the test harness.
Refactoring	Refactoring means to improve the design of existing code without changing the system's observable behavior.
Pair Programming	Pair programming is where two developers sit at the same workstation and share development tasks.
Collective Ownership	Collective Ownership enables anyone to improve, or change, any part of the code at anytime.
Continuous Integration	The components of the system are built or integrated many times each day.
40-Hour Work Week	Consistent quality and performance cannot be maintained with overtime-heavy teams. XP mandates a regular work hours to ensure quality.
On-Site Customer	The customer representative is on-site and forms part of the team.
Coding Standards	Coding Standards are a group of conventions that everyone agrees to develop under.

We will revisit the XP practices in Hour 6, "XP Practices in Action," explaining how they are used and their interactions, but for now you should have an adequate sense of their coverage.

XP's Key Features

We've explained the values, principles, activities, and practices of XP, so what then differentiates XP from other methodologies? Figure 2.3 displays the key features of XP.

FIGURE 2.3
XP features are separated from other methodologies.

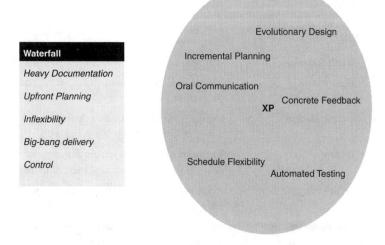

Concrete Feedback

Most development methodologies employ some kind of feedback between developer and customer. As we discussed in Hour 1, developers often "go dark" during the construction phase of a project, leaving customers wondering if they are building the right thing. These non-Agile approaches usually incorporate documents that describe progress, state, and the quality of the software. The major problem with this is that the feedback doesn't give any real, definite sense of the software itself. With XP the feedback is taken early and is concrete, based on metrics that describe the state of the system. Build cycles are very short and the customer can see numbers such as unit tests passed and user stories completed; these indicate the exact status of the software itself (rather than documents, reports, and other deliverables that are simply reflections).

Incremental Planning

XP's incremental planning approach quickly comes up with an overall plan. The plan is broken down into releases and iterations. Planning happens during the Planning Game which we'll go into in more depth during Hour 8, "Planning Your Software Release with XP." Usually, development methodologies require concentrated, detailed planning at the start of the project. In essence, XP says "let's plan what we know now and then replan from time to time as change happens."

Schedule Flexibility

Because XP's incremental planning produces a roadmap with pencil, the customer can alter the direction of development as work progresses. It's quite conceivable that functionality that seemed high value at the start of the project might slip in priority or might even be dropped entirely. Passing control back to the customer is a powerful differentiator between XP and other typical RAD approaches.

Automated Testing

Automated testing involves the use of testing tools that can be scripted or programmed to repeat test tasks. XP relies on automated testing to give feedback on the software's status. You will learn later how these tools work, and how you can use them in your own environment. Automated tests are necessary to XP because they encourage simple design, make collective code ownership more manageable and less risky, and foster pair programming.

Oral Communication

In the past, software developers have learned to distrust verbal communication. Instead, they look for sign offs, written confirmations, change requests, and documents. The XP environment is totally different; there is one team (including the customer) in which developers work in pairs. Pair Programming refers to a fundamental XP practice where developers share the same computer and program together. This concept will be explained in Hour 11, "Software Development with Pair Programming." It does require a much higher degree of communication than most developers are used to. There is a reliance on oral communication in XP; team members simply must talk and listen effectively. XP teams work in open workspaces, removing any physical barriers that separate team members. The use of shared spaces further enhances oral communication.

Evolutionary Design

Ordinarily, customers are expected to decide what they require before design can begin. In non-Agile methodologies the development team comes up with a complete design, which is then signed off by the customer (this design will cover most if not all the solution). No such up-front design exists in XP where all the team requires is the metaphor (see Hour 6 for more on this concept), or high-level statement, for the system. XP developers postpone design decisions until they are required, the dependence on simplicity and feedback ensure that the resulting system is not cobbled together.

Investigating XP's Extreme Aspects

One of the criticisms aimed at XP and its proponents is that there is nothing new with the methodology. To a degree this is true if you look at the elements of XP in isolation, but the power of XP comes with the synergy of the practices. XP is mostly best practices, or common sense, taken to extremes. In Table 2.5 we see how certain, common practices are expressed in XP.

TABLE 2.5 Common Practices When Used by XP

Practice	XP Practice
Testing	Most methodologies employ testing as a separate phase in development. Even after developers complete some unit testing, software quality problems can occur during customer tests. XP says that rather than wait for a milestone test (perhaps months in advance), why not test all the time? Even better; write the test before you develop the code, and then add these test cases to a test suite and run them continuously.
Code reviews	The idea of code walkthroughs or inspections is not new and has its roots in industrial engineering. Software engineers have long used peer reviews to ensure quality, consistency, and maintainability. XP uses the practice of pair programming to create an environment where code reviews are happening constantly. As one developer is writing code the other is checking, reviewing, and considering wider implications.
Simplicity	Every system architect understands and values the principle of simplicity. Simple systems are easy to extend, work faster, are easier to communicate about, and simpler to maintain. In XP the team works to keep reducing complexity until they have the simplest design that works.
Integration testing	Those developers who have worked on teams are familiar with the pain and problems caused by integrating the code base together. In XP integration occurs many times a day until it becomes the norm. The question of how often to integrate then becomes more around how often the customer and development team can sustain the level of change. A strong test suite, code standards, and pair programming guides this process. The use of automated build tools simplifies this even further.
Short iterations	The concept of building applications more frequently has been around since the advent of RAD. In XP, iterations are measured in minutes and hours, as code is quickly turned around, integrated, and tested. Both customer and developer alike are quickly able to see the impacts of design or code change.

How Does XP Differ from Other Development Approaches?

By now you have a good sense of how XP is more dynamic, flexible, and simple than the methodologies we looked at in the previous hour. Some of the XP practices could be implemented within, say, a RUP project, but none of the approaches discussed combine all of XP's features. Table 2.6 demonstrates how XP differs from existing software development lifecycles.

TABLE 2.6   Comparing XP with Other Development Approaches

	XP	Waterfall	Staged	MSF
Requirements	User Stories	Functional Specification (FS)	FS	FS
Planning	Incremental (Planning Game)	Detailed	Detailed Stage Plans	Vision/Scope High-level
Design	Metaphor (evolutionary)	Detailed Design	Detailed + Stage reviews	Detailed Design
Build	Continuous Integration	Linear	Linear	Daily build Automated tools
Test	Test First/Automated tools	Unit testing, Acceptance tests	Unit testing, Acceptance tests	Unit testing, Acceptance tests
Deploy	Platform specific	Deployment Guides	Deployment Guides	Deployment Guides

Reviewing Table 2.6 we can see that XP tends toward more of a dynamic style of software development. At first glance it would appear that XP is not that extreme after all! Remember though that XP takes best practices to extremes. For example, all development methodologies have some form of unit testing, but with XP developers write, test *first,* and then execute after each system integration! So, contrary to any bad press XP has received; we're not throwing the baby out with bathwater!

Summary

In this hour, you have learned how XP emerged from real-world experiences of software engineers driven by the desire to build quality systems that met the expectations of customers. Unlike methodologies that have gone before, XP is founded on values and principles. We saw how these values are expressed through solid, simple best practices. Passing control back to the customer is powerful differentiator between XP and other typical RAD approaches.

The power of XP comes from the flexibility and quality that it combines; the focus is truly on giving customers exactly what they want. During the next hour you'll learn how XP overcomes the common problems faced by software development.

Q&A

Q What degree of acceptance is XP receiving in the wider software development market?

A XP is rapidly gaining traction in consulting, development, and business markets. Large consulting firms are either implementing XP wholesale or integrating the methodology into their e-business solution lines. Companies as diverse as Motorola and Caterpillar have seen real benefits from using XP in their internal projects.

Q Is XP connected with any particular development language or vendor?

A No. XP was initially used in what was primarily a Smalltalk (object-oriented language) environment. Since its release to the wider development community, Java users have been the main users of XP. Microsoft developers have constructed their own tools using both COM and .NET platforms.

Q Is Extreme Programming aimed mainly at developers?

A No, but it was created by developers! The entire project team, both business and technical, can benefit from this new approach.

Q Can I pick and choose the XP practices?

A The effectiveness of XP comes from the use of all 12 practices together. You can use a practice outside of the XP context, but you will not receive maximum benefits in productivity or quality. In Hour 19, "Retrofitting XP into Your Project," we will investigate how you can retrofit XP into an existing environment.

Q How is conformance to XP measured?

A There is no XP certification at the moment. Keeping to the principles and values is the best way to indicate your closeness to XP. It is possible that new practices could be added to the 12 that XP has at present.

Q Where can I find case studies of successful XP projects to show my boss?

A The best case studies and reports are on the Internet. Try these links as starting points:

- `http://www.c2.com/cgi/wiki?TopLinkForJavaUsageExperiences`
- `http://www.xpuniverse.com/2001/xpuPapers.htm`

The book *Extreme Programming—Examined*, by Succi and Marchesi (Addison Wesley) has collected case studies.

There are some common objections that are raised when people hear of XP for the first time. Some of these are listed in the following table and have included both the objection and corresponding answer.

TABLE 2.7   Common Objections to XP and Refutes

Objection to XP	Refute
"I can't work in an open area with others. I won't be able to concentrate."	XP development is done with pairs sharing the same workstation. Interactions are guided and monitored by the coach (project manager); the open space is not an excuse for noise!
"I don't want to work at the same PC with another programmer because he'll get the credit for my work and that's not fair."	You will all get the credit for the team's work! The increased interaction with other team members enhances your position, in the sense that pretty soon everyone knows what kind of work you produce. The end result is that your visibility is raised beyond programming; the customer *knows* that you made a difference.
"Fitting good requirements on note cards is impossible."	The user story is a starting point; it begins the conversation between developer and customer. The level of requirements is much lower than on a typical Waterfall project. The user story may have supporting information that can be attached; you're not limited to the space on the card.
"Customers shouldn't be allowed to talk to developers—that makes change control impossible."	Exactly! We don't want to control change, but rather embrace it as a fact of life and learn how to develop with this understanding. It's a whole new way of thinking!
"There's no way to write a test harness before the system design exists."	Technically, it is possible to write tests first and the xunit family of test harnesses can help you here. (We will discuss this more in Hour 13, "Using XP Development Tools.")
"You have to anticipate the customer's needs —otherwise the system won't be scalable and you'll have tons of rework."	Anticipate or is that *guess*? If you build your system simply and abstract out components, scalability will be improved. Rework comes when you have to change the code that you

TABLE 2.7   continued

Objection to XP	Refute
	developed in anticipation. Who pays for this anyway? Why would a customer ever pay for functionality that she may never use?
"Limiting Internet development teams to a 40-hour week is unrealistic in this day and age of 'first to market.'"	Working consistently longer hours will reduce quality and ends with the project taking longer. The advent of the Internet fits XP perfectly; build what we need right now and let's put off the fancy widgets until we have the need. The whole world will know if your site fails because of poor quality!

Workshops

This workshop tests whether you understand all the concepts you learned today. It is very helpful to know and understand the answers before starting tomorrow's lesson.

Quiz

1. What are the four values of XP?

2. What does YAGNI mean?

3. Why is XP extreme?

Answers

1. Communication, Simplicity, Feedback, and Courage.

2. You aren't going to need it.

3. XP practices, for the most part, are commonly used, or best practices, that are taken to extremes in terms of application and speed.

Activities

1. Consider your last or current development project. Are you already using some XP practices? Investigate whether you can start to use say, pair programming, today.

2. Reviewing the 12 XP practices, separate them into team, organizational, and individual practices.

Hour **3**

Overcoming Software Development Problems with XP

Before we go more in depth with XP it is helpful to have a solid understanding of what key problems XP overcomes. Some of these were hinted at during Hour 1, "Setting the XP Landscape." In this hour we'll uncover the major software development problems and see how XP resolves them. By the end of the hour you will have learned

- How you can control your project's outcome with XP
- What the key risks are with software development and how XP mitigates them
- How XP projects produce quality software products
- How XP embraces change during development

Uncovering Software Development Problems

In this section we will uncover some of the most common problems with software development. Then, we will isolate four variables that you can use to control the outcome of your project. Before I explain what these are and how XP manages projects differently, let's dig a little deeper into why software projects go bad.

The Software Development Crisis

In Hour 1 we discovered how software engineering was born in the late 1960s as a response to the rising level of project failures. Something had to be done and rigorous control appeared to be the answer. Thirty years later software development still struggles with bad press from what seems an endless list of project failures and cost overruns. A 1995 research article from KPMG reported on the causes and effects of project failure. The top reasons for software project failures were

- Project objectives not fully specified
- Bad planning and estimating
- Technology new to the organization
- Inadequate or no project management methodology
- Insufficient senior staff on the team
- Poor performance by suppliers of hardware/software

The Denver International Airport (DIA) Baggage Handling System is one of the most publicized and dramatic examples of a *software runaway*. The images of luggage littered throughout the baggage claim area, dismembered, and spat out by the hugely complex automated system, became headline news during 1994–95. The idea was to take an existing, simple baggage-handling system that worked well and scale-up to a more complex, integrated system. After stumbling through delay after delay, the airport finally opened on February 28, 1995, with more than $300 million spent on the automated baggage system for United Airlines. The vision to develop a completely integrated system, serving all airlines had failed. Shifting goals, technical challenges, politics, and personnel change had all combined to derail the project.

| NEW TERM | *Software runaway* is a project that goes out of control primarily because of the difficulty of building the software needed by the system. |

Your software development projects might not approach the complexity of the DIA baggage handling system, but you can learn lessons from such spectacular failures. Some industry pundits claim we are in the midst of a software "crisis" where the chances of completing a successful project are extremely poor.

The software runaway article is available from: "Runaway Projects—Causes and Effects," *Software World* (UK), Vol.26, No.3, 1995, by Andy Cole, KPMG.

To summarize, your project is liable to drift into runaway if you lack a development strategy that is highly flexible, open, and scaleable. XP attacks this risk at the root by embracing change and accepting it as the norm. The practices support dynamic development that weeds out defects in quality as they occur.

The Death March

Software runaway projects are typically started with a good chance of success, but the wheels fall off during development. Increasingly developers are being dragged, tricked, or happen into a new style of software project: the *death march*. Edward Yourdon devotes an entire book to this subject (*Death March—The Complete Software Developer's Guide to Surviving "Mission Impossible" Projects*, 1997), for now we'll gain an understanding of how XP can aid you in not just *surviving* but *overcoming* the death march.

New Term   *Death march* is a project that after objective analysis has greater than 50% likelihood of failure.

Death march projects start with little chance of success; they are doomed to fail. Apple spent years developing what was to be its new operating system, code-named "Pink," all the while continuing to treat it as a two-year endeavor. Expectations were not adjusted when it became clear development could never be completed within a two-year time frame. Pink was eventually dissolved with seven years worth of effort wasted. Whether this project was a runaway or a death march is immaterial; it was a failure. Yourdon lists some of the typical reasons for death march in his book:

- Politics—Internal or personal factors result in impossible constraints being established ("the project must be completed by 1 May"). These constrains are either never questioned or issues are swept under the carpet with the smokescreen of "its just politics."

- Naive promises—Senior management makes promises to customers or marketing without checking with the development team.

- Naive optimism—Developers with little experience or maturity, underestimate the effort involved. When committed they lack the confidence to retract their estimates.

- The "Marine Corps" mentality—Developers understand the impossibility of the task ahead, which becomes some kind of weird challenge. This do-or-die mentality is fueled by a lethal mix of inexperienced team members, weak project management, and a general gung-ho attitude.

How can XP help with a death march? One obvious way is the XP practice that mandates a 40-hour work week. XP allows change to the scope of the project, but not the cost, time, or quality.

The Four Control Variables in Your Project

There are four variables that you can control in your software project: time, cost, quality, and scope, as shown in Figure 3.1.

FIGURE 3.1

The four variables of development.

What then are the impacts of controlling your project using these variables? The customer chooses three of the four and leaves you to manage the fourth. Which is the best control variable? Table 3.1 lists our variables and the side effects of controlling each.

TABLE 3.1   The Four Control Variables and Their Effect

Variable	Effect
Time	Too little time will certainly impede the quality of the product because there's not enough time to listen to customers, code, or test. On the other hand, extending the timeframe (not common) might not yield the answer you expected. The role of the development team is to implement changes as quickly as possible so that the customer can give feedback. Quality might be improved by lengthened timelines, but, as we will discuss later in this chapter, there is more to quality than bugs.
Cost	Can throwing money and resources at the project save you from disaster? Adding more resources to a project that is already late will only succeed in making it later. The customer needs to fund development to the estimated level, but should not expect that pouring money into a project in strife will cover issues.
Quality	The worst of our control variables! Reducing quality can appear to quicken development time, but in the end we've only succeeded in moving testing into the hands of our end users.
Scope	The standard procedure with software development is to only begin work after the scope has been agreed to and signed off. Tying down requirements and scope is an uphill battle in this model. Customers want to make sure they throw in everything they *think* they want and *might* want in the future.

How do we overcome software development issues and challenges with XP? We allow the scope of development to change, fix the other variables, and develop using the 12 XP practices.

> Allowing scope to change does not mean an unlimited-length project! The key word is *change*. If the customer adds a new feature request they will have to remove something of equivalent size. This is quite different from scope creep where the customer continually adds requests that the team never planned for.

Controlling Risk with XP

By now you should have a definite sense that software development is a risky business, surrounded by uncertainty and change. There are however, some common risks with software development that we can highlight:

- Schedule slips—As the work progress it becomes clear that the delivery date is unreachable.

- Project cancelled—This is more of a problem when the project size is larger. The customer has been spending huge amounts of money for no perceived business value and they finally pull the plug.

- No business acceptance—The system was developed far from the end users and failed to work the way they wanted. The cost or pain of changing the business was too high.

- Technical complexity—The tools or platforms chosen are untried and prove too difficult to integrate.

- Defect rates high—The quality of the system is shown to be very low, defects are either overlooked or not tracked. When in the hands of the user the system is buggy and defect-ridden. Litigation, rework on commercial impacts are the result.

XP addresses these risks head on by building quality into the software and delivering working software in very small release cycles. Before we tackle our risks, let's review an example of how *not* to run a software development project.

INCIS: A Case Study of a Software Disaster

In 1994 the New Zealand Police awarded a tender to IBM for the development and delivery of its Integrated National Computerized Information System (INCIS). INCIS was slated to be the first law enforcement information management system in the world to link all aspects of police work at a national level. Five years and $67.5 million later, the project had been scrapped, $15 million over budget and with little, if any, real result. As you'd expect with a disaster of this scale, there was no single root problem. There were some obvious contributing factors:

- Complexity—The project was both technically and operationally extremely complex. The level of this complexity was greatly underestimated. This risk was never highlighted or dealt with.

- Technical problems—Initially IBM developed their client machines under OS/2; in 1996 they switched to Windows NT at an estimated rework cost of $3.5 million.

- Unreasonable deadlines—Deadlines were not based on real estimates of time to complete; politics and marketing set impossible dates that were never met.

- Overly optimistic, blinded management—Any issues raised by development staff were typically squashed under the "think positive" regime.

- Big Bang approach—Almost all the work had to be completed before the users saw the system. The idea was to replace the old system with a single cut-over. A pilot was run for part of the system, but the results were ignored.

- Silver bullet syndrome—Politicians and management placed their faith in technology and tools such as high-level computer languages to overcome obstacles. Due to the length of the project some of these technologies, such as OS/2, became obsolete.

- Waterfall approach—The functional specification ran to more than 4,000 pages and had more than 900 variations over the lifetime of the project. It wasn't until the users actually *saw* the system that they understood what those 4,000 pages spelled out. Naturally, numerous changes were requested late in development, and with the Waterfall approach, this was expensive.

What can you learn from this software disaster? Software development needs to be done in a dynamic, change-friendly environment, and the software itself is the best form of specification. The project managers on the INCIS project made the mistake of confusing *documentation* with *communication*.

For the official report into this software disaster see
http://www.justice.govt.nz/pubs/reports/2000/incis_rpt/schedules/
schedule_6.html.

Averting Disaster with XP

You now know the all-to-common risks associated with software development, and you've learned how one project (INCIS) failed because of some of them—namely, Waterfall development, unreasonable deadlines, single release approach, and complexities inherent in the technology. XP has direct ways of mitigating and overcoming these risks. Table 3.2 lists our risks and explains how XP deals with them.

TABLE 3.2   How XP Mitigates Risk

Risk	Mitigation
Schedule slips	XP has very short release cycles; any slippage or change is very small. The highest business value features are delivered first and the customer can actually *see* the software (not merely documentation about the system).
Project cancelled	In an XP project, since the most important work is done up-front, if the project is cancelled, the XP team/company at least achieved some functionality. This is unlike most software projects, where teams spend the first six months in planning, and if its cancelled, the company is left with nothing to show for it. The XP approach reduces budgetary risk.
No business acceptance	The customer is part of the development team on a full-time basis. They select the functionality being delivered and can guide as necessary. There is no need to create buy-in because they developed the solution with the rest of the team.
Technical complexity	The XP practice of continuous integration means that the team is at ease with integrating the complete system, and there is no "big bang" before delivery. The value of simplicity drives code quality through practices such as code standards, pair programming, collective ownership, and refactoring.
Defect rates high	The use of automated testing and test-first programming establishes low defect counts as a way of life. Issues with functional defects and cosmetic changes are uncovered early by the on-site customer.

Yes, software development is risky, but with XP we have a structured environment where we can expose and deal with issues before we have another project disaster on our hands.

Improving Quality with XP

XP is very strong at producing high-quality software. What is quality? Quality is ultimately subjective and depends on the situation. A high-quality medical software product has a completely different set of expectations and requirements from, say, a consumer-marketed software game. To define what quality is we need to think of it from each stakeholder's point of view. Table 3.3 lists the common stakeholders with a software product and their definition of quality.

TABLE 3.3   Stakeholder Definitions of Quality

Stakeholder	Definition of Quality
User	The person who directly interacts with the software product. As the end user of the product he has concerns about functionality, robustness, performance, usability, and reliability. They need their application to ease their workload and can be trusted to operate consistently.
Customer	The person or department that purchases the software (these are often NOT users). They might be the project owners and define the functional requirements of the system. They are not concerned about usability and to a lesser extent, performance. Customers consider costs, supportability, availability, and manageability.
Investor	Investors in a product development scenario and those stakeholders that fund the complete product cycle. They are concerned about service costs (the overheads required to support the product) and intellectual property. They expected that the software might be reusable or perhaps form the start of a new product line. Their vision is more long term than other stakeholders.
Developer	Developer includes all those people actively involved in the core software development of the product. They are concerned with defect rates, conformance to internal standards, performance, and technical quality.

Quality, then, is in the eye of the beholder and means different things to each stakeholder. There are, however, some key attributes that we can use to explain quality. Table 3.4 lists some of these quality attributes and details about how XP enables quality.

TABLE 3.4   Attributes of Quality Showing How XP Enables Quality

Attribute	Description	XP Practice(s)
Usability	The ease of use of the system from the end user's point of view	On-site customer
Scalability	The capability of the software to handle increasing capacity (users, amount of data, and so on)	Testing Continuous Integration
Availability	The percentage of time the system is available for use by the users	Simple Design Refactoring Testing
Maintainability	The measure of how economic the costs of repairing defects is	Testing Collective Ownership Code Standards Pair Programming
Supportability	How easy the system is to upgrade or patch while running	Simple Design Testing Continuous Integration
Functionality	How close the system's features meet the customer's requirements	On-site customer User stories Metaphor
Extendibility	The ease at which new features can be added to the system	Simple Design Small Releases Continuous Integration
Mean Time Between Failure (MTBF)	A measure of system reliability— the average time between failures	Testing Collective Ownership Code Standards Pair Programming

Users of XP achieve quality software products (covering all the aspects of quality) with the combination of its 12 practices.

Managing Change with XP

We've seen how projects spiral out of control. Huge budget blowouts such as the DIA baggage system are all too common. Studies by software measurement experts such as Quantitative Software Management (QSM) show that costs associated with development grow over the life of the project. Figure 3.2 illustrates the costs of development.

FIGURE 3.2

The rising cost of development.

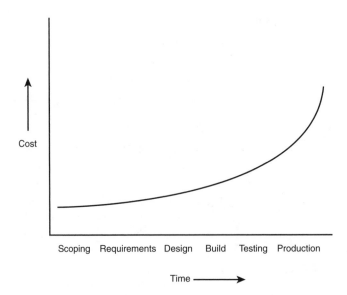

See Q&A section at the end of this chapter for more resources on software quality.

The simple correlation between time and cost explains why software projects spend so much time in up-front planning. Measurements taken by QSM prove a definite link between time spent in careful planning and requirements gathering up-front and lower costs. When development starts the burn-rate of the project accelerates and costs can sky rocket. This explains why Waterfall approaches effectively tie the hands of the customer *before* work begins. Without sign off and fixed scope, the customer could request changes during development, and change at this stage is costly and difficult. This makes perfect sense as changing requirements *before* construction involves changing documents; no real work has been done yet!

Contrary to what you might expect, spending more time in development does not always lower the defect rate. In fact, there is an optimal time to spend; you need a fine balance between time and quality. See *Applied Software Measurement* by Capers Jones (1991) for more on this.

XP offers a completely different paradigm: What if the cost of change could be flattened? What if the cost to change your software project was the same during construction as that during requirements gathering? This is exactly what XP does! Before explaining how this happens let's consider what the implications of leveling out the cost of change. Figure 3.3 shows how XP equalizes the cost of change.

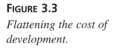

FIGURE 3.3

Flattening the cost of development.

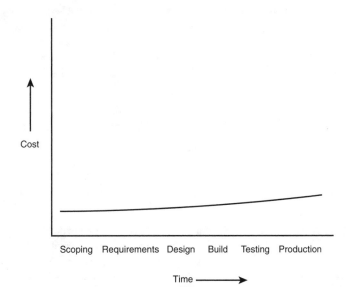

3

If the cost of change could be leveled, the need to specify exact requirements would be removed. The development team could leave some questions unanswered and begin construction based on what is known *now*. Also, we'd no longer feel obliged to demand that the customer "crystal ball gaze" about their possible future requirements. The project would be more like a journey whose final destination is not known. If the customer is directing with the team quickly delivering business value for feedback, it can work.

To summarize, XP accepts change and seeks to flatten the cost of change over the life of the project. This way you can postpone decisions until later, when they may or may not be required. Table 3.5 lists some key ways XP levels your cost of change.

TABLE 3.5   XP Cost Flattening Practices

Practices	Approach
Objects	Using object-oriented programming techniques means developers are able to simplify code with data hiding, abstraction, and other features.
Message-based protocols	Message-based protocols enable the development of systems that decouple your systems from those you interface with. You can effectively draw a line in the sand separating your development from the outside. Emerging standards, such as XML, are frequently used as a soft, yet robust, interface.
Simple design	Building and developing only those features required by the customer is rooted in the idea that simplicity is best. Automated testing and object-based tools enable simple design.
Automated testing	The automated test harness is a constantly growing framework of tests that run against the system. The tests were written before the code and are executed returning hard defect metrics. Developers can change code with courage, as their test suite will quickly report on code quality.
Refactoring	Simplifying code is second nature to XP developers as they refactor existing code and have consistent practice with redevelopment. Rather than be tentative about replacing a poor performing module or class, they have an attitude that expects change.

These practices will not on their own be a *guarantee* that development costs can be flattened, but they do allow a new style of high-speed, confident development to occur. In reality, XP practices and standard software development best practices work *together* to maintain a level development cost throughout the life of your software product.

Summary

How does XP overcome software development problems? By the working together of all the 12 XP practices, the sum of these is greater than their individual capabilities. Synergy of practices enables a new way of thinking about risk, change, and quality. Development can begin with confidence, and the results clearly seen by the entire team. Now we are ready to learn about the XP lifecycle and how it works in action.

Q&A

Q **Reading about project runaways and failures seems to imply that tighter project management with more control would reduce risk. Is this the case?**

A More aware project management is always a good thing, and you can draw the conclusion that *control* is a key to success. The problem with this is that control only works when you know exactly *what* is required and *how* to solve it. The mindset is that we never know exactly where the development path will take us. With this in mind we need a more flexible—not more rigid—approach. Not that XP is formless or uncontrolled, the business control is placed firmly back with the customer, and developers are left to use automated, smart ways of doing their work. In that sense, XP is more controlled (in a software-engineering sense) than a Waterfall approach.

Q **What are some good resources for further study on quality, project management, and risk?**

A Quantitative Software Management (`http://www.qsm.com`) has some excellent studies on software metrics. Software Testing Quality and Engineering (`http://www.stqemagazine.com`) is probably the most accessible journal covering these issues. For general project-management topics try `http://www.gantthead.com`. InformIT has a broad ranging library of software engineering articles at `http://www.informit.com`.

Q **Surely allowing the scope to change would result in scope-creep and projects running wild?**

A The key word is *change*; the scope can be altered, but the amount of work the team can do remains the same. This means that if the customer wants to add some new functionality, they can, but they have to remove another feature of similar effort. This assumes the team size remains the same; it is possible that more resources can increase the team's throughput. This kind of thinking can be a slippery slope. There is a real limit to how your team can grow and yet maintain output.

Q **Will XP solve all the project risks and challenges covered in this hour?**

A Using all XP practices together can either mitigate or eliminate all the risks we've covered in this hour. It's not a silver bullet; personnel issues, contractual problems, and technical problems can still derail your project. But with XP you're quickly getting working software into the hands of the customer; this gives you a huge advantage over other non-Agile methodologies.

3

Workshop

This workshop tests whether you understand all the concepts you learned today. It is very helpful to know and understand the answers before starting tomorrow's lesson.

Quiz

1. What variable does XP use to control the project?

2. How does XP handle the risk of schedule slippage?

    a. Enables the customer to change deadlines as the need arises.

    b. Deadlines are not managed in the normal way, so this is not an issue.

    c. Development continues with small releases to the customer; therefore, any change is exposed quickly.

    d. By use of the XP practices of Pair Programming and refactoring.

3. What is the effect of flattening the cost of development?

Answers

1. Scope. The cost, quality, and time are fixed allowing scope to change.

2. c.

3. Decisions can be postponed until they are needed. Development can begin quickly and developers can work at top-speed.

Activity

1. Review one of the project failures covered in this hour and investigate how XP practices might have been applied. Consider whether using XP would have averted, or at least mitigated, the failure.

PART II

Understanding XP in Action

Hour

HOUR 4

The XP Development Lifecycle

In the previous hour, we explored how XP overcomes the common problems associated with software development. You learned how using XP practices together is one of the keys to solving these problems. The focus of this hour will be gaining an understanding of how the overall XP process works.

In this hour you will learn

- What the XP project lifecycle looks like
- How customers define business value and direct the project
- How customers and developers collaborate in defining the system
- How to separate the software into releases and iterations
- How development occurs during the iteration
- How to deploy your software with XP
- How ongoing maintenance is handled on an XP project

Overview of an XP Project Lifecycle

In XP the foundational premise is that the customer and developer should work *together* to produce software that has real value. The customer directs the development team on how to deliver the business value throughout the lifecycle of an XP project. The customer is actively involved during the life of the project. In the last hour we learned how change and uncertainty are accepted on a XP project; we expect change to happen. Figure 4.1 demonstrates how the XP cycle is a process of continuously defining and building value.

FIGURE 4.1

XP customers define value; developers build and deliver value.

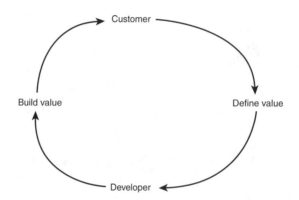

At the one level it could be said there is nothing new here. All development is about customers defining value, and the developers delivering value. The difference with XP is that this loop happens very quickly. The team is building a small piece of functionality every few minutes, hours, or days. This enables the customer to drive the project with adjustments and corrections. (Waterfall approaches would result in the customer waiting for months or years before value was actually delivered). Table 4.1 outlines the XP lifecycle:

TABLE 4.1   The Phases of XP

Phase	Description
Exploration	Project inception, high-level user requirements, technical prototyping
Planning	Prioritization of work, breakdown into releases, and first plan
Iterations	Testing and development of the system. Includes iteration planning where low-level work breakdown occurs. End users may work here at refining interface, ensuring usability.
Productionizing	Deployment of software into the customer's production environment.
Maintenance	Ongoing maintenance, patches, and enhancements.

Broadly speaking, XP projects involve breaking down the customer's product vision into releases and then segmenting those releases into iterations. Planning is seen as an evolving process that's refined and tuned over the life of the project. Figure 4.2 shows how this works.

FIGURE 4.2

XP releases are made out of iterations.

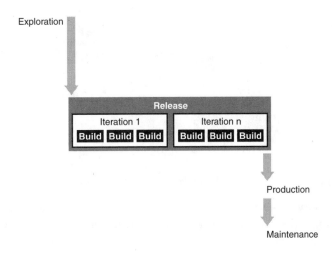

During the iteration there are multiple *builds*, which occur regularly during the day as the team integrates new code. The number of builds is dependent on the type of technology used and the development style the team adopts. What is the main difference between the release and iteration? The release is where the team hands working software over to the customer, whereas the iteration has an internal focus. It enables the on-site customer and developers to measure and adjust progress.

NEW TERM *Build* is the process by which the components of a system are integrated into a whole for testing.

Figure 4.3 illustrates the iterative nature of an XP project.

After exploration, the team begins a cycle of release planning and continuing iterations until the software is deemed complete and ready for production. Production or release is where the complete software is moved into a live or working environment. Production is important because it means the business can start to get some real value from their new software. Another facet of productionizing your software is that the costs associated with failure are much higher; this explains the care most customers take to cover final acceptance testing.

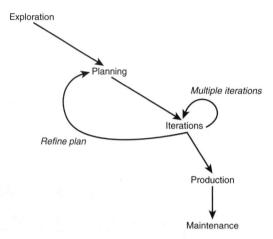

FIGURE 4.3
The XP project life-cycle.

Exploring User Requirements

Exploration is where discovery of the system vision and mission occurs. At this stage of the project the customer is charged with coming up with a vision statement. This vision statement should be around 20–30 words in length and leads into development of the system metaphor. Customers and developers work together in this phase, exploring technical options, defining requirements, and completing a list of *user stories*.

NEW TERM   A *vision statement* is a high-level statement that describes the goal of the system. For example, the purpose of this new system is to sell books via the Internet.

NEW TERM   The *system metaphor* is how the team conceptualizes the system and is typically written in language that is relevant to the business domain. For example, the system is like a virtual bookstore where customers (users) can come in and browse, search, or buy books.

NEW TERM   A *user story* is the tool that captures user requirements. User stories are similar to use cases and are written by the customer in nontechnical language. Most user stories are around 3–4 sentences long.

Writing User Stories

In this inception phase, the customer develops primary high-level user stories, and developers estimate time to implement. There's an implicit understanding that any estimates at this stage are rough and will be refined at the iteration level as the project progresses. In some cases, developers *spike* solutions (spend time prototyping and researching technical issues) to get a more accurate estimation figure. Technology specialists or consultants might be used to validate high-level approaches, and they can also help in spiking. The concept of spiking is a simple, yet powerful tool in aiding the team to both understand effort and the typical development approach they will take. Sometimes the technical team will separate into a number of pairs, each of which will investigate a particular technical option.

 NEW TERM *Spike* is exploring effort by developing prototype code. Spiking is not spending time on general technical research; it has a specific goal in mind.

At the end of the spike the code is thrown away, leaving the development team with a common understanding of the way forward. The length of a spike can be measured in hours, but more commonly is a matter of days. As work progresses developers may "down tools" during development to spike difficult technical problems, this is an exception rather than on a regular basis.

> The code generated during a spike is often thrown away because the quality is not good enough to reuse. When spending time with the spike, developers are focused on writing code as a research mechanism not detailed design.

Estimating and Discovering

The exploration phase is mostly about discovery. Customers discover what they want, and developers discover their probable approach and estimates. As developers are spiking solutions, they are also estimating and tracking. This works simply by developers estimating the time to complete their spike tasks; they execute the spike and compare it to their estimate. This way the exploration phase has the added benefit of allowing the team to fine-tune its estimation skills. These skills will be vital when iteration planning starts.

Spiking in the Real World

I came across the need to spike a solution the other day. We were developing a data warehouse and needed to load large amounts of data from raw text files into our database. My pair programming partner and I spent a few minutes at the whiteboard designing a possible solution. At first we needed to understand whether the technical solution was realistic, and then from this estimate, the time to complete our task.

We soon realized we had two options, one using built in database-specific loading tools, and the other low-level custom development. We took a fixed period of time (less than an hour) to quickly build a working model that could at least answer the question "will our custom loader work?"

4

By the end of our spike we knew exactly what direction to take with the development. As a bonus we discovered that we had network issues that would more than likely affect the main loader.

 The exploration phase can be compared to the development of a business case and project charter. However, in XP, developers undertake actual programming work as they spike solutions. This is not the case in a classic development project.

The length of the exploration depends on the nature of the project and the technologies at play. The need to spend time spiking is reduced if the development team uses familiar tools and techniques. The total length of the phase then might be either a few weeks or months depending on scope and requirements.

The output of exploration will be the system metaphor and the first list of user stories. The team now knows roughly what is required, how they will do it, and where they are going. This is likely to change as work progresses, which is why you have selected XP!

Creating the Project Plan

Planning is a short phase in which customers and developers agree on features for the first release. Features (user stories) are delivered in a way that makes both business and technical sense. Table 4.2 lists the responsibilities of customers and developers during the planning stage.

TABLE 4.2   The Responsibilities During the Planning Stage

Role	Responsibilities
Customer	Defines user stories
	Decides what business value the stories have
	Decides what stories to build in the release
Developer	Estimates how long each story will take to build
	Warns the customer of technical risks
	Measures the development team's progress

Table 4.2 was adapted from *Planning Extreme Programming* (2001) Kent Beck and Martin Fowler.

Planning involves give and take between customer and developer, but there is a balance between technical feasibility and business value. Developers might generate their own "zero business value" user stories for the infrastructure work that supports the core system. An example of this would be the establishment of test and build environments. Doing this ensures that all the work the team is doing is estimated and tracked.

The XP practice "Planning Game" is the primary tool used for planning. The Planning Game involves customers and programmers working through user stories, estimating, and prioritizing.

Calling the XP planning practice the *planning game* can be problematic to management. Is XP all fun and games? Some large consulting firms shy away from the use of some XP descriptors such as this and rename them according to their own internal conventions. Issues such as this will be covered in Hour 18, "Implementing XP in Your Organization."

The Planning Game is an event that is informal, lightweight, and pragmatic. User requirements are written on index cards and are handled/discussed during the session. XP encourages the use of index cards for both user stories and planning. The use of index cards is not mandatory and the team might choose to use other software-based collaboration tools.

Some XP users take the middle ground and write stories using a word processor, and then print them out. The problem with this is that handling sheets of paper during the Planning Game is cumbersome.

The output of this phase is a release schedule—not a work breakdown structure. The customers and developers now have a common understanding of what the release will contain. The next step is to plan individual iterations.

Dividing Releases into Iterations

The release is reduced to a number of iterations with a typical length of one to four weeks. The initial iteration focuses on the architecture components required providing a baseline system. This can be called a "zero business value" iteration because the user stories are more likely purely technical and have no direct business benefit to the customer.

Subsequent iterations should deliver business value that continues to grow over time. The customer picks the stories they want, and developers complete the build. The "customer can change her mind" approach can be frustrating to developers. The only consolation is that the iteration is time boxed. *Time boxing* means that the scope doesn't change—just the user stories being developed. The customer is unable to change user stories during the iteration. The point is that the length of the cycle is so short that the risk or possibility of change is less.

NEW TERM   *Time boxing* is a technique for planning and controlling software development projects. Each timebox has a fixed duration, typically one to four weeks. The central principle in timeboxing is that the delivery date is not moveable—some work product must be delivered on the appointed date.

The Iteration Process

The iteration is where the real work of development happens. At the start of the iteration a planning meeting is called to enable the team to break down work into programming tasks. The customer selects user stories from the overall release plan, placing priority on those with the highest business value. Failed acceptance tests from the previous iteration will also be selected. Figure 4.4 shows the process inside a iteration.

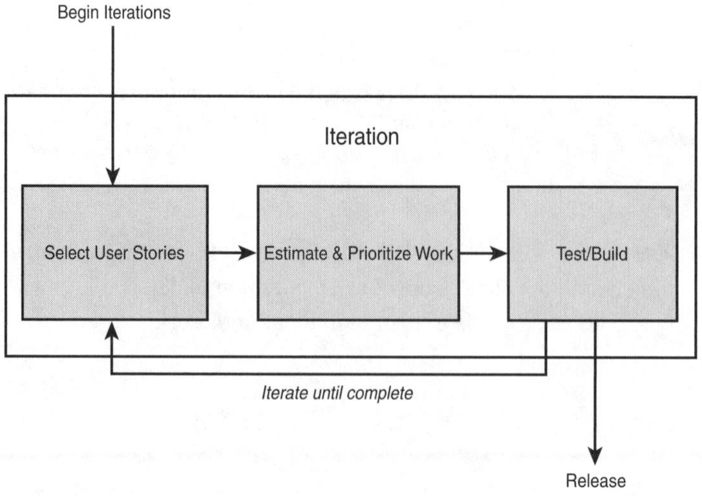

FIGURE 4.4
The XP iteration life-cycle.

Begin Iterations

Iteration

Select User Stories → Estimate & Prioritize Work → Test/Build

Iterate until complete

Release

The customer can opt to perform usability testing as work progress, which is particularly important in the cases where the software product is consumer facing. In the case of a public Web site the interface must cater to varying user skill and experience levels. Leaving usability until the release point is not as effective as building in usability as development continues. There are no hard and fast rules on how to manage your interface development while working in small iterations. You might decide that a full-time user group is warranted. Be warned however that they will quickly become expert users and this could reduce their value as "generic users."

User stories are generally too high-level to execute as programming tasks, so the next step is to break out the actual development tasks needed to support the story. Developers work together to investigate the tasks that they will need to execute. The tasks are written either on the back of the story, on separate task cards, or on some other tracking mechanism. In Hour 10, "Gathering Requirements with User Stories," we give some examples of user stories.

The typical length for a task is around one to three ideal programming days in duration. Ideal programming days are how long it would take you to complete the task if there were no distractions. Longer tasks need to be further broken down into smaller units.

We will cover measurement techniques used to estimate work and throughput in later chapters. There are numerous ways of measuring effort; the important thing is that the metric you use is tracked and repeatable.

Developers sign up for the tasks, and then estimate how long their own tasks will take to complete. As with estimation in general the best practice is for the developers who *estimate* the work to actually *do* the work.

Measuring Throughput

XP measures throughput (the amount work the team is completing over time) by *velocity*. The reality is that estimates will be inaccurate during iteration zero. This is because the team is new; clarity around requirements might be missing and toolsets are being bedded down. Both customer and developers should recognize this at the outset. The key is to track actual output against our estimates, and then we can begin refining the accuracy of future estimates.

As development progresses, the team is working in pairs on tasks that are linked back to user stories. The programming pair marks the task as complete on the central planning wall. See Hour 13, "Using XP Development Tools," for an example of using a planning wall. Daily standing meetings are used as forums to quickly expose issues and get status on the whole team's progress. Outsiders from the wider customer or development teams might make guest appearances at these meetings. They quickly get a sense of where the project is at and how well the team is working together.

Developing and Testing

Developers begin work on a new task by writing the test first and adding it to their test framework. Programming continues in pairs with each partner taking turns to "drive" the keyboard from time to time. As classes or components are completed they are added to the integration machine. The integration machine is a workstation that has been designated solely for build or integration work. During the iteration, the developers are using continuous integration supported by automated build frameworks.

At the end of the iteration, customers perform the acceptance tests they've written. Any user stories that fail acceptance will be fixed during the next iteration.

Deploying Software into Production

At the end of the release, the product is verified and certified for deployment into the customer production environment. This is also the point where a usability expert would assemble sample users to conduct acceptance testing on the latest build. Testing on real users ensures that the flow of the interface supports users in accomplishing their tasks. Any issues discovered that hinder user productivity must be reconciled and mean the build is not yet complete.

This phase might involve some system or application tuning, depending on the target environment. Tuning can be executed in the *staging environment*, assuming that it mirrors production. (Customers normally refuse developer access to production code, anyway.) The goal is not to continue functional evolution, but to stabilize the system.

NEW TERM *Staging environment* is the customer's software environment that mirrors, or replicates, their live environment. Staging is used to perform final prerelease tests and performance checks. Software development will typically have these environments: development, test, staging, and production. Neglecting to establish separate environments leads to chaos at deployment and maintenance times.

In theory, any system developed using XP can be deployed into production as early as the first iteration. (Iteration one might be a purely technical phase where the team establishes the base system.) The customer will select the deployment iteration depending on business value and external factors, such as data migration or legacy system integration.

The timing of deployment will likely be dependent on external constrains, not the team's ability to produce software quickly enough.

The deployment approach requires a degree of planning and risk management as the development team is now entering the customer's production environment. In productionizing your system you need to be aware that operations staff will require deployment guides or other supporting documentation. Any documentation the development team writes will be in keeping with the lightweight approach of XP; it should be enough, but no more.

Whether big bang or phased migration is used for deployment is a decision that should be made by all the relevant stakeholders: developers, customers, operations, and users. Table 4.3 compares these approaches.

TABLE 4.3 Comparing Deployment Approaches

Approach	Description
Big Bang	Single cutover after system completion. This approach is used when an existing system is being replaced and managing a transition period is too complex or expensive. Deployment is simpler, but the risks are higher and failures can be critical.
Phased	The new system is rolled out in discrete pieces of functionality. This works well where the system can be logically divided into sections. Rolling out the system over a prolonged period can lower risk, but it does expose the business to longer-term upheaval.
Parallel	This involves running both the new and existing systems side by side for a period of time. The high cost associated with multiple data entry and reporting tends to outweigh the risk reduction aspects of this approach.
Green field	The system is deployed into an environment where no system exists. This could be a startup or a new business line that now has supporting software products. This is the ideal scenario for deployment because the risks are lower and integration issues with other systems are minimal.

NEW TERM *Big Bang* is deploying a system using a single cutover or go-live event.

Maintaining the System After Release

After the deployment your system enters an ongoing status of maintenance. With XP you've been used to constantly evolving, refactoring, and refining the system. The ability to patch or upgrade the system is aided by your established and verified automated test platform. This means you can go ahead and freely make changes to code with confidence.

Deployment requires more care now that you are dealing with a production system. You will need to create data migration and system patching strategies. There will be an impact on development team output as developers juggle their time between production support and new work. This is a fact of life, so rather than ignoring this less-than-ideal state, the team will record and measure their new throughput. Estimates for the next or current iteration will be adjusted accordingly.

Summary

Over the last hour you've learned how XP tackles planning, development, and rollout. The project starts with a period of mutual discovery and research between the developers and the customer. It's clear that the customer defines and describes business value (what's important), whereas developers estimate and complete the work required to deliver this value. The project is divided into short periods of activity called iterations, which is where developers write tests and code; it's also the place where usability testing may occur. The XP lifecycle is very resilient to change, enabling the customer to make course corrections, as required.

In the next hour we will learn about the roles on an XP project and the responsibilities throughout the lifecycle.

Q&A

Q Where is the customer sign off in the XP lifecycle?

A XP does not need formal sign off on requirements to be effective because it requires the customer and developers to agree on the requirements during planning. The customer does get to verify/certify the XP team's output when doing acceptance testing.

Q We are already developing with another non-XP approach. Can we transition to XP midstream?

A Yes. The ease of transition depends on numerous factors, including current project status, toolset, customer relationship, and type of project. Changing midstream would tend to imply that your project is in trouble or the time taken to learn XP is offset against your expected gains.

Q Where is the design stage in XP?

A Design is an ongoing process not a once-in-a-project event. All developers are designing as the project moves forward.

Q Is the customer a single person?

A Not always. The single person view is simplistic and is used here to aid in understanding the lifecycle. More frequently, you'd expect to find that the customer is actually a group of individuals for each relevant business area.

Q To what extent do XP developers interface with end users to determine usability and acceptance?

A The development team should communicate and learn from end users as they work on their user stories. Corporate branding of your Web site poses real challenges. You can't expect the marketing department to evolve their graphic design as development continues. Branding might be a case where up-front should occur before developers start work. There's no reason why the team can't use XP planning techniques in this up-front piece as they work through graphic design issues. As with any Web integration work, there will be some give and take of visual design and page structure when developers start work. Some design elements are easy in PhotoShop, but not so easy to code!

Workshop

This workshop tests whether you understand all the concepts you learned in this hour. It is very helpful to know and understand the answers before starting the next hour's lesson.

Quiz

1. What practice does XP use to enable project planning?

2. Why have a "zero business value" iteration in your project?

3. How do developers work on user stories?

   a. The work is estimated by the technical lead who assigns work.

   b. Each pair is assigned work at the iteration-planning meeting.

   c. The user stories are broken into tasks; developers estimate the tasks and work on them in pairs.

   d. The project manager tracks throughput and assigns work based on developer performance.

4. Why measure development team throughput?

   a. Developers use the information for billing purposes.

   b. We need to understand how many user stories can be completed within the iteration.

   c. The information is used to help refine future estimates.

   d. Customers use throughput to measure how close the project is to completion.

Answers

1. The Planning Game

2. To enable the development team to build any underlying infrastructure

3. c.

4. b. and c.

Activities

1. Compare and contrast the attitudes of customers and developers in XP versus Waterfall development.

2. Consider the importance of human, relational aspects of development under XP. Are these factors more important in XP than in other methodologies and if so, why?

Hour 5

Understanding XP Team Roles

In the last hour we discovered what the XP project lifecycle looks like. We saw how customers and developers worked together to build software. Now we need to get a firm grip on how the roles work during the XP lifecycle. In this hour we'll go further into the roles found in an XP project. You will learn

- How collaboration works in an XP project
- How XP develops software using the "one team" concept
- The rights and responsibilities for roles
- What the core XP roles are
- What the secondary XP roles are

How XP Roles Work Together

Most software-development methodologies list the described roles of participants on the project. Often these are quite static and can denote status or importance; for example, "project manager," "program manager," or "solution architect" carry some serious weight. XP sheds these lofty titles and instead relies on the synergy between team roles to create success. Roles are not frozen or set in concrete; you could be a "developer" one moment, and the "tracker" the next. Getting the job done and building what the customer wants is where the team is headed. XP works, in part, by collaboration between the team members. Let's make a start at understanding why effective collaboration is so crucial to the success of the project.

The Importance of Collaboration

Software development is never an individual pursuit. At the very least there is one customer and one developer, and how they work together will ultimately determine the success of the project. XP, with its reliance on values and principles leans more on people than process to achieve excellence. In their book *The Wisdom of Teams*, Katzenbach and Smith define a team as "a small number of people with complementary skills who are committed to a common purpose, performance goals, and approach for which they hold themselves mutually accountable." Steve McConnell, in his book *Rapid Development,* specifies the characteristics of a hyperproductive team:

- a shared, elevating vision or goal
- a sense of team identity
- a results-driven structure
- competent team members
- a commitment to the team
- mutual trust
- interdependence among team members
- effective communication
- a sense of autonomy
- a sense of empowerment
- small team size
- a high level of enjoyment

Reading through this list we can draw parallels between the characteristics of XP and hyperproductive teams. The sense of teamwork, autonomy, and empowerment are all significant factors in making XP projects a success.

What is collaboration? One definition for collaboration is a *purposive relationship*, which involves individuals coming together to solve, create, or discover something. James Watson (Nobel Prize winner and codiscoverer of the double helix) once said, "Nothing new that is really interesting comes without collaboration." If your desire is to build software of excellence, quality, and reliability, you need to value the importance of collaboration. Stephen Covey describes, in his book *The Seven Habits of Highly Effective People*, how rather than seeing personal differences in terms of *yours* or *mine*, we can *synergize* and thereby create a third option. The synergy mindset in your project will break down walls between customer and developer, allowing the creation of world-class software.

The book *No More Teams! Mastering the Dynamics of Creative Collaboration*, by Michael Schrage is an excellent resource for further study into collaboration.

True collaboration comes when the team "jells" as a unit. What does it mean to jell? A team that jells is strongly knit together both relationally and goal-wise. Productivity with the jelled team exceeds that of the team that is held together by mere process rules. One thing is for certain: You know when you *don't* have jell!

Solving Problems as One Team

At the heart of XP is the belief that people are more important than process. XP does outline a process we can follow, but it's the empowerment of individuals, guided by practices, that maximizes results. We learned during the previous hour how the XP project moves along from exploration, planning, development, and release. In planning we saw how the roles of customer and developer are clearly defined. Broadly speaking, customers define what requirements have value, and developers build that value.

At first, XP described how a single customer interacted with the development team to create the solution. In reality, this is seldom, if ever, the case. The single customer view is possible in the case where the business domain is narrow or the customer representative has expert knowledge. Figure 5.1 illustrates this model.

The obvious advantages to considering this method of development are the number of interactions are reduced and decision-making is simplified. A problem with the two teams, however, is that there are more roles than just developer and customer in software development. We have designers, testers, modelers, information architects, users, and so on. A more accurate view is to think of two groups within the one team. Figure 5.2 illustrates this.

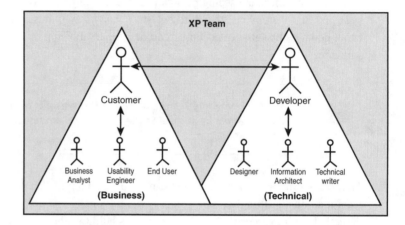

Working together as one team implies an open relationship between business and technical sides that enables collaboration. A customer that insists on signoff and manages the team strictly to the terms of the contract rather than its intent or spirit, probably won't work well inside a collaborative environment.

Table 5.1 breaks out the core roles on an XP project into the two groups.

TABLE 5.1   XP Roles and Responsibilities

Group	Role	Responsibilities
Business	Customer	Funding, direction, business lead
	Manager	Schedules meetings, interfaces with customer and management on project, clears road blocks for the team, ensures meeting process is followed
Technical	Developer/programmer	Estimates stories, defines engineering tasks, implements stories (writes code and unit tests)
	Tracker	Tracks project progress, initiates actions if tracking problems occur, gathers metrics
	Coach	Ensures XP is being followed, mentors, leads technical team, lends help where required

Rights and Responsibilities

Extreme Programming is a simplifying process that boils software development down to the basics. What do we really need to do? The rules of engagement for our XP project can be expressed as a series of *rights*. These rights are crucial to enabling software development to be successful. Interestingly enough, during any project team members have unspoken expectations of how they believe the project will run and what requirements will be placed on them. Expressing these expectations gets these feelings, hopes, and desires out on the table. Rights go hand in hand with responsibilities. Lists of the customer's and developer's Bill of Rights follow.

Customer's Bill of Rights

1. You have the right to an overall plan, and to know what can be accomplished, when, and at what cost.

2. You have the right get the most value out of every programming week.

3. You have right to see the progress in a running system, proven to work by passing repeatable tests that you specify.

4. You have the right to change your mind, to substitute functionality, and to change priorities without paying exorbitant costs.

5. You have the right to be informed of schedule changes in time to choose how to reduce scope to restore the original date. You can cancel at any time and be left with a useful working system that reflects investment to date.

Developer's Bill of Rights

1. You have the right to know what is needed, with clear declarations of priority.

2. You have the right to produce quality work at all times.

3. You have the right to ask for and receive help from peers, superiors, from other experts and customers.

4. You have the right to make and update your own estimates.

5. You have the right to accept your responsibilities instead of having them assigned to you.

These rights were adapted from *Extreme Programming Installed*, by Ron Jefferies, Ann Anderson, and Chet Hendrickson. The Wiki Wiki starting point for rights can be found at http://www.c2.com/cgi/wiki?CustomerBillOfRights and http://www.c2.com/cgi/wiki?DeveloperBillOfRights.

5

The rights listed here aren't set in stone, and you will naturally evolve your own. Whatever rights are defined, you can be sure that agreement and acceptance of them will smooth teamwork and defuse arguments.

Now, let's look at the core roles in XP.

Customer

The customer defines what our project is, the business value, and our direction as we move through the project. In actuality, this is not a single role or person; we use the term "customer" throughout this book to cover the people who

- Define business value
- Write user stories
- Write or specify acceptance tests
- Might be the end-user of the system

The customer will have expert knowledge of existing business process and issues and will give clarity on what problems the new system is resolving. Their level of technical skill is less critical than their business background and knowledge. Our "customer" can wear many hats during the XP project. Table 5.2 lists some of these additional or secondary customer roles.

TABLE 5.2   Additional Customer Roles

Role	Description
User	End user, usability testing, workflow design, and functional testing.
Acceptor	Users from the customer who run acceptance tests.
Gold Donor	Has first-hand experience of the system and is able to clarify issues for the technical team. They will often be the users who will benefit when the new system is implemented. Sometimes this role is also known as the *Storyteller*.
Gold Owner	The primary source of funding for the project who provides the resources required to complete it. Classic project management usually refers to this person as the project *owner* or *sponsor*.
Planner	Planners work at defining, specifying, and managing deployment of the system into production. They typically have a firm grasp of wider business impacts, including product release cycles and marketing. They will sometimes manage deployment slippage.

The book *A Practical Guide to eXtreme Programming* by David Astels, Granville Miller, and Miroslav Novak has a very good section on roles within XP. The Wiki Wiki starting point for roles can be found at `http://www.c2.com/cgi/wiki?ExtremeRoles`.

Coaching XP Teams

XP introduces the concept of a *coach* who is the primary facilitator of communication in the team. The coach knows where the team is going, not in an absolute sense, but in a way that asks the question: Are we still doing XP? Doing XP means expressing its values and using its practices.

The coach needs to have excellent soft skills and technical astuteness because she leads refactoring efforts at both a design and method level. From time to time she might be called on to pair program, providing a mentoring role.

No member of the team needs to demonstrate total commitment to guarantee project success as much as the coach. Not to be confused with a classic project manager, the coach must be technical and relevant to the team she leads. There is no room for the coach to hide behind a wall of project plans and documentation. If you're the coach you need to be attuned to object-oriented techniques, patterns, and the dynamics of XP development. The following lists, in no particular order, some of attributes required of the coach.

- Strong understanding of XP
- Awareness of broader development and process techniques
- Confidence
- Leadership
- Sense of humor
- Ability to balance the perspectives of both a long-term vision for the project with the short-term problems of the here and now
- Problem solving
- Mentoring
- Integrity
- Balance
- Object-oriented background (very useful)
- Relevant language experience (Java, Smalltalk, C++, and so on)

5

A new approach as radical as XP can raise some upper-management eyebrows. With this in mind, the coach might also need to explain the approach and be ready to demonstrate its value. As we've found in our study of XP, *value* is easy to measure: Customers get the functionality they want, when they want it. That's value!

In smaller or new implementations of XP the role of coach and manager sometimes become blurred. The role of the coach is more in charge of clearing *XP* roadblocks, whereas the manager is removing *project* obstacles. The acquisition of equipment and workstations falls into the realm of coach. The coach is concerned with the team: Are they doing XP? Doing XP in this context refers to following the 12 core practices. Think of the difference between the coach and manager in a sports team where the manager negotiates the business end and, while on the field of play, the coach is king. Whether you are a coach or a manager is fundamentally less important than whether you have individuals who are guiding the team in development (play), and others who establish the basis for success (resources). XPers don't let titles such as coach siderack them from completing user stories and delivering value.

Who do you call when you're sick? Same as you've always done; the office manager and the on-site lead or senior team member.

Developer

What do Extreme programmers look like? Extreme programmers have stripped away anything that hinders the development of *code*. Program code is how developers deliver the customer's user story and XP enables the technical team to focus on just that. Developers on XP projects have to do the following:

- Estimate user stories
- Perform spikes where necessary
- Write unit tests (using test frameworks)
- Write code
- Participate in planning meetings
- Participate in daily standing meetings

The Daily Routine

The developers are the engine room of your XP project and manage to squeeze a great deal of activity into their busy days. It will be useful to gain some insight into what a typical day consists of for the average developer during the iteration. Figure 5.3 gives you an idea of the daily routine.

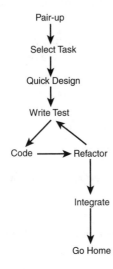

FIGURE 5.3
An XP developer's daily routine.

These daily developer tasks are during actual development and don't include planning meetings.

The diagram has simplified the process somewhat by removing the many points of communication between developers and other team members. The most notable communication is the clarification and feedback that the programming pair will seek from the customer. Table 5.3 helps explain what these activities mean.

5

TABLE 5.3 The XP Developers Daily Tasks

Activity	Description
Pair-up	Developers work in pairs, sharing each workstation. Your pair might already be established if you're still working on a task, otherwise you'll need to find another developer from the team to pair-up with.
Select Task	Assuming, you're not still working on a task, your pair will need to select the next engineering task to work on.
Quick Design	Design at this level means "how are we going to solve this task?"
Write Test	Begin the task by writing a test case and check that this test fails before coding. Expand your test to cover everything that could possibly break. Seek clarity from the customer team where required.

TABLE 5.3   Continued

Activity	Description
Code	Write the code to complete the task. The goal is to write only enough code to ensure the component passes your test case.
Refactor	Revisiting the code, look for areas of simplification and improvement. Stop refactoring when simplicity has been achieved.
Integrate	Add the complete component to the integration or build machine. Verify that the integrated class passes tests. If integration problems continue, discard the code and start again tomorrow.
Go Home	In keeping with the XP practice of 40-hour weeks, go home at 5 p.m.

Table 5.3 was adapted from Extreme Programming—Explored, by William C. Wake.

Mapping XP Practices to Developer Tasks

The list of developer activities is fairly succinct, as you'd expect from XP; they are directed toward pure development as opposed to process. XP practices guide developers in delivering the business value that customers want. Table 5.4 enumerates the practices that developers use.

TABLE 5.4   Practices Developers Use

Practice	Usage
Testing	Developers write tests before they code, and then add these to their test framework. These test frameworks then allow the team to automate testing tasks. Typical test tools are Junit (for Java) and VbUnit (for Visual Basic).
Refactoring	Developers consistently revisit existing code to simplify. This lowers defect counts, improves readability, evolves design, and enhances extendibility.
Pair programming	Developers share the same workstation and take turns writing code, reviewing, and thinking.
Collective ownership	In XP, all developers own the source code for the system. Pair programming and code standards help this to work. Any developer can change any code, at anytime.
Continuous integration	The system is built as each completed class or component is integrated. Automated tools can be used to sense coded changes, and then run the rebuild.
Coding standards	Coding standards and guidelines enrich the quality of the system, putting a halt to arguments during pair programming. These standards usually include style guidelines, although not mandatory, will bring a consistent approach to development work.

We will continue to interchangeably use developer and programmer. Some argue that these are distinctly different roles, but we will ignore these arguments for the purpose of learning XP.

Tester

The role of the tester is to complete functional testing, ensuring the system works as expected. The exact boundaries of the tester vary from project to project. Rather than being an external QA position with an outsider's view, he will be part of the team, probably writing tests with the customer. The good news for the tester is that with XP he is less likely to have to wade through heavy defect counts. Developers have been testing the system as code was developed.

Tracker

The role of the *tracker* is to gather metrics, such as, user stories or tasks complete, and disseminate them to the team. A tracker needs to decide what metrics are meaningful for the team; meaning, those that are the best at indicating the project's status. Information overload with "number of methods that have fewer than 10 lines of code" or the like won't add any value, and important metrics are lost in the haze. The tracker should keep the metric count low (less than five), and definitely include something about the last build status, number of stories, velocity, and so on. XP projects favor the use of simple tools, such as Post-It notes and whiteboards, for tracking purposes. Nothing precludes the use of software-based tools, such as a project Web site, and something such as the Wiki Wiki collaboration tool is ideal.

5

Using Wiki Wiki will be covered in Hour 10, "Gathering the Customer's Requirements with User Stories."

The tracker's responsibilities are clear:

1. Get metrics.
2. Make the metrics public, favoring simple tools (Post-It, whiteboards, and so on) over snazzy groupware products.
3. Check with the team to make sure that the metrics are valuable.
4. Keep the historical results.

The key aspect to remember with tracking in XP is that it ought to be unobtrusive and light. The job as tracker is not to act as the XP police, but to sift through the team's output and report on the team's progress. The role is part-time in nature, given the simple and light approach XP takes.

Manager

The manager or "big boss" is the person who champions the project both internally and to the wider customer community. A manager is concerned with clearing roadblocks for the technical team and running interference (from customer or technical management). The manager deals with the organizational obstructions that hinder the core work of the team. She is able to stay above the detail and is aligned with the team's core values. Whether the manager sits on the technical or customer team is less important than knowing that *someone* is able to lower any noise the team has to deal with. This noise might take the form of so-called mandatory procedures or internal compliances issues. The manager has the power to deflect outside interference from the team. Initially, developers might be slow to value the role of the manager. This will change when they have benefited from the manager's roadblock removal powers!

The Wiki Wiki starting point for tips on XP managers is at
`http://www.c2.com/cgi/wiki?ItManager`.

Other XP Roles

Over the last few pages we've covered the main roles found in an XP project; there are a few others that you'll read about in the XP community. We will go ahead and mention them here. Table 5.5 lists these other XP roles.

TABLE 5.5   Additional XP Roles

Role	Description
Consultant	Outside expert who gives advice on a technical issues.
Build Master	Engineer who sets-up and configures build and development environment, supplies tools and maintains overall software development environment.
Analyst	The business analyst who understands any business impacts and can provide a bridge between business and technical groups. They may assist in the creation of user stories.

TABLE 5.5 continued

Role	Description
Operator/Support	The support staff is in charge of production control, system change control, migration to live environment and IT standards compliance.
Project Manager	The project manager is the customer's project manager or program manager, covering broader aspects of the project (integration into the business, training, and so on).
Doom Sayer	The doom sayer exposes risk and is sometimes referred to as the "risk officer." Ideally, all team members should be pointed out risks to the team as they see them arise.

Summary

XP has built-in practices and roles that make collaboration work. We've seen how XP establishes rights for developers and customers, clearly defining expectations, and responsibilities up-front. XP roles are hinged around customer and developer, with the other roles supporting these two as they work together. Developer's daily work is centered on key XP practices; in the next hour we'll uncover these in depth.

Q&A

Q Does XP only work well with superstar or expert level developers?

A XP accepts both junior and senior skill sets. One common practice is to mix juniors and seniors during pair programming, which has the benefit of quality mentoring.

Q Is there any special training required before team members join the project?

A Everybody can profit from learning the XP basics before starting on the project. Holding a project induction or startup session also helps to introduce team members. Interpersonal skills are an area that any XP user would do well to brush up on.

Q Can developers write user stories?

A The ideal is that customers express requirements in their own words. Developers might have a tendency to *solve* the story while they write, but if they have strong business knowledge they might aid the customer. Failing to take the time to understand the customer's requirements might result in some key aspects being overlooked. The quality of your stories is a good measure of how this is working.

5

Q What is Wiki Wiki?

A Wiki Wiki is Web-based collaboration tool invented by Ward Cunningham
(`http://c2com/`). Numerous versions of Wiki Wiki are downloadable from the
Web, we will explain more about the tool in Hour 10, "Gathering the Customer's
Requirements with User Stories."

Workshop

This workshop tests whether you understand all the concepts you learned in this hour. It
is very helpful to know and understand the answers before starting the next hour's lesson.

Quiz

1. What kind of metrics should the tracker capture?

    a. The customer will define these

    b. Number of user stories and velocity

    c. Whatever metrics the tracker decides will indicate the project status

    d. Wiki Wiki has these built-in

2. What is the primary activity for the customer role?

    a. Help collaboration

    b. Define business value

    c. Write engineering tasks

    d. Manage the customer-side project

3. What is the coach's primary role?

    a. Manage the progress against the timeline

    b. Help customers define user stories

    c. Ensure the team is doing XP

    d. Remove organizational roadblocks

4. What is unusual about the XP developer's average day?

    a. They work a set eight hours

    b. They write the test before the code

    c. They spend a great deal of time talking to customers

    d. They choose their own work

Answers

1. c.

2. b.

3. c.

4. b.

Activities

1. Visit the Wiki Wiki Extreme Programming site at
   `http://www.c2.com/cgi/wiki?ExtremeProgramming` and begin your own journey
   of discovery.

2. Compare your existing role to those found in XP. If you're a developer, how does
   your average day compare to an XPer?

3. Create your own diagram that maps XP roles against the lifecycle.

5

Hour **6**

XP Practices in Action

In this hour we will study the 12 XP practices that you will use in your project. We will cover

- What the XP practices are
- How the practices work together
- The programming, team, and process aspects of the practices

Understanding How XP Practices Work Together

XP has 12 core practices that describe how the team will develop the system. You might notice that most of the XP practices are already in use and are recognized as software engineering best practices; what's new is using them in a concerted way. A good example of how this works is by taking a practice such as "collective ownership of code." In isolation using this practice could lead to chaos because anybody can change the system without constraints. In XP, however, pair programming, coding standards, and testing all balance collective ownership. Therefore, the weakness of a particular practice is mitigated by the other balancing practices.

The other aspect of these best practices that distinguishes XP is how they are taken to extremes. A common practice is done in a more intensive, rigorous manner, pushing the practice as far as it can go. We could separate the practices into three categories, listed in Table 6.1.

TABLE 6.1 XP Practices Separated by Category

Category	Practice
Programming	Simple design, testing, refactoring, coding standards
Team	Collective ownership, continuous integration, metaphor, coding standards, 40-hour week, pair programming, small releases
Processes	On-site customer, testing, small releases, Planning Game

Table 6.1 was adapted from Extreme Programming—Explored, by William C. Wake.

As you can see there is some crossover between the three areas. Unlike most software-development methodologies, XP has specific practices that describe how actual coding is done. Practices such as testing and pair programming offer easy-to-follow, practical guidance to developers.

XP is not just mechanical assembling of practices, but is built on values and principles. We can group our XP practices together, reflecting how they relate back the principles of XP. Table 6.2 lists the XP practices and relates them to the underlying core principles.

TABLE 6.2 The Values and Principles of XP

XP Principle	Related Practice
Fine scale feedback	Test Driven Development
	The Planning Game
	On-site Customer
	Pair Programming
Continuous process rather than batch	Continuous Integration
	Refactoring
	Small Releases
Shared understanding	Simple Design
	System Metaphor
	Collective Code Ownership
	Coding Standards
Programmer welfare	40-Hour Week

Table 6.2 was adapted from Extreme Programming Core Practices, Portland Pattern Repository. February 12, 2002, http://www.c2.com/cgi/wiki?ExtremeProgrammingCorePractices.

To summarize, the 12 XP practices work together, complementing each other. The sum of the parts is greater than the whole. Now, let's look at each practice in turn.

The Planning Game

The Planning Game enables us to quickly come up with a rough plan, and then refine it as the project continues. We could say that the Planning Game is a *meeting*, but as everyone knows—developers hate meetings! The Planning Game is a vital point of interaction between customer and developer; it's quite literally cards on the table time. The meeting takes place with the team working through a stack of index cards that contain the user stories. User requirements are written on index cards and are handled/discussed during the Planning Game. Using index cards might seem a little "Back to the Future" initially, but it is a highly effective tool. The simple utility of the cards connects customers and programmers to meet their common goal. Using index cards is by no means mandatory in the Planning Game, and you might find other tools, such as Web applications, can be effective. Whatever tools you choose, there is a clear separation of responsibilities during the Planning Game. Table 6.3 shows the responsibilities of each team member.

TABLE 6.3 Responsibilities During the Planning Game

Business	Technical
Define scope of the release	Estimate how long each user story will take
Define the order of delivery (which stories are done first)	Communicate technical impacts of implementing requirements
Set dates and times of release	Break down user stories into tasks and allocate work

Planning happens often and is done with an expectation of change. How can you start development with a rough plan? Even with our rough plan we have a more accurate picture than most because the customer and development team worked together to create it. The people who are *doing* the work are the same people that *estimated* the work. Problems and questions are dealt with early during the Planning Game, short-circuiting issues as they arise. We planned expecting change and involved the entire team in the process; therefore, we're on track to succeed! The XP practice of small releases works with planning as well. We can quickly gain feedback into how good our plan is, and if we need to adjust we can manage at a much finer level.

We will go in depth on both iteration and release planning in Hour 8, "Planning Your Software Release with XP" and Hour 9, "Developing Software in Iterations."

6

Small Releases

The only way to ensure that you're developing the software that the customer expects is to keep release cycles as short as possible. Even though the release will be small it should still deliver business value to the customer. As part of release planning, the customer works with the development team to define user stories and the order of implementation.

Another benefit to small releases is that the development team can use each release as a checkpoint where they measure estimation accuracy. During the planning stage developers estimated user stories based on their expected throughput and difficulty. We can now compare *planned* to *actual*, using these lessons learned for the next iteration.

Small release cycles are workable because we are building the most important user stories first, and our automated environment makes frequent integration painless.

How the customer defines the release is covered in depth in Hour 8, but for now we know enough to understand the value of small releases in controlling and managing.

Metaphor

When building a system for our customer, we'll be hamstrung without a common set of terms to use in communication. Sometimes the business domain is relevant enough to enable us to use the native language directly: books, orders, customers, suppliers, and so on. Pretty soon the team evolves its own form of "tribal language," which is used to describe user stories and development. A good metaphor is a powerful aid in unifying the technical and business teams.

Another reason to use metaphors is that they make technology easier to understand for the customer. There is no special training course that teaches the business team members to understand developer techno-speak. Customers are going to have to use their own words soon enough as they write user stories!

How can you start development with just a metaphor as your architectural guide? This works a few ways, the prime way being the quick feedback the technical team gives to the customer. With the short cycles we are using in XP the customer quickly gets a measurement of how well our metaphor is working. Customer involvement in your project is key to success as we discovered while looking at project failures. If you want strong involvement from your customer, they will need to be comfortable speaking to you about the system. Developers often miss this aspect as they overwhelm the business with their software-engineering jargon. Is it any wonder that customers don't speak up at critical meetings or junctures? They might have no idea what you're talking about!

An example of a metaphor is when the team is developing a foreign exchange dealing-room system. The customer will be using words like "swaps," "options," "basis point," "interest rate risk," and so on. The team aligns their language around the language of the customer, which might go down to the level of individual components or modules.

Often customers will think and express ideas based on what they can *see*. The struggle is to firm up the intangible thoughts into something that the team can build. From a user interface perspective the metaphor may extend to visual cues on the screens or forms. Amazon's online site (`http://www.amazon.com/`) was originally limited to the selling of new books. The user selected the book they wanted by clicking on the image of the book cover.

Finally, using metaphors keeps with the XP values of simplicity, communication, and feedback.

Simple Design

Most software architects would agree with simplicity of design as a foundational tenet. But what is simplicity, and how do you achieve it? XP has a very clear definition of what *simplicity* means:

- Runs all the tests
- Contains no duplicate code
- States the programmer's intent for all the code clearly
- Contains the fewest possible classes and methods

Critics claim that XP is weak in design as it lacks a design phase. The difference between XP and Waterfall is that with XP there is no big design up-front or BDUF. In the world of Agile development, viewing design as a one-time event is simplistic and narrow. BDUF is too frozen, static, and doesn't allow for the reality of real-world change, ultimately locking in development. The thinking in XP is that design is a continuous process that happens at both the conceptual and physical levels. This makes perfect sense when you consider the change is a given in XP and we're never quite sure what is around the corner.

6

As XP developers we're building and designing things that are as simple as possible, doing all we need today. The tendency to add in features "just in case" is more likely to result in spaghetti code than delaying design. As you get more familiar with XP you'll come across some new acronyms and sayings such as YAGNI. YAGNI stands for "You Are Not Going To Need It," and in essence means don't add anything because you think you *might* need it. Chances are that you won't and you wasted time either solving problems that don't exist or adding features that no customer is paying for! To develop with restrain could be one of the hardest things to learn for developers who are new to XP. Only do what you need to do *now*.

Testing

XP has added a new twist to testing: rather than test after development, XP developers write the test *before* coding. Developers write unit tests that test each method and every thing that could possibly break. When they've written all their tests for that component, they write only enough code to pass the test. Writing tests such as this gives us a complete suite of tests for our system and we write the simplest thing that could possibly work. Work on the class continues until it passes all the tests in the suite. At this point the code is checked into the development team's source code control repository.

Testing in this committed way gives developers confidence in their code, and is the basis for refactoring. Refactoring without a test suite results in tentative development because we're never quite sure what will break if we refine untested code. In fact, refactoring without a test suite is fairly risky business and the old adage "if it ain't broke don't fix" is true. This means you will be stuck with the code you deployed because changing for the sake of improvement is a hard sell to both developers and customers.

The tests we've written will be added to our automated test harness or framework. Using an automated test harness enables us to run tests continuously as integrations occur. Doing this also gives you the flexibility to run after hours and stress tests. With automation, both business and technical teams get constant feedback on the state of the system with solid, real metrics.

Testing is good—we know that, but how do we get developers to write tests? XP developers work in pairs and use automated test frameworks such as Junit and VBUnit to write unit tests. Sharing the testing task and the use of tools lessens the chore of test writing. We'll learn how to use these tools in Hour 14, "Unit Testing with Java Tools" and Hour 15, "Unit Testing with Microsoft Tools."

Refactoring

Refactoring is the technique of improving code without changing functionality. Refactoring is an ongoing process of simplification that applies to code, design, testing, and XP itself. Rather than just saying "you should keep trying to make your code better," you will need a repeatable process to guide refactoring. In some ways, you've always done some form of refactoring as you review your code and make changes and improvements. The problem is that it's haphazard and is left until the team has spare time. In XP, developers will be refactoring during the entire process of development.

The standard reference on refactoring is Martin Fowler's *Refactoring: Improving the Design of Existing Code.*

Why refactor? Because you're an XP developer it means that your code should be the simplest thing that could possibly work. Inevitably, your initial code might tend to be overly complex which is true even of a 20-line function. We learned early on in this book how software is a craft more than a science, and you constantly cycle through code-run-refine as you go along. Refactoring has given your simplifying, improving process a name. In Hour 21, "More on Refactoring Techniques," we will cover examples of specific refactorings you can use; skip to that chapter now if you want to get a head start today with refactoring.

Pair Programming

With XP, developers working in pairs do software development. Two developers share the same workstation, taking turns using the keyboard. Does this mean half the output? No, development speed is not impacted by how fast you can type! The work of programming includes coding, thinking, designing, testing, listening, and talking. The following benefits are derived from pair programming:

- All design decisions involve two minds
- At least two developers are familiar with that part of the system
- There is less chance that tests will be missed
- Switching pairs enhances knowledge sharing even further
- All code is reviewed all the time
- One developer is looking at detail while the other is looking at the conceptual

Figure 6.1 shows pair programmers at work, huddled around their workstations.

6

FIGURE **6.1**
Pair programmers at work.

We will walk through more on how to pair program in Hour 11 "Software Development with Pair Programming."

Collective Ownership

Collective ownership of code reverses the isolated development models of the past and means that any person can change the application code at anytime. Here's the catch: If you own all the code, you are responsible for all the code as well. The good news is that so is everybody else on the team. Pair programming supports the idea of collective ownership, as well.

The opposite of collective ownership is where *individual* developers are assigned as "module owners" or "subsystem owners." This has a ring of control and safety about it. However, the truth is quite the contrary where key team members hold information in their heads and might inadvertently hold the project team to ransom. One sick day or vacation can throw the entire team out as they try and overcome integration problems with missing team member's code. The "it's not my code" defense is not only frustrating, but works against any sense of team that you've managed to establish.

If your project uses collective ownership, and not the other XP practices of pair programming, testing, and coding standards, your efforts will end in chaos.

Continuous Integration

Consider the normal pattern with development: Developers work on their part of the system, and then when completed, *integrate* with the whole system. The longer the time period between integrations, the more conflicts you'll see, and the effort to integrate will increase. In less rigorous engineering environments, developers work for weeks or months and only integrate at delivery time. As you can imagine, results are disastrous with developers scrambling to build the system for the first time! Nightmare stories of all-night build sessions are all too common.

The extreme of delayed integration is *continuous* integration. Calling integration continuous is perhaps a little misleading, more of an over statement to say that we should integrate as much as possible. The practice of daily builds is simply not good enough to withstand the speed of XP development.

How continuous integration works in practice is that developers work on a module, class, or component until complete. Then they integrate (add to the integration machine), run tests, fix problems, and move onto the next task. Development tasks are small, and the smaller the better. This bite-sized development fits our object-oriented environment where developers are working on objects, not complete applications. XP tools such as Ant and Nant enable integration at this speed. We'll cover these in more depth in Hour 16, "Automating Your Software Development."

40-Hour Work Week

In XP, development is high in communication and boasts impressive speed. Developers are working in an environment where the stress of change is ever present. Working on XP projects means consistently driving quality and performance throughout the life of the project. How do you maintain quality with overtime-heavy teams? The answer is you can't; defect rates begin to climb, tempers flare, and communication deteriorates. Remembering that an XP core principle is that quality of work can never be compromised, we're going to have to control how many hours developers clock and still maintain high standards.

In the IT industry, workers are increasingly busy and the important is being squeezed out by the urgent. How much of your average day is spent on trivial issues, wading through broadcast emails, and interminable meetings? If energy could be directed exclusively toward the project for eight hours per day, ignoring anything outside of the project, 40-hour work weeks could be successful.

Sustainable Working Hours

The idea of the 40-hour week is that team members should work the hours that they can *sustain* quality. Sustainable workload could be 40 hours or thereabouts. Each country or culture has differing acceptance of reasonable working hours. The important thing is to recognize what a reasonable work week should be, and then come to an agreement with the team on that number. Tremendous power comes from committing to this up-front and then having the integrity to follow through during crunch time.

Exposing the Overtime Black Market

Establishing a policy of sustainable hours also removes the "black market" in project time. This refers to the very dubious practice of price-fixing the contract (effectively locking the team into charging no more than eight hours per day) while still allowing management to lean on the team to work extended, unpaid hours. For those employees paid on a salary, they are losing personal time for no reward.

Long Term or Short Term

Studies have shown that productivity can actually improve when working between 60–80 hours per week. Younger team members can sometimes be more easily encouraged to work excessive overtime. Youth and enthusiasm enables them to survive this extra work in the short-term and management can view them as expendable. Working after hours with similar die-hard colleagues also lends to the general atmosphere of life on the edge. Senior players who've seen it all before have probably gone home while these volunteer overtime workers continue development. The next day is often spent in rework and recovery from the previous late night. Figure 6.2 shows the increased productivity with increased overtime.

FIGURE 6.2

Productivity increases over time.

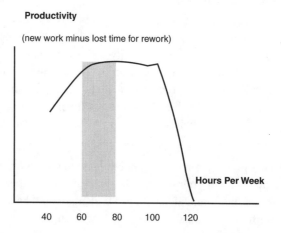

So, short-term gains are possible from working teams harder, but what are the longer-term impacts? Longer working hours over a prolonged period is going to result in staff turnover and poor quality. Exhaustion in an XP team breeds crankiness and irritability, and keeping communication open and positive with your customer will become impossible. If we are using the other XP practices and spending our day on what we *know* is important and solving problems simply, why would we need more than eight hours per day?

On-Site Customer

In earlier hours we learned that lack of ongoing customer involvement was a common thread between the project failures and runaways. The RAD methodologies we covered during our first hour were an attempt to bring the customer back into development. With RAD, developers prototyped the application with customers or users, it was then signed off and development began. This method has serious drawbacks, not the least of which is the lack of flexibility; the customer is still locked in while development carries on at full speed.

With XP, we get extreme about customer involvement. we'll mandate that the customer be on the project full-time for the duration and be located on-site with the team. On-site then means on-site! Remember that we're developing with one team, a team that includes customers. Look at it this way: How could your team develop any other way? If developers are coding from user stories that lack detail and call for clarity, they will have to speak to the customer.

Another feature of XP is the high level of communication and feedback that the team thrives on. Talking, listening, questioning, and so on. How could you do this when not sitting side-by-side with your customer?

> The customer could include, users, business experts, and any other customer-side resource.

The customer will be taking part in the Planning Game, working through business requirements, prioritizing, and defining. When development starts the customer will be entering into ongoing conversations as developers begin coding.

Coding Standards

6

Coding standards have long been recognized as a best practice when developing software. These rules apply to most languages and cover several aspects of coding. The overall purpose of coding standards is to produce software that has a consistent style, independent of the author. This, in turn, results in software that is easier to understand and maintain.

In most cases these standards are documented and formalized as part of company's technique of developing software. We can separate coding standards into various categories:

- *Mandatory*—Those standards to be adhered to by all team members.
- *Guidelines*—Those considered best or good practice and often describe the general approach toward development.
- *Recommendations*—These rules are considered good practice and should be used at all times unless there are exceptional circumstances where valid justification can be given.

If you're using XP you will be developing in pairs, each taking turns and at the keyboard. Before coding starts, you will need an agreed upon set of rules on how to attack development. This removes petty arguments about formatting, naming, and such. Without coding standards the swapping of pairs would become difficult because you'd be forced to learn every other developers style and approach.

So, coding standards are not just a best practice—they grease the wheels of the development team and ensure that everybody wins.

Aspects of Coding Standards

There are a number of different aspects that coding standards seek to define, some of the key ones are listed in Table 6.4.

TABLE 6.4   Types of Coding Standards

Standard	Description
Formatting	Formatting includes the use of white space, indention, and length of statement lines in code. Some standards might include, for example, common editor setup and handling for tabs versus spaces for indentation.
Code structure	Code structure includes overall project layout (files, and so on), classes, resources, and other source file types.
Naming conventions	Naming conventions specify how developers name their methods, classes, variables, events, and parameters.
Error handling	Error handling describes how objects handle errors, reporting, and logging
Comments	Comments are an English description in the code that explains the logic of the code. (Quality code should be self-documenting by default.) The use of quality commenting gives quality code better maintainability and easier understandability.

Where to Go for Coding Standards

If you want a head start on creating your own coding standards a good place to start is the relevant development communities. Both Microsoft and Sun offer their own versions of coding standards. Other vendors, such as Borland and IBM will have their own guidelines for effective development. That's not to say that Microsoft's coding standard is any better than yours is; the important thing is to have a standard and then conform to it. To help you in defining your own standards we've included links to the Sun Java and Microsoft .NET coding standards in Table 6.5.

TABLE 6.5 Coding Standard References

Coding Standard	Web Link
Java	http://java.sun.com/docs/codeconv/html/CodeConvTOC.doc.html
Microsoft .NET	http://msdn.microsoft.com/library/default.asp?url=/library/ en-us/vsent7/html/vxconcodingstandardscodereviews.asp

A good practice to use when applying coding standards to your project is to create just-in-time standards. With just-in-time standards you decide on standards and guidelines, as you need them. Using a tool such as Wiki Wiki (a Web-based collaboration application) developers agree on naming conventions and so forth as the need arises. The principle with this approach is that if no standard exists for your task quickly convene an on-the-fly meeting and agree on one together. When the standard is agreed to, add it to your Wiki Wiki site for the project.

An on-the-fly meeting is where developers spin their chairs around in a circle or gather at the whiteboard. XP has the entire team sitting in the same work area, so this is practical.

Summary

We've covered a lot of ground in the last hour! Some of the XP practices are in use today by the mainstream development community; ideas such as increasing customer involvement have long been seen as important. It's the extreme aspect of these practices that makes XP a highly flexible development approach.

We also learned how the synergy of the practices is what makes XP work; the weakness of a given practice is mitigated by another.

Now we're ready to learn how to lead an XP project!

6

Q&A

Q **Can I use the practices in isolation and what are the risks of doing this?**

A Yes, you can use any practice on its own, but the inherent weakness in that practice needs to be mitigated.

Q **What is the best practice to start with today?**

A It depends on where you are in your lifecycle. Some teams have changed project approaches midstream and used the XP programming practices inside the context of an existing structure. Developers should try unit-testing tools that can be used across development styles as soon as possible.

Q **Where can I find some more facts about the costs and benefits of pair programming?**

A The home of pair programming is `http://www.pairprogramming.com`. There is an excellent article on the costs and benefits of pair programming at `http://collaboration.csc.ncsu.edu/laurie/Papers/XPSardinia.PDF`.

Q **Is XP simply the name given to the 12 practices? What is the glue that holds it together?**

A No. We started learning about XP by looking at the values and how it overcomes common development challenges; it's these values that are the "soul" of XP.

Workshop

This workshop tests whether you understand all the concepts you learned in this hour. It is very helpful to know and understand the answers before starting the next hour's lesson.

Quiz

1. How does developing with only a rough plan work?

   a. The customer manages progress and so improves the plan if necessary.

   b. The planning practice is supported by the use of small releases; the team can make adjustments as they go.

   c. This is poor practice and should be avoided by the use of the Planning Game.

   d. XP developers are generally more skilled than the average and so need less guidance.

2. Which of the following are aspects of simple design as defined by XP?

   a. The system is easy to change.

   b. The system passes all the tests.

   c. Can be modeled simply using cards or whiteboard.

   d. The system contains no duplicate code.

3. Why does refactoring need testing to support it?

   a. It doesn't, but can be improved by testing.

   b. Developers need a way of determining what impacts their changes have had on the system.

   c. Without testing developers have no way of knowing what needs to be refactored.

   d. Testing tools can also be used for refactoring.

4. What are the three categories of XP?

   a. Planning, process, and people.

   b. Core, support, and optional.

   c. Programming, team, and process.

   d. Process, development, and testing.

5. What is the idea behind using a metaphor to describe the system?

   a. It forms a bridge between customer and developer.

   b. It allows for greater flexibility.

   c. Better communication speeds development.

   d. Using tools such as Wiki Wiki are much easier to use with metaphors.

Answers

1. a.
2. b. and d.
3. b.
4. c.
5. a.

6

Activities

1. Visit the xUnit testing frameworks download page at `http://www.xprogramming.com/software.htm`. Find your relevant language tool (Java, C++, Visual Basic, .NET, and so on) and begin experimenting with the tool, today.

2. Create the coding standard for your development shop. Use resources from Sun, Microsoft, Apple, or your language vendor.

3. Investigate how you can implement an XP practice on your current project. If you're a developer, consider pair programming. Could you use it today? Research more on the costs and benefits before approaching your manager!

PART III

Running Your XP Project

Hour

HOUR 7

Leading Your XP Project

In this hour you will learn how to lead your XP project. If you're a project manager or team leader, you'll need to gain a firm understanding of the differences between managing and leading in XP. In this hour we will cover

- How the XP values relate to leadership
- The importance of people to the success of the project
- What it takes to be a leader in an XP project
- What is team building, and what it means for an XP project

Using XP Values to Run Your Project

You can think of your software development project as consisting of two parts: the process of managing the work and the actual programming itself. Some of the XP practices are clearly developer-related, such as Pair Programming and refactoring. Others, such as The Planning Game are tools you can use to lead or manage. In this hour we'll consider the kind of approach you'll need to adopt as you start to lead XP projects. A great place to begin this is by revisiting our XP values and principles with respect to leadership.

- **Simplicity**—Lead using simple tools that work such as cards, whiteboards, and Web applications. As a leader you'll search for practical solutions and not be afraid to move furniture or do whatever it takes to clear the way for the team.

- **Communication**—XP practices such as Pair Programming require communication to work. XP recognizes this and seeks to remove barriers between team members. As a coach you'll be watching interactions, listening for fluctuations in tone, and generally getting a sense of the team. Improving the team's communication, most of which is verbal, falls on your shoulders.

- **Feedback**—Feedback is happening all the time between customer and developer, and leaders need feedback, too. Is your leadership effective? Are team members who are new to XP growing under your mentoring?

- **Courage**—The team will quickly learn to respect you as you display courage, fighting for the rights of the team. If your customer or management is new to XP, they might be skeptical or even negative. Expect pressure to come on you to "bend the rules" as the *new* comes into conflict with the *old*.

Leading your XP project means no hiding behind project plans, status reports, and emails. The team expects you to be technical and relevant enough to add hands-on value as well. Starting your XP project could be a little uncertain, a little loose for you if you're used to a more structured approach. Structure isn't a bad thing at all, as long as the team is doing the simplest thing that could possibly work. So, we can apply our XP programming approach to leadership on the project. If you as a leader can demonstrate integrity and ability, your team will follow and together you'll reach success. The starting point is to recognize the unique nature of your people. They make the difference.

Trusting Your Team

XP is not a set of dry documents or dogma, but a living thing. In software development, one success factor that stands out is that the people on the project can make the difference between success or failure, the victory parade or ignominy. The way you view people or, more specifically, your people will directly affect the way you will manage or lead them. If your perception is that your people are basically lazy or untrustworthy, this will drive you to manage and control them. That control could take the form of detailed prescriptive processes that are dictated from on high. Rigorous methodologies use this tactic.

Clearly, XP doesn't hold the view that people are resources that can be switched in and out at will by project managers. Managing a project by the numbers is attractive, but unrealistic at the least. It's your people then, not a best practice, tool, or process that create success. People are still required to implement even the perfect methodology. The methodology alone cannot be a substitute for skill or attitude.

A better approach is to trust your team and, where necessary, provide checklists to prompt their memory about process or procedure. Your colleagues are highly skilled individuals who will flourish with freedom not petty restraint.

The complaint that XP projects don't have enough documentation might be true if you believe that the tacit knowledge held within the team can be captured on paper. XP makes no pretense on this and instead encourages the team to jot down the "memory joggers" in simple tools such as Wiki Wiki. XP fits a recent trend away from the more is better, to simple, clear tools. In his book *Simplicity: The New Competitive Advantage in a World of More, Better, Faster* by Bill Jensen, the author argues that *simplicity* is power not *information*. Businesses are seeking clarity of vision and direction; this is where XP stands out as a great enabling approach.

Leading Your XP Team

Most development methodologies have an extensive list of managers: project managers, product managers, program managers, QA managers, and the list goes on. In XP, we are more interested in leading rather than managing. What is the difference between these two? Leadership is focused on direction (where we are going), whereas management is focused on speed (are we getting there the fastest way). Management works fine when the process is consistent and repeatable. Unfortunately, software development isn't that clear-cut, hence the reason to use an Agile approach such as XP! Table 7.1 lists the different aspects of leadership and management.

TABLE 7.1   The Difference Between Leadership and Management

Leadership	Management
Focus on vision, direction	Focus on speed
Effectiveness	Efficiency
Derives power from values and principles	Organizes resources to secure objectives

 Table 7.1 was developed, in part, from *Principle-Centered Leadership*, by Stephen Covey, Fireside Books.

7

Your role in leading XP projects is to give direction, guide relationships, and grow synergy. Empowerment is an overused word nowadays, but it is exactly what you need to do for your team; enable them to be their best. Clearing blockages that hinder team members, giving them both the freedom and power to create. Empowering individuals on the team doesn't mean removing the safety harness, and then saying "jump!" By using XP practices you're placing real, workable tools into the hands of the team.

Keep in mind that your authority is, in one sense, given to you by the team, and they can just as quickly take it away. Using the title on your business card as a form of authority will ultimately leave you as a lame-duck manager, ignored by the team. A leader is someone people follow. What will it take for the team to follow you?

Being a Leader Your Team Will Follow

For project success there should be cooperation between leader and team. Leading by virtue of your title or sheer presence isn't going to cut it in the long term. There is a period of time at the start of your engagement, where you must win the right to lead. The team is asking the question "should I follow you?" How does the team size you up? By what criteria are you being judged? The bottom line is that they want to know why they should trust you. What are your motives, values, and skills? Let's look at each of these aspects in turn:

- **Motives**—What are your real motives? Are you interested in your own success first? Do you think in terms of the team's success or your own?

- **Values**—What are your core values? Is your commitment to the XP values and principles more than just skin-deep? Do you influence others around you to work by principles? Do you stick by your principles when the heat is on?

- **Skills**—Are you creative? Do you have technical skills that are relevant to the problem domain? Are you able to offer the team practical help toward achieving the project vision?

Assuming, you're a new leader to the team these questions may take time to answer. A more likely scenario is that you are known as part of the wider company, and therefore they might have at least a secondary view on you're character. In the final analysis, the team decides to follow you after you've proven to have integrity. Time will tell.

Intolerance

Leading your XP project isn't all group hugs and snacks, there is a form of rigor. XP rigor is the passionate adherence to its core values of feedback, communication, simplicity, and courage. Process-heavy development enforces strictness around the approach; we are interested in the values and principles. David Maister in his book *Practice What You Preach*, studied successful, high-performing companies and found a number of common success factors. One of these factors is the complete intolerance that these successful companies have for core value infractions.

Here is a list of some things that should not be tolerated:

- Abuse of power
- Disrespect of any kind
- Anyone who is abusive
- Backstabbing
- Bullying
- People who call in sick when they're not
- Cruising
- Dealing in blame
- Gossiping, whining, and complaining
- Lack of teamwork
- Management through intimidation
- Screaming
- People who try and make their own rules

 For the complete results of David Maister's survey read his book *Practice What You Preach*, The Free Press, 2001.

The interesting thing to note about the list of intolerable acts is that they are primarily concerned with relationships. Gathering a group of individuals, and then fashioning them into a team, is an intensive, time-consuming process. Protecting your team relationships and its adherence to core values is vital to your ongoing success.

The question is in light of your values as a team, what will you refuse to tolerate? If you're a leader, the team will learn more from watching how you live out your values than a thousand emails, words, or presentations. Building a team without this integrity is simply not possible.

What Kind of Leader Are You?

There are numerous different styles of leadership and management. What kind of leader will your XP project thrive on? We've already covered some of these: integrity, technical astuteness, and humility are all aspects of leadership that will gain the respect of your team. Let's go ahead and review three styles of a leader.

7

The Uninvolved Manager

The uninvolved manager relies on hackers or experts to meet impossible deadlines. This manager might put her trust in a single "super-developer" who also has extensive business experience. The team assists or supports the prime developer as she leads the charge. This is a very abusive and negative environment where promises are made to upper management, and then are imposed on the team. Somehow the work gets done by either long work hours, reliance on key people, or luck. This is a workplace where turnover is high and developers exit as soon as possible. The manager is also likely to be nontechnical and have no understanding about what the team is doing and the challenges it faces.

This manager can never lead an XP project and in fact would have no interest in the level of commitment XP calls for.

The Controlling Manager

The opposite of the uninvolved manager is the manager who must control every aspect of the project. He views his role as dictator and demonstrates complete lack of trust in the team by his attitude. He forms the hub through which all communication must flow; he setup all kinds of processes to ensure he remains the center. Even worse is when this kind of manager has some degree of technical skill and insists on rubber-stamping the team's decisions. The manager quickly becomes the bottleneck, by then the team has already established its own secondary lines of communication, otherwise work would grind to a halt.

Strange to consider is that from their viewpoint the controlling manager is acting in a perfectly reasonable manner. Control on this scale might have functioned in a waterfall project, but is destined to fail with XP.

The Team Member Manager

The team member manager is seen as part of the team and *not* the center. The manager has probably come up through the ranks, has clearly recognized development skills, and a proven track record. She sees her role as just that, a *role* and doesn't confuse that with position or power. In fact, she delights in empowering team members because she remembers how it felt to be sidelined while decisions were made about her future.

The XP leader who is secure in her own technical skills and is also aware of her own shortcomings will be readily accepted by her colleagues. If you're a leader, how do you galvanize the team as a unit? Team building is your new focus.

Building Your Team

A team is more than a group of individuals on a project organization chart—a team has to be built. Team building means actively helping people to succeed and dealing with people as individuals, not as replaceable units. Taking a diverse group of people, and then getting them to work together—that's team building!

People have a tendency to see the project in terms of their own skills, background, or role. The challenge is valuing the person's uniqueness, and then aligning that with the team's goals. The goal of your team building is an effective team where team members significantly relate to each other to accomplish shared objectives.

Here are a few characteristics of effective teams. Team members

- Share common goals.
- Enjoy working together.
- Have commitment to achieve their goals.
- Are different people concentrating on a common effort.
- Have high team morale and spirit.
- Show exceptional creativity.
- Have a degree of competition and conflict.
- Are interdependent.

An effective team is one where the whole is greater than the sum of its parts!

Creating Your Team Culture

Team building isn't an item on a project plan or a one-time event. Effective team building is a continuous process that starts as soon as the team is assembled—you have to *create* your team. There is some front-loaded activity as you might instigate a project kick-off meeting that sets the tone for the rest of the project. The project kick-off meeting is where introductions are made, the vision is explained, and goals agreed upon. It might also be the forum to discuss roles, but in XP these are fairly dynamic and change throughout the project.

The chance of any formal team building activities for the team is remote, so you'll need to integrate them into the overall project. Whatever forms your team building takes, it will need at least the following:

- Clear objectives and agreed goals
- Openness and healthy confrontation

7

- Support and trust
- Sound practices
- Appropriate leadership
- Regular reviews
- Individual development
- Sound intragroup relationships

Who will be on your team? You will not always have the pick of the bunch and, if XP is new to your company, seasoned veterans will be hard to find. Rather than look for a prescription of what steps you should take in team building, be aware of the human and unspoken aspects of your team. Keep your ears and eyes open, get a sense of the atmosphere and the culture, this will aid in building that "jell" you seek. As a leader, you might call yourself "coach," but titles should be held lightly and you will need to prove yourself just as much as any rookie.

It's not reasonable to expect that team building will consist of a few pats on the back and a dozen doughnuts. If you're aware of the barriers to team development, you avert disaster before it strikes. Here are some things to watch out for:

- Differing outlooks, priorities, interests, and judgments
- Role conflicts
- Unclear project organization
- Lack of team definition
- No team input into personnel selection
- Poor leader credibility
- Lack of team member commitment
- Communication problems
- Lack of senior management support

When you look at your team do you see developers, engineers, and programmers or do you see influencers, creators, and comedians. Understanding what technical skills your team members have is easy, but when you're team building it helps to see beyond skills and toward *roles*. Let's separate the roles in which people function into constructive and destructive. Table 7.2 lists these roles for us:

TABLE 7.2   Team Member Roles

Constructive Roles	Destructive Roles
Initiators—"Let's do this…"	Aggressor—Criticizes and deflates the status of others.
Information seekers—"Don't we have some better information?"	Blocker—Rejects the views of others.
Information givers—"My experience is…"	Withdrawer—Holds back and will not participate.
Encouragers—"That was a great help…"	Recognition seeker—Seeks attention by controlling discussions.
Clarifiers—"I believe we are saying…"	Topic jumper—Continually changes the subject.
Harmonizers—"I believe we are all saying the same thing…"	Dominator—Tries to take over the discussion.
Gatekeeper—Helps others participate: "We haven't heard from…"	Devil's advocate—Brings up alternative view points. Can be positive or negative.

Team members will quite possibly function in either constructive or destructive roles from time-to-time. This is quite natural, but the important thing is being aware of patterns of behavior.

Motivating Your Team

After, you've created your team's culture you'll want to make sure that you nurture and cultivate motivation. Team building won't be completely effective until the team members are motivated to do the work required. One motivator is the overall value or importance of the project; working on a worthwhile project will lift the morale of the team. Conversely, building software that the team knows is destined for the scrap heap after a year will not motivate anyone! The synergy of the team is elevated to another level once the value of the project is fully established in their minds. This kind of group or team motivation helps the process of pulling the team together into a unit. Your role if you're a leader is to clearly express the value of the team's work. This isn't a one-time deal and you'll want to reaffirm how worthwhile the project is, which doesn't mean announcing how important the software is every chance you get! Instead, feedback your customer's positive comments about the team's direction; describe the part the software plays in the customer's broader plans. Here are some simple steps you can take towards motivating the team:

- Present the project as a challenge—describe the project in terms of the unique or special nature of the work (never been done before, and so forth).

- Give regular feedback—Make sure the team is kept informed about the projects progress, include customer comments.

7

- Use rewards—senior management should reward the extra work the team is putting in.
- Encourage professional development—Allow and encourage team members to attend conferences and specialized training events.
- Provide a good working environment—Create a project space that reflects the nature of the project, allow relaxation of corporate standards where applicable and supply food!

We can summarize our motivator list with this comment: Use the carrot not the stick! Managers that threaten, trick, manipulate, or cajole workers might get short-term results, but the low team morale will soon cancel out these gains.

Summary

There's a lot to think about in this hour! XP requires new kinds of leaders. Leaders with the courage to stand by their values, even when the going gets tough. The secret of success with your XP project isn't in the application of the 12 practices, but rather in harnessing the power of your people. Taking a group, and then turning them into an XP-focused team takes integrity, hard work, and commitment.

The next hour will see us start our project and plan the release with the team.

Q&A

Q What particular skills should I brush up on if I want to lead XP teams?

A Read books that focus on the softer aspects of leadership, in particular those written from a values standpoint. Stephen Covey is a good general author to start with. Also, any books about EQ—Emotional Quotient would be worthwhile. Classic, project-management books tend to labor on the process side.

Q XP seems a bit too "touchy-feely," is this true?

A There is a definite emphasis on the human side of development work, but it is at heart still an engineering approach. The close proximity in which people work combined with high communication, elevates the importance of the people factor.

Q Is XP leadership democratic, and are the leaders weak?

A No, there is no democratic process to electing leaders in XP. There are times to direct your team members clearly and bluntly. There is a huge difference when doing this from a position of respect.

Workshop

This workshop tests whether you understand all the concepts you learned in this hour. It is very helpful to know and understand the answers before starting the next lesson.

Quiz

1. What is the difference between leading and managing?

    a. Leaders are more interested in the human-side.

    b. Fundamentally they are the same, with the exception that leading is more dynamic.

    c. Managing works best in controlled projects.

    d. Leading is focused on direction, whereas managing is focused on speed.

2. When considering you as a leader, what question should the team ask?

    a. What is your level of technical skill and flexibility?

    b. What are your motives, skills, and values?

    c. What is your level of experience with XP?

    d. Are you a team member manager?

3. What is an effective team?

    a. One that completes the project under budget.

    b. One where the leader has used XP values correctly.

    c. One where team members significantly relate to each other to achieve the shared goal.

    d. One with a high-level of constructive roles.

4. What is the best place to start team building?

    a. The project kick-off.

    b. The project room, so all can be involved.

    c. Start anytime, the important thing is to start.

    d. During The Planning Game.

5. What is your primary role as a leader?

    a. Interface with the team and management.

    b. Ensure the team is doing XP.

    c. Empower the team to succeed.

    d. Clear technical roadblocks.

7

Answers

1. a.
2. b.
3. c.
4. a.
5. c.

Activities

1. Sit down today and write down your personal core values. Monitor yourself over the next week and determine if you are remaining true to these?

2. Think about your team (as a leader or member). Using the criteria for an effective team, measure your team. Is there anything you can do to begin team building?

3. Revisit the constructive and destructive roles mentioned earlier in this hour. Which deconstructive role(s) have you exhibited before? Pick a constructive role and over the next week, practice it at work.

HOUR 8

Planning Your Software Release with XP

In this hour you will learn how to plan your software release with XP. You'll discover how to quickly create a flexible and simple plan. In this hour we will cover

- How release planning works in XP
- How XP uses the release to enable customers to control development
- How to estimate development work
- How to break the release into iterations

The Basics of a Software Release

Once you have the tools and understand the roles and the core values of XP, you're ready to begin developing! The customer will have a broad idea about what business objectives and goals they are hoping to meet with their project. It could be that they are drawn to using XP because their direction is not certain, or they want to manage their risk by developing in small releases. Using small releases is one of the 12 XP practices, and it enables the customer to steer the team in small stages as they move from concept to final product.

Planning is not just an up-front activity in XP; it happens throughout the life the project. With the underlying premise that we should come up with a plan quickly and then change it when the need arises. You will see a pattern with planning in XP:

- Customer defines requirements (user stories)
- Developers estimate effort
- Customer prioritizes the work
- The plan is agreed upon

The Planning Game is the XP practice where this work takes place. There are three primary stages where the planning cycle is acted out, and Table 8.1 describes them:

TABLE 8.1 The XP Planning Stages

Stage	Description
Scoping	This occurs during the Exploration phase of the XP project. It enables the customer to get a quick sense of the size of the project and can result in a go/no-go decision.
Release	Customer breaks the entire project down into releases based on business value.
Iteration	Each release consists of a number of iterations that slowly builds towards the release. The team builds an iteration plan taking user stories from the release plan.

In this hour we will investigate how the release is scoped and planned. In Hour 9, "Developing Software in Iteration," we'll spend time on the iteration stage of XP. Now, let's look at how the team assembles a big picture view of the project.

Scoping the Project

If your customer is still at the conceptual stage, he requires more help from the technical team to decide if the project is worthwhile. The business might be working through a cost-benefit analysis to determine the Return on Investment (ROI) for the proposed project. The customer must answer the question "should the project go forward? He will probably have a pretty good idea about the benefits of the new software, the cost or price still remains unclear.

It has been said that *cost* is always too high, the key is to express the price in terms of an *investment*. The technical team may be able to help the business derive benefits from the *pain* of the existing system or the *gains* expect from the new system.

A simple, robust way of arriving at a decision is the Kepner-Tregoe (KT) decision-making methodology. The KT method works by assigning weights and criteria to your options, and then scoring them accordingly. This scientific, mathematical approach takes away emotion from the decision-making process. Read more on this in the book *New Rational Manager* by Charles Kepner and Benjamin Tregoe, Princeton Press, 1997. Kepner-Tregoe can be found on the Web at `http://www.Kepner-Tregoe.com/`.

Before a decision can be made on the future of the project the business will need

- User stories
- Estimates to complete
- Budget
- Constraints

To get to the go/no-go decision the team executes the Planning Game at a high level.

The role of the business is to define value and the order of development. They know what they want to achieve at a high level and now need the technical team's input to reach a conclusion. Definition of requirements is done through user stories, which are simple functional requirements. The role of the technical team is to clarify these user stories, and then estimate the effort to implement. Table 8.2 lays out the process for you:

TABLE 8.2   The Steps in Creating the Big Plan

Write user stories	The customer writes high-level requirements down on cards in the form of stories.
Organize the stories	The team lays the stories out on the table and organizes them into features and constraints. Constraints are items such as "credit card should be authorized in under 10 seconds."
Estimate the stories	The team takes a very rough high-level estimate on how much effort is required to deliver the stories.
Calculate the cost of the release	Using an estimated throughput or velocity and cost of resources, calculate the cost of the release.

Finding out who will represent the business and act as the "customer" is very important. The customer representative should have an in-depth knowledge of the business domain, some appreciation for the value the software can bring, the ability to make decisions, and a commitment to the success of the project.

It will help you to visualize this if we walk through an example. Let's take an imaginary customer whose goal is to sell books over the Internet. Sounds familiar, doesn't it? Table 8.3 outlines the customer's vision for the software.

TABLE 8.3 Example Project Vision

Vision
To sell books on the Internet, providing the means for customers to find books, accept payment, and deliver the order.

Let's keep going and break down the vision into some high-level user stories, and then supply estimates. Table 8.4 lists our stories.

TABLE 8.4 Example High-Level Feature List

User Story	Estimate (Weeks)
Search and list books	6
Payment and transaction handling	6
Order processing	4
Inventory management	6
Customer management	5
Total	27

Our customer's feature list raises a lot of questions, but the urge to delve more into detail should be resisted. At this point we're not attempting to nail-down exactly what the customer wants, just the big picture. If the development team is estimating in days or hours, this is a sure sign that the technical team has drifted into detail.

Estimation at this level does not take dependencies into account; estimate as if each story is completely isolated. Dependencies will be covered and accounted for later, our concentration at this stage of planning is on business value and deliverables.

Release Planning

Breaking the project down into smaller, bite-sized pieces enables the customer and technical team to make corrections in midcourse. The *Release* in XP is akin to a product-release cycle and is driven by business issues. Product-release cycles are when the customer rolls out a new version of the product or system to the end users. This holds true for external and internal software users; in the internal project, your XP project can form part of an overall program of work. An example of this is the development of a new HR system, where training, internal marketing, and migration are all aspects of the project. Your XP project is required to sync-up with the rest of the program. In this scenario the customer comes to the XP project with an end date in mind: "this project must be completed by the end of the financial year!" Understanding where the constraints on your team come from is half the battle.

The end of the release is when the technical team deploys the software to the business' environment. The end users get their hands on the software, and the business starts to receive benefits. Developers work in shorter cycles called iterations, still producing software that has business value to the customer. The short iteration helps the technical team improve their estimates, and they can also remain open to change.

Release planning has a number of activities, which are similar to the exploration or scoping stage; they are as follows:

- Writing user stories for the release
- Estimating the size of the release (how much effort it will take)
- Estimating the number of iterations it will take to complete
- Prioritizing of user stories (which ones will be done first)
- Writing the initial release plan

Activities in release planning are very similar to those that were done during the exploration stage. The difference is that release planning is a more accurate with a finer level of detail. The resulting release plan is still just a roadmap or starting-point, and you can expect it to undergo revision from time to time. Let's now take a look at each of these release-planning activities in turn.

Writing User Stories for the Release

As you learned earlier, customers write down their functionality or features as user stories. You should realize that your customer is unlikely to have a detailed knowledge of use cases, UML, or some other requirements notation, and will be more comfortable with her native language. That's not to say that use cases are bad, per se. Your customer *could* write her stories using a use-case format. The problem is use cases are a bit of a kludge in XP, and they capture far too much detail for release planning. User stories are little more than a title and 25 words of text, whereas a use case will identify a range of users and model their behavior as they use the system. XP team members will discover the "fine print" as they go along. The user story is little more than a placeholder.

> A use case is an approach used to identify, clarify, and organize customer requirements. The use case is made up of a set of possible interactions between systems and users. Users are called "actors," which are followed through various scenarios as they move toward their goal.

The technical team is solving the customer's business problem with technology. Enabling the customers to express requirements in their own words is a powerful tool in closing the communication gap. The story should be simple, and in XP we know what that means: The simplest approach that could possibly work. As a guideline, user stories should follow these principles:

- They should be understood by the customer
- They should be one or two sentences long
- They should represent a concept and not be too detailed

Table 8.5 gives an example user story.

TABLE 8.5   Example User Story

Title: Book Search
The system should enable users to search for books by name and return a list of matches.

The use case for this story would be considerably longer! Many questions are left unanswered by our user story in Table 8.5:

- Does the user have to be known by the system?
- Is there a limit to how many books that should be returned?
- What fields should be returned?
- Should the search be exact, wild card, or fuzzy?
- How fast should search be?

We can expect that more questions will be uncovered as development starts. The important thing to remember is that during planning we only need enough information to estimate the work.

A user story is an agreement to talk about a feature in the future. The story on the card begins the conversation between customer and developer. The technical team isn't trying to pin the customer down, we're going to trust that we can get the answers we need when we need them. You can see why XP mandates an on-site customer for the length of the

8

project. Development using high-level requirements necessitates a lot of questions and answers when work begins. User stories will not work if the customer or developer has a sign off mindset where he won't move forward until requirements have been locked down. There's a degree of trust between the business and technical sides. It will be a very real struggle for your team to use XP if you're building software in a combative environment where customers hide behind a wall of deliverables.

Estimating the Size of the Release

Developers estimate how long user stories take to implement using *ideal programming time*. Ideal programming time is how long the story would take if there are were no distractions, you know exactly what to do, and there are no other overheads. Ideal time is not the same as *calendar* time. Originally, XP estimation used load factor as the adjustment factor applied to estimates. Load factor is a common software development concept and is simply actual days to complete divided by estimated days. Figure 8.1 illustrates this.

FIGURE 8.1
Calculating load factor.

$$\text{Load Factor} = \frac{\text{Actual Time to Complete}}{\text{Estimated Time To Complete}}$$

Projects usually have load factors of around three, and you could use this as a starting point for deriving your *velocity*. Velocity is now the popular metric used in tracking progress for XP projects. Velocity is the measurement that tells the team how fast work is getting done. Figure 8.2 illustrates the estimation cycle.

FIGURE 8.2
The estimation cycle.

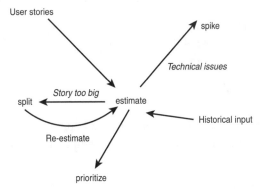

Figure 8.2 shows how developers need to spike a solution if technical issues arise from the story. Spiking, as we covered earlier, is when the developer performs some directed research on a technical topic. An example of this is when there are two methods to use in

interlayer communication for an n-tier solution, for example SOAP or COM+. Knowing the probable solution to the story affects its effort. The spike might last for a few minutes or a few hours.

Estimation is notoriously difficult, but numerous methods and tools are available to aid in this odious task. One thing all estimation has in common is the need for a *seed number*. This seed number could be something such as "lines of code," "number of classes," "number of subsystems," and so on. Here's the catch, without doing detailed analysis and then locking in the customer, you're seed value is a guess, too! XP backs away from the use of expensive tools or complex spreadsheets, taking the "keep it simple" approach.

Realizing the estimation is more art than science (or should that be magic!), we'll take the following approach:

- Use what happened in the (recent) past
- Learn and track our estimates

Using "yesterday's weather" is what Kent Beck (in *Planning Extreme Programming*) calls estimating based on the past. Yesterday's weather means that we track how many story points (or whatever metric you're using) we did last iteration or release and assume we will do the same in the future.

Your initial estimates won't be accurate because you have no history to fall back on; expect them to be wrong. You might as well come clean on this at the start. Here's where small releases and short cycles help because you can swiftly refine your estimates.

> Keep this in mind when calculating cost. Work is done by pairs of developers, so one day of ideal time equals daily rate times 2.

Without a seed or starting point, how do you begin to estimate? One simple, effective way is to look through your stack of user stories for one that is similar and take this as your basis. Is it twice as hard as your new story? Apply the factor that you believe makes sense. You're estimating as a team, so the group will even out any wild fluctuations in estimation.

Whatever measurement you do use; ideal programming time, perfect engineering days, story points, and so on, it's important to track actual against estimated. After you've picked a metric, stick with it. In time, the team will be able to balance individual estimation techniques: the pessimist versus the optimist.

Estimating the Number of Iterations

After the size and length of the release has been decided upon we need to divide it into iterations. Each iteration should be as short as possible because we are building working software as quickly as we can. The best indicator the customer has to whether the technical team is on track both delivery- and feature-wise is to shorten the build cycle. Typical iteration lengths range between one and four weeks, with the average being three weeks. Iteration planning does carry an overhead, which can limit how short your iteration is.

The drive is to deliver business value to the customer with each iteration, however, your team can request time to establish infrastructure or similar zero business value work. It's quite possible that the technical team will require this first iteration to build base infrastructure, such as the test framework or development environment. Keep the purely technical iteration narrow in its focus, and build the bare minimum to establish the working environment. The good news from the customer viewpoint is that they control the length of this iteration.

 Arguments abound in the XP community about whether any iteration should have zero value to the customer. So much the better if you can roll some business value into the first iteration.

Prioritizing Release Features

Now that you have the estimated user stories it is time to order them for implementation. An important facet of planning within XP is that dependencies between stories are not considered. The idea is that stories can be built in any order. The challenge is more around how the user will test functionality rather than whether the team can deliver.

There are two sides to ordering: business and technical. The business is concerned with building the stories that give the greatest business benefit. Incremental development such as XP enables customers to push their most requested features out the door as soon as possible. The alternative of this is to tie up key functionality with less important enhancements so that the customer eagerly awaits the "real" work while other stakeholders slow down delivery by adding features. This is compounded when the department is spending its entire budget on your project, and everybody wants to get a piece of your development action.

The Planning Game is not the forum for debating business value with the customer; he knows what has value to him. Besides, it's his money anyway. A gentle nudge or clarification could be useful, especially if the customer got his ROI numbers from another consultant. This consultant may have been envisioning a different solution than you!

The technical team looks at ordering from the angle of risk: Does the solution look reasonable? Has the team had experience with this kind of development before? Are there too many external, supplier dependencies? Does the customer want you to use beta software? Does the technical team want to use beta software? An exploratory spike can allay some of these fears: "Now, I have a good idea of how to solve this and I can estimate." At the end of the day software development is still risky, and short release cycles mitigate this as we discovered in Hour 3, "Overcoming Software Development Problems with XP."

XP is unique in that it downplays the importance of system interdependencies; for example, can you build the search screen without a database at the backend? The reality is that modern development enables you to separate components to a greater degree. In the previous example you could write a middle-tier component that acted like the database until the required tables were in place. That being said the developers might want to point out glaring problems or obvious conflicts. For example, writing our middle-tier mock component might take too long—indicate this to the customer and let her make the call.

The best tool to use with ordering is your faithful pack of index cards. Shuffle, handout, scribble on, tear up, and generally handle these cards. The consensus is that software tools are cumbersome in the group setting and are best utilized for tracking. You can select any tool that works for you, just make sure that the tool doesn't become the master.

Ordering of the stories is complete. Let's see what our release plan looks like.

The Sample Release Plan

The output of release planning is a schedule that outlines what stories will be in the release and the order of delivery. Table 8.6 is the release plan for our fictional project.

TABLE 8.6   Example Release Plan

Story	Effort	Iteration 0	Iteration 1	Iteration 2	Iteration 3
Database setup	2	X			
Test framework setup	1	X			
Search for books	3		X		
List books	3		X		
Accept payments	3			X	
Validate payments	3			X	
Shipping order processing	3				X
Receiving order processing	3				X

There are some interesting things to note with our release plan. For example:

- We've added a zero business value iteration to establish our environment. This will be half the length of the other iterations.

- For the purposes of this example we've used a velocity of six. That is, the team can implement six ideal programming units or points.

- Our initial user stories were too long, so we asked the customer to split them.

- We planned three iterations worth of customer stories; in practice we'd shy away from planning this far out. The common pattern is to plan for two iterations; that is, the next one and the one after that. The release plan will be altered as we finish iterations.

- We left stories such as customer relationship management out of the example, but they would come back into focus as the project progresses.

You can store this plan using your planning cards, or you might want to enter the plan into a simple tool such as Wiki Wiki. The advantage of capturing the plan electronically is that reporting and tracking will be easier. The index cards are better for planning.

Summary

In this chapter you've learned how to break down the customer's requirements into releases and iterations. XP uses a similar approach to planning for scoping, release, and iteration; clearly separating the roles of customer and developer. The customer is firmly in control of the business direction of the project, whereas the development team estimates effort to implement.

The challenge of how to estimate software development effort is handled simply by the use of the "yesterday's weather" concept. Rather than rely on complicated estimation formulas, XP opts for measuring and estimation using velocity. Velocity is the measure of how much work the team is getting done on the project.

Now that we have our release and the first few iterations mapped out it's time to go into iteration planning.

Q&A

Q How can I get a start with velocity on my first release?

A You could use a seed value of three as the multiple against estimated work. For example, one week estimated effort would give for three ideal engineering weeks. Use the first iteration to get a real number as soon as possible.

Q User stories seem very high level. Where are the actual development tasks tracked?

A Development or engineering tasks are decomposed during the iteration. Developers sign up (in pairs) to work on these.

Q Are XP software development estimates very scientific or accurate?

A If XP was a single, monolithic development cycle that lasted for months or years, its estimation style would not work. Estimating works in XP because iterations are so short, estimates are tracked and refinement is swift. Each project and team is different, and XP allows for this in its estimation style.

Q How long does release planning take?

A Ranges are from a few hours to a couple of days.

Workshop

This workshop tests whether you understand all the concepts you learned in this hour. It is very helpful to know and understand the answers before starting the next lesson.

Quiz

1. What is the role of the customer in the Planning Game?

    a. Provide funding and ownership.

    b. Business direction and writes user stories.

    c. Write user stories and prioritize work.

    d. Write user stories, define business value, and order of implementation.

2. Why would the technical team need a spike?

    a. To investigate technical options and refine the estimate.

    b. They aren't used in planning.

    c. To ensure the Planning Game runs at maximum velocity.

    d. As an input into "yesterday's weather."

3. With regard to XP what is "yesterday's weather" concept?

    a. Specialized XP planning technique.

    b. Using tracked velocity as guide in estimation.

    c. Equalizes estimates for all stories.

    d. Works with load factor in estimation.

4. Why have an zero business value iteration?

   a. To enable the team to practice their XP skills.

   b. To ensure the estimates are accurate before work begins.

   c. These should not be used.

   d. To enable the development team to establish the technical environment.

5. Why would a user story be split?

   a. If it was longer than two sentences.

   b. To allow the iteration to be split.

   c. For estimation purposes.

   d. To increase velocity.

Answers

1. d.

2. a.

3. b.

4. d.

5. c.

Activities

1. Here's the scenario: Your customer needs a new system. Invent this imaginary system (in basic form) and create user stories for it. You may use existing functional specifications from your company in place of the imaginary system if you like.

2. Using the user stories you created in Activity 1, complete our sample release plan using a velocity of nine. Hint: This means you can only assign nine ideal engineering points to each iteration.

Hour **9**

Developing Software in Iterations

In this hour you will learn how to build software in an iteration. We'll look into how to break down the customer's high-level user stories into tasks for developers. Then we'll discover how to monitor and control progress. In this hour we will cover

- How to break down the release into an iteration
- How to break down the user stories into tasks
- How developers estimate and sign up for work
- How the tracker measures progress
- How to write acceptance tests for user stories

Breaking Down the Release into Iterations

After release planning is concluded we have a stack of index cards that contain user stories, and we are ready to begin development. Software development happens inside of the *iteration*. The iteration is a time box between one to four weeks and is the building block that the customer uses to implement her software. The development team and customer gain confidence that the software is on track by breaking down releases into short iterations. Figure 9.1 shows how the iteration begins with planning, proceeds into development, and then is released to the customer for acceptance testing.

Figure 9.1

The XP iteration cycle.

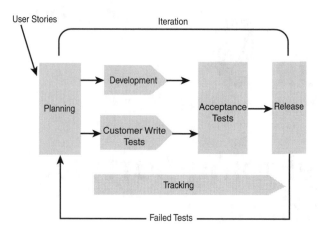

The inputs to our iteration are new user stories and failed acceptance tests from the previous iteration. We estimate how many user stories we can accept into the iteration by using the team's velocity. As we discovered earlier, *velocity* is the measure of the team's throughput, or how fast work is getting done. How fast work is being completed is also affected by the customer's ability to test new functionality and other external factors such as third-party suppliers. We will cover more on measuring velocity later in this hour. A number of activities occur in the iteration, and they are listed in Table 9.1.

TABLE 9.1   The Activities in the Iteration

Planning	Selection of user stories, breakdown into tasks, task estimation, and assignment.
Development	Developers work through tasks in pairs, writing tests first, coding, and then integrating.
Customer writes tests	Customers start writing acceptance tests when planning is complete.
Acceptance tests	Customers run acceptance tests.

TABLE 9.1 continued

Tracking	The tracker monitors progress through the individual engineering tasks that make up the user story.
Acceptance	The customer accepts all new functionality that passes QA. Items that fail the tests are fed back into the next cycle.

Brainstorming Tasks with the Team

The team enters a new iteration with a collection of user stories that the customer wants to implement next. Think back to the release planning meeting; the customer mapped-out the functionality she wanted to see implemented over a series of iterations. Developers provided high-level estimates for these stories, and the first batch has been picked for your iteration.

The customer's user stories will have to be broken down into more manageable chunks before work can be assigned to the development team members. Stories are divided into tasks that describe discrete development activities.

> Tasks are not limited to developers, and might include graphic design, documentation, or other work items. In traditional software development, often these experts are not allowed to interface with the technical team, and this disconnect affects the quality of their output because they are not aware of the latest changes to the product.

Decomposing the stories into tasks is a group effort. The best approach is to brainstorm through the list with the team. The goal of this session is not a detailed solution for each problem, but rather to gather enough information to enable accurate estimation. As developers investigate the stories, they will be clarifying their understanding with the customer and uncovering dependencies. Figure 9.2 illustrates an example user story, broken down into tasks.

Our example leaves some unanswered questions such as "what is the file format?" "What is the log format?" and "who is the user?" These questions will be answered soon enough when development starts. At task breakdown time the conversation might go something like this:

Developer A: Okay, let's tackle the customer import story. Is this the regular customer file that we process at the moment?

Customer: Yes and no; it does come from the mainframe, but I think the format is a little different.

Developer A: It's still straight CSV, right?

Customer: Yes, the format difference is more around the lack of century on dates.

Developer A: You mean the source is not Y2K compliant? We'll need to consider how to handle this. But for now we know and love CSV, so the import ought to be straightforward.

Customer: Lucky we only have a million customers!

Developer B: Really! This might affect how we process the import. Should we spike this now before we estimate further?

Developer A: No I don't think so, we used BulkImporter class on the last project to load more data than this. Let's call it a task and carry on.

FIGURE 9.2

User story broken down into tasks.

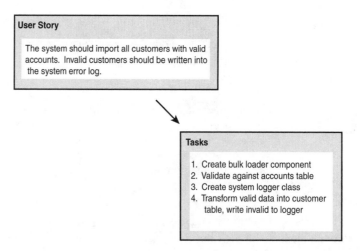

There are some interesting things in our sample dialogue:

- It looks like the source system has some data integrity issues. We can assume that, if it's not Y2K compliant, other problems might come up with the load. We're going to have to resist the temptation to dig into detail at this point. Knowing that it's a CSV text file is enough. We're familiar with loading and parsing these.

- The customer gave us some free information about the size of the file (we would have asked this question anyway). Again, we needed to have an awareness of the size issue, thankfully one of the team had some experience with our loader.

- The customer was involved in this process, this may or may not be necessary and your jargon might scare him away. Closing the loop early is a strong argument for having the customer present throughout task breakdown.
- The developer's considered a spike to analyze how the load would be implemented, after the customer specified the size. In this case, there was enough tacit knowledge in the team to short-circuit the need for any more exploration. If a spike is called for, it's best to time box at a few minutes or hours.

This should give you a sense of how task breakdown happens.

The development team could have technical tasks that require work in the iteration and these should be treated as regular tasks. The attraction to add these "zero business value" tasks is strong and should be controlled; the customer's software is paramount. Documentation or online help are examples of tasks that are, at first glance nonbusiness, but this is not the case. Creation of the online help should be treated as part of the story like any other task. Hopefully, everything the team is doing has some value to the customer! By zero business value we mean there is no direct observable benefit to the customer; low-level error handling is important to the system, but perhaps not very important to the customer!

One approach to handling these technical tasks is to create a "bucket" user story where the tasks can live or, alternatively, work as hard as possible to tie the task directly to a user story. There's something satisfying about aligning everything the team does to the customer's business value.

Signing Up for Work

After the team has broken down the user stories into engineering tasks that can be easily implemented and tracked, the question becomes who does what? The team decides together by signing up for tasks, thereby accepting responsibility for its completion. An effective way of doing this is to list the tasks on the whiteboard, and then "feed the tasks to the sharks!" The leader might need to guide this session to ensure that workload is shared evenly through the team. Generally, this will not be a problem, and developers will take a turn at the boring stuff from time to time.

An important thing to note here is that developers estimate the task after they sign up and are using their own velocity as the estimation benchmark. They look at the previous iterations or similar work and reflect on how long the tasks will actually take. (The tracker might be able to help refresh tired memories.) All development in XP is done in pairs, so your estimations should take this into account. For example, working on a database-intensive task with a recognized RDMS guru would reduce your estimate.

Comparing developers with one another is counter productive and should be avoided. A higher velocity might indicate a different style of estimation rather than personal performance issues. The question is: Are you consistent with your estimates, and are they increasing in accuracy?

Any estimation will be in ideal engineering days or units and will also include time taken to write unit tests. Short-circuiting test writing is a definite no-no in XP. It makes no sense to say "I've finished, except for the tests," when you write the tests first!

Here is an interesting quirk to our task estimation: The task estimates might not equal your original user story number! This is quite okay and indicates the lower level of granularity we're now using. Development of some stories may need to be held off until the next iteration if the revised estimations are greater than the team's velocity.

Task estimations are best captured in a simple spreadsheet. Some XPers have used Wiki Wiki for tracking, and then parsed through the text to remove numeric data.

 Wiki Wiki stores pages as text, and then reformats into HTML at the Web browser. This makes numerical analysis more difficult.

Writing Acceptance Tests

The customer is the final arbitrator on whether the software meets her requirements. It's possible that the team's unit tests pass 100% and still fail to deliver what the customer wants. The risk of developers missing the mark is significantly reduced by the use of XP practices, but it still remains. You *think* you're on track, but how do you *know*? The answer is to get the customer (or business) to write and run acceptance tests. The customer should be writing these as soon as possible; they flow naturally from the user story. While developers are working on their development tasks, the customer (or business) will be writing tests. Figure 9.3 illustrates the acceptance testing workflow, demonstrating how customers write tests while developers implement. Tests that fail are fed back into the next iteration.

Let's take a look at our user story from Figure 9.2, and then write the matching acceptance test. Table 9.2 describes our user story.

FIGURE 9.3

Acceptance testing workflow.

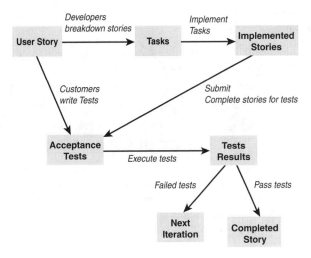

TABLE 9.2   The Example User Story for Acceptance Testing

Import Customers
The system should import all customers with valid accounts. Invalid customers should be written in the system error log.

Acceptance tests should follow the general guidelines listed in Table 9.3:

TABLE 9.3   Acceptance Test Outline

Initialize	Known conditions and/or data are staged into the system to prepare it for testing. The data should be traceable to a known verifiable source, such as dataset, that has been quality checked and placed under software configuration management.
Execute	The tester walks through the test script, following the actions verbatim and recording the results.
Verify	The output or behavior of the test is verified against the expected result.

Some XP projects use business analysts, or something similar, to write acceptance tests for the customer. This can be as simple as interviewing the relevant user or customer representative, and then using this detail as the basis for the acceptance test. The XP approach to user acceptance is a little different from the norm where tests are written on small pieces of functionality (user stories). It might be that these tests are aggregated at release time into a complete end-to-end test suite.

Using this outline we can create an acceptance test for the user story in Table 9.2. Table 9.4 is our finished test.

TABLE 9.4 Example Acceptance Test

Initialize	Taking the sample data set load file (`customers_small.dat`)
Execute	Execute the load customers option on the master import screen
Verify	After load is completed validate that customer master has the eight correct customers, and the system.log lists the two invalid records. Please see attached spreadsheet for the customer list.

> The first column (initialize, execute, and verify) is not part of the acceptance test, but was left on the example for simplicity.

The resulting acceptance test is easy to write and understand. We can expect the need for some supporting notes to describe where test data is and the expected result data. The power and usefulness of acceptance tests becomes more apparent after we automate. All tests should be automated, and our example test is an obvious candidate for automation.

Automating Your Acceptance Tests

You learned earlier how automating unit tests is an integral part of the XP development cycle; the same is true for acceptance tests. Realistically, customers will need help scripting their tests. You can automate interface tests using capture tools such as Visual Test from Rational Software Corporation, but these can quickly develop a life of their own. They typically capture the screen and then use this as a basis for screen image comparisons. Using GUI interface–testing tools such as Visual Test can mean that any alteration in interface will require a test script adjustment. This can become very time consuming. Automation should strike the balance between functionality and overhead.

Business analysts could use simple office automation or scripting tools to load and run tests. These need not be difficult to devise and will become invaluable as the product grows in complexity. At release time, regression testing will create unwelcome overhead if automated acceptance tests don't exist.

It's in the development team's interest to help the customer automate his tests. Spare developers (uneven pairs or developers finished with their tasks) can lend a hand at scripting tasks. After automation is established, extending to new tests is much easier.

In our example, the customer could use an Excel spreadsheet to hold customer test data, run macros to load the data, execute your component, and then verify the results. File-based tests such as this, where output is compared against a golden log (known good data) are easy to automate.

Tracking and Steering the Iteration

Tracking the iteration is how the team and customer know progress and throughput. Rather than get weighed down by detailed metrics and reports, the team will opt to measure by a handful of key indicators. *Extreme Programming Installed* expresses tracking in four broad areas:

- Resources—Planned versus actual resource usage: number of developers, number of customer team members, hardware, and other resource related metrics
- Scope—Number of stories: total completed and new ones in the pipeline
- Quality—Number of acceptance tests passed, changes over time
- Time—User stories planned against actual on the release plan

Gathering and reporting metrics can get out of control. The temptation to add every possible measurement into tracking set should be resisted. In true XP style we're looking to capture just enough metrics and no more. The tracker should devise graphs that display story completion and defect measures. Unit tests results will always be 100%, therefore, reporting on these is easy! Logging detailed source measures such as number of classes, lines of code, and method counts are more useful, post project. Capture these for historical purposes after the release; don't consume tracking time with these. Review Figures 9.4 and 9.5 below for an example of the kind of charts you could use when tracking.

FIGURE 9.4

User stories completed chart against the burn rate.

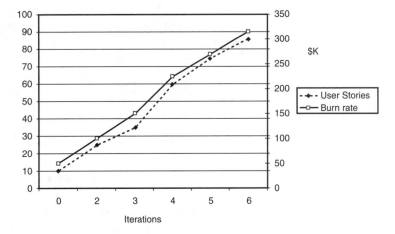

The chart illustrated in Figure 9.4 compares the user stories completed against the *burn rate*. The burn rate is how fast the development team is spending the overall project budget. It's very important to measure burn rate in a fixed-priced contract because it indicates to the development team whether they are on track to complete the project within budget constraints. See the note on calculating cost variance for another approach to burn rate. The user stories completed chart is useful to both the business and development sides of the team because it indicates the velocity of the development team. We could expect that burn rate will track the user story throughput, but this is not always the case because stories have different efforts. You might choose to switch the user story axis for perfect engineering days or whatever effort measurement you're using. As it stands the chart is useful to both the development team and the customer, but you might not want the customer to know your burn rate!

Classic project management measures cost variance (CV), which is another way of tracking expenditure and, therefore, schedule. CV is equal to BCWP–ACWP), where

- Budgeted cost of work performed (BCWP): The value for completed work measured in terms of the planned budget for that work.
- Actual cost of work performed (ACWP): The actual cost incurred for the work performed within a given time period.
- Burn rate is a simpler way of tracking how fast the project is being consumed.

FIGURE 9.5

Acceptance tests passed for each iteration chart.

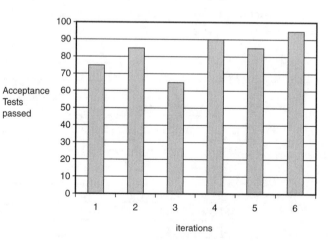

The chart in Figure 9.5 indicates how many acceptance tests are passing for each iteration. Beyond making the team feel good (or bad!), what real benefit does this chart have?

One useful aspect is that it exposes troublesome modules or areas of the system. For example, if during iteration you noticed a drop in the number of acceptance tests passing, you can take this as a cue to dig a little further. On a larger development project, you might break down tests by area, which would highlight the area that should be targeted for refactoring. So, think of a drop in test scores as smoke; your mission is to find the fire! It's debatable whether you should bother with a suite of charts that displayed detailed results for the whole acceptance test suite. Start with the high-level, simple approach and investigate further if the need arises.

Tracking will often have external and internal views, and you should recognize these and report on what makes sense based on your context. One important common denominator is that milestones should be *binary* in nature; that is, done/not done as opposed to percent complete. Display tracking results is best done with printed output fixed to the wall in the project room. Electronically, Wiki Wiki works well for textual or numerical output. It is essential to use your project Web site if displaying status online.

So, track only what's necessary to measure how fast or well the team is implementing the customer's stories.

Handling a Slip

What does the tracker do if she sees developers fall behind? It could be that they are not behind at all, but that they got their estimates wrong! The question is will the task cause the user story to miss the iteration. Remember we have a fixed window of time in which to operate and if the task spirals out because of unforeseen difficulties it might have to be rescheduled for the next iteration. This is the worst case. In all probability, there is another developer available to help, and she can bring fresh eyes to the problem. If the task is clearly too big, a split is possible with another pair chipping in.

Working in small iterations, tracking, and using daily standup meetings all help to mitigate task slippage. A slip is not the end if the world, but the iteration end date cannot be moved.

Steering the Iteration

Steering the iteration is about maximizing throughput through the cycle. If velocity is dropping it might indicate issues that can be resolved by adding resources or pairing back stories, or it might indicate an estimation inaccuracy. Remember that the team is learning how to estimate as iterations progress, and that slippage might simply point to a bad estimate. As always, learning and refining are the keys.

The idea behind the concept of steering in XP is that we make many small course corrections, rather than a few major ones. Kent Beck compares this to driving a car, which involves almost constant adjustments to either speed or direction. Even if you set the cruise control you still have to steer! It falls to the lot of the tracker to highlight when these course corrections need to be made. If you're looking for a complicated process you'll be disappointed! The XP project is steered by measuring and controlling velocity; how fast *are* we going, and how fast *should* we be going?

Measuring and Controlling Velocity

Development progress is measured during the iteration against the engineering tasks. It falls to the tracker to monitor the team's velocity. The tracker is expected to be "light on her feet," and unobtrusive as she questions developers on their progress. The two main questions that developers are asked are

- How many ideal engineering days or units have you worked on your task?
- How many more units do you estimate it will take to complete the task?

There has to be some way of interpreting ideal days or units back into calendar time, and applying a load factor is one effective approach to doing this. This load factor is derived over time from your particular project. You could take three as starting factor and refine from there. The tracker should be gathering metrics that make sense in relation to the project, and then using these to get a sense of where the project is headed. Figure 9.6 demonstrates how we can get a baseline velocity.

FIGURE 9.6
Baseline velocity formula.

$$Velocity = \frac{iterationLength * No. Developers}{LoadFactor}$$

Working with an iteration length of three weeks gives us a baseline velocity of eight. Figure 9.7 walks through this example for us.

FIGURE 9.7
Example velocity calculation.

$$8 = \frac{3 * 8}{3}$$

Iteration Length = 3 weeks
Number of Developers = 8
Load Factor = 3

An interesting, yet vital, facet of the tracker's role is that she can gain tremendous insight into the project by simply asking her tracking questions. She does this by keeping her eyes and ears open, using her EQ or soft skills: "How did the team member respond to my innocuous questions?" or "Do they seem overcome or blinded by workload?" Tracking isn't only concerned with entering numbers into your spreadsheet; numbers don't always tell the whole story.

The daily standup or standing meeting is another forum where issues can be exposed.

Standup Meetings

XP saves developers from the dreaded meeting cycle by minimizing development overhead. The team meets daily for short, focused, informal meetings to keep everyone in touch with progress. The best approach is to gather the team together once a day, and while standing in a circle, go around each person in turn. The meeting lasts around 10–15 minutes and is best attended with your beverage of choice in hand. This is not a detailed problem-solving session and any issues that are raised can be taken offline afterwards. The standup is invaluable for quickly synchronizing the team. Management or interested observers might drop by, and they can learn more from 10 minutes taken here than any report.

How vital is the standup? The alternative is a more structured meeting, with agenda and minutes. Such a meeting could realistically only take place once a week, and there's a lot of water under the bridge in the meantime. So, the standup is a great way to close the loop in a low overhead kind of way. Developers are likely to avoid the hour-long project meeting at all costs! The result is a poorly attended meeting that has little real value and can become mere window dressing.

Closing the Iteration

The end of the iteration is quite clear; it's the end of the time box! Closing the iteration is where the customer performs the acceptance tests and either accepts or rejects. Criteria for acceptance are based on the customer's level of satisfaction with the user story. Remember that we're developing within a release that has multiple iterations, and that minor issues can be resolved in the future. User stories that fail the "save order details" test will be rejected, whereas cosmetic quibbles might be overlooked.

Any stories that fail customer acceptance will be fed back into the next iteration. The risk of failure is reduced by constant customer involvement during development; they have seen the functionality grow over the iteration and have been subjected to a lot of questions. Testing time is not the first time they have seen their implemented functionality!

Summary

Over the last hour we've seen how the iteration is where the real work of development takes place. The customer is still very much involved in steering, planning, and testing. The tracker assembles some simple measures that accurately indicate progress both to the team and external audience. The customer selects stories, and then grades each complete story using his own acceptance tests.

The customer is still very much in the driver's seat!

In the next hour we will go into greater depth about user stories. You know *what* they are, but the next hour will explain *how* to write them and the tools you can use to create them.

Q&A

Q What is the best tool to use for automating Web browser tests?

A There are some unit test tools such as httpUnit, but they are suited for developers. Rational and Compuware are two leading software vendors that enable the user to capture and then replay actions.

Q What level of detail should I write in my acceptance tests?

A XP acceptance tests tend to focus on the "happy path," which is how the system operates with good or correct data. Some QA departments like to extend this to so-called "monkey testing," where random data is entered and output observed. Keep in mind that the development team has written many more unit tests that have tested everything that could break. These have all passed at 100%. The bottom line is the tests should satisfy the customer that functionally has been delivered; they write the tests and the story.

Q Can I add resources if velocity is falling?

A Classic project-management theory states that adding resources to a project that is late will make it later! A better approach is to defer stories or switch pairs. If the trend is falling velocity, you could add resource in the next iteration. Remember that this will change the chemistry of team; you're not developing by the numbers!

Q What if the customer refuses to write acceptance tests?

A There is a very real chance that this will happen. Offer the services of analysts or developers to act as scribes or translators. They might not be willing to *write*, but they might *talk*. Writing tests is collaboration between the team, but the customer must *own* the result.

Workshop

This workshop tests whether you understand all the concepts you learned in this hour. It is very helpful to know and understand the answers before starting the next lesson.

Quiz

1. What happens to failed acceptance tests?

    a. Like unit tests, they should pass 100%.

    b. The team must not let the story fail; they should work until the test passes.

    c. The story should be split and tasks that pass can be accepted.

    d. They should be fed back into the next iteration.

2. Taking a load factor of three, what is the velocity of six developers with a four week iteration?

    a. Not enough data to say.

    b. eight.

    c. 12.

    d. six.

3. Why is it important to automate acceptance tests?

    a. Development speed is easier to maintain.

    b. Repeatability and reliability of results.

    c. Reduces customer testing time.

    d. Enables the team to integrate the tests into the testing framework.

4. What are the four areas that the tracker should focus on?

    a. Testing, defects, team morale, and automation.

    b. Measurement, results, feedback, and quality.

    c. Resources, tests, quality, and time.

    d. Scope, quality, time, and resources.

Answers

1. d.
2. b.
3. b.
4. d.

Activities

1. Create some charts using Excel, or a similar spreadsheet, to display results of tasks, user stories, and acceptance tests. Experiment with stacked-bar, scatter, and line styles.

2. Write script of Excel macro to complete the customer's acceptance test in Table 9.4.

HOUR 10

Gathering the Customer's Requirements with User Stories

In this hour you will learn how to gather requirements with user stories. User stories are a new, lightweight way of capturing your customer's requirements. In this hour you will learn

- How user stories are used to gather customer requirements
- What the essential elements of user stories are and how to write them
- What tools you can use when creating user stories
- How to merge user stories into your existing requirements approach

Writing Your First User Story

Understanding the customer's requirements is vital to the success of any project. In earlier hours we talked about how various approaches attempted to close the loop between requirements and development. In a classic Waterfall project the customer defines his requirements through *functional specifications*. These are usually detailed enough for both estimation and design purposes. Development will not start until the functional specification is signed off. Sign off is effectively saying, "This document describes *exactly* what I want you to build." We know from experience that this tactic is fraught with problems, not the least is that the written word can be poor at conveying abstract concepts. Another challenge is that often the customer or user needs to *see* something to gain insight into what is possible.

So, instead of forcing the customer to explicitly define the requirements up front, XP allows for evolution. The user story can be described as a placeholder for future requirements. Customers are opening dialogue with the development team about what they want and are using the story as the starting point. Requirements evolve both as developers learn more about the business domain and customers realize the possibilities and constraints.

What if the customer won't write the user stories? This is a similar problem to the one we faced in the last hour with acceptance tests. Don't get hung up on who physically has the pen in hand and does the writing. It could be that the customer talks and explains while a scribe converts this into stories. We should learn from the customer why they are reluctant to write, and then endeavor to allay their fears.

Whoever does the actual writing is less important than who *owns* the resulting stories. The stories have to be an expression of what is in the mind of the customer. The customer will make the final call on whether the story is close enough to his understanding. It has been said that understanding what user stories are is easy; the hard part is writing them! In the next section we'll walk through the process.

Where do you start with the story? Try the name. Name the story something that captures the user's goal in a few words. Avoid using numbers or arbitrary key sequences. A name such as AZ124 smacks of a system-generated entity; remember we are creating a bridge between *people*. Using verb-object construction for the title will be easiest to understand. The customers will name the story anyway, so let them use whatever makes sense from their viewpoint. The story has a short life and there are only a few per iteration. The team's focus is this iteration's stories. Having a small set of requirements enables the team to hold the names and stories either in their heads or on an easily displayable chart.

The user story isn't the place to describe functionality in detail. Think of it as sign on the way to our destination. Table 10.1 lists the parts of the user story:

You could argue that the *estimate* is not truly part of the user story, but it's included here because the practice is to attach the estimate to the story.

TABLE 10.1 The Elements of the User Story

Element	Description
Name	A short description that the team can use when discussing, estimating, and tracking the story.
Text	The body of the story that describes the concept of the story in a few sentences.
Estimate	Preliminary estimate generated during the Planning Game.

Your user story text should be two or three sentences long. If you're struggling to find the right level of detail for the story you can use the *testable* benchmark. By this we mean, "is the story testable, or can I write a test to verify the story." The ink will still be wet on your user story when it's time to write the acceptance tests! To be testable implies that some known good input and expected results exist. Table 10.2 reads like a reasonable user story that clearly could be tested. It still needs some supporting documentation, so leave it out of your story because it will only add clutter at this stage.

TABLE 10.2 Update Customer Profile Sample User Story

Update Customer Profile
Customers call in and request changes to their details. The system should enable the user to update all customer fields. SSN is the primary search key to be used.

Table 10.3 is an example of a user story that could be a challenge to test:

TABLE 10.3 Customer Profile Ease of Use Sample User Story

Customer Profile Ease of Use
The existing customer profile screen is very hard to use. The interface should be redesigned to increase usability.

Is the user story in Table 10.3 testable? As it stands, this user story will be very hard to test! Usability metrics can be used to directly measure this, but more obvious metrics such as screen access or error counts could be used. It could be that the story simply needs more supporting documentation to explain what the goal of "ease of use" really means. User stories that describe softer measurements, such as usability, require some care while writing.

The customer can write stories on paper or electronically. The customer could be apprehensive about this new approach, after all, sliding a stack of index cards across the table and then asking that they "just write user stories" might be a little threatening. Take time to walk through examples of stories; write some together and let the customer become more familiar. The best way to become familiar with the cards is to ask the customer to scribble a few and tear them up. Being allowed to tear up the cards is liberating!

XPers favor index cards; they are simple, easy to handle, and cheap! The limited space on the cards also helps to keep the description short.

Selecting Tools for Writing User Stories

XP makes a convincing argument to write stories on index cards. Putting this to one side, there will be some XP users who would rather use electronic storage. The distributed XP team might actually need to reflect stories to a wider audience. One approach is to use a word processor and, in either a single document or individual files, capture stories. However, as familiar as the word processing approach is, it falters in planning because the customer can't easily sort the stories.

If you insist on using a word processor you can extend the use of the story to include the supporting documentation. Figure 10.1 displays a typical Microsoft Word–based user story.

FIGURE 10.1

Using a word processor for writing user stories.

Acme Project

Story Number: AC101
Story Description: An administrator should be able to search for and
                       update user profiles.

Developers:
Date Started: 10/10/2002
Date Completed:

Task	Description	Estimate
1	Build search API interface	1.5
2	Create admin search screen off admin main	2.5
3	Extended user object	3

Comments:

Date	Comment	Developer
10/12	Need John to explain his API model!	

Code Complete   Y/N
Integrated   Y/N
Actual Hours

Capturing User Stories with Wiki Wiki

Wiki Wiki is a Web-based collaboration tool that enables users to freely edit and create information. Originally developed by one of the founders of XP (Ward Cunningham) it has quickly spawned numerous clones on a wide-range of platforms. Wiki's are typically operated in either a document or thread mode. This refers to the way the Wiki is used and has nothing to do with the interface; there is no document mode button. When used in a document mode, the Wiki can be used as a kind of shared notepad where any user that has access to the site can edit and add text. Using a page in the thread mode is similar to the good-old bulletin board; users discuss topics and ideas in a rambling, free way.

> Think of a Wiki as kind of shared notepad, where users can search a virtually unlimited body of text.

The Wiki Wiki philosophy is to minimize features in the tool and to give uncontrolled access to content. It relies on the Wiki Wiki user community to self-police. Truly erroneous pages can be deprecated (deleted) by the administrator.

> For a complete list of Wiki Wiki clones visit
> http://www.c2.com/cgi/wiki?WikiEngines.

Wiki Wiki works by storing user content in some kind of backend database and then converting this to HTML when the user requests the page. Formatting and links are implemented through a very simple set of basic style; for example, `ThisIsAWikiLink` would create an internal link. Creating links is through the use of mixed case, also known as camel case. The training course for Wiki normally lasts about 10 minutes.

Wiki Wiki is an ideal tool to implement if you need to distribute user stories. In our example we are using Openwiki, which is a Microsoft Active Server Pages (ASP) version of Wiki Wiki. For now I'll demonstrate how it can be used easily with user stories. Figure 10.2 shows our starting page for user stories.

10

FIGURE 10.2
Wiki Wiki user stories starting page.

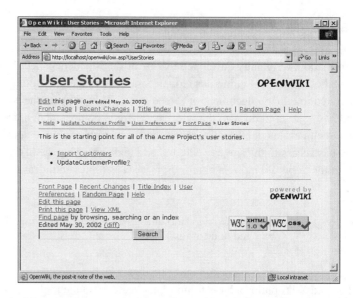

Acme project only has one user story at the moment. We begin by editing the page and add the `UpdateCustomerProfile` user story. This title corresponds with the index card user story name. Mixed or camel case is used to indicate a link inside Openwiki. After saving the page you'll see the user story name with a "?" next to it. Click this and you'll enter the UpdateCustomerProfile page, as shown in Figure 10.3.

FIGURE 10.3
The UpdateCustomerProfile user story page.

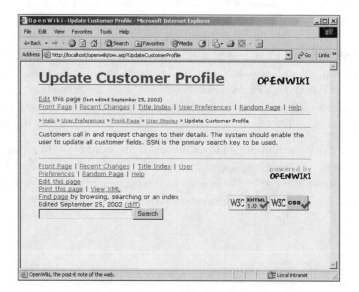

From here you can transfer the text from your index card into the UpdateCustomerProfile page. You might decide to add the estimation to the story at this point, but its value is only used in planning. Decide whether it adds any value in your situation. Perhaps a secondary estimation summary page or an extra column on the user story list page will suffice.

Your story is now captured in Wiki Wiki. The logical next step is to add the underlying task detail after the iteration planning starts. These engineering tasks can still be written on the flip side of the index card, or they can be entered directly into the Wiki. Figure 10.4 illustrates how developers can add their tasks to the story.

FIGURE 10.4

The UpdateCustomerProfile user story page with engineering tasks.

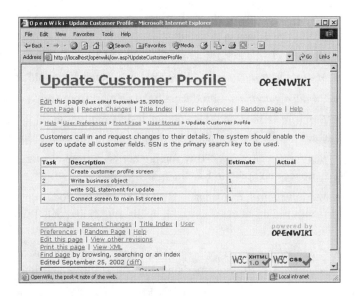

Again, there are no hard and fast rules about the level of detail that you capture for your tasks. In the example the following columns were added and are listed in Table 10.4:

TABLE 10.4   User Story Task Column Descriptors

Column	Description
Task	A task sequence number. Use this if it helps in reporting.
Description	One line description for the task. Create a Wiki link to a child page if you need more detail.
Estimate	The estimate complete in your measurement type (ideal engineering days, and so on).
Actual	The actual time it took to complete the task.

You might decide to add a column for the task owner, but only include this column if it adds value. If the team is small you will know the owner's name! For tracking purposes you could add a current effort column, but the visual wallchart is generally better for tracking status.

Sample User Stories for Gathering Customer's Requirements

For people new to XP, it can be hard to visualize what user stories look like. In this section we will list and demonstrate some examples to help jump-start your own writing.

- *Accept credit application*—Enables customers to enter personal details online and process their loan application.
- *Book hotel*—Search for a hotel by city and book a room.
- *Migrate user accounts*—Move all user accounts from old email server to new.
- *Produce data mart*—Produce ABC data mart from core data warehouse.
- *Fuzzy name search*—The existing system requires exact last name matches. Create a new search feature that uses close matches and smart search logic.
- *Buy foreign currency*—Buy foreign currency from clients. Use daily rates against currency and apply to base margin.
- *Version control documents*—Extend the existing document management solution to require validated users to check documents in and out. Track and record version differences.
- *Cross-sell media*—Display matches from other, nonbook, media when the user searches. Use the customer's buying patterns to establish a subset.

 The cross-sell media story looks like it might need a split! Cross searching and the second part (business intelligence about buy patterns) seem to be too complex for a single story. This is a good example of a *splitable* user story.

- *Print tax form*—Print all relevant tax paperwork.

Hopefully these examples give you a sense of the level of detail and style in the user story. The best way to learn is by doing and practicing writing lots of stories!

User Story Variations

There are other variations on user stories that can be useful as you migrate from your existing approach to XP. If you find that your customers are initially hesitant about specifying everything with user stories, you can build a bridge to them by looking for a middle ground. Let's take a look into three of the common scenarios you might face: use cases, functional specifications, and prototyping.

Comparing User Stories and Use Cases

The Rational Unified Process (RUP) gathers requirements with *use cases*. Use cases describe a sequence of actions a system performs and the results of those actions. There is wide-spread acceptance of use cases as a mechanism for defining requirements if they are practiced in your environment. It will be useful to compare use cases with user stories.

Use cases are much more structured than user stories; Table 10.5 lists the components of use cases:

TABLE 10.5   The Elements of a Use Case

Element	Description
Actor	An actor is a person or other entity external to the software system being specified who interacts with the system and performs use cases to accomplish tasks. Different actors often correspond to different user classes, or roles, identified from the customer.
Description	A brief description of the use case or a high-level description of the actions and the outcome of executing the use case.
Preconditions	Any activities that must take place or any conditions that must be true before the use case can be started.
Postconditions	The state of the system at the conclusion of the use case execution.
Frequency of Use	Estimate of the number of times the use case will be performed by the actors per some unit of time.
Normal Course of Events	A detailed description of the user actions and system responses that will take place during execution of the use case under normal, expected conditions.
Exceptions	Any anticipated error conditions that could occur during execution of the use case, and including definitions of how the system is to respond to those conditions.
Includes	Any other use cases that are included by the use case.

TABLE 10.5   continued

Element	Description
Special Requirements	Any additional requirements, such as nonfunctional requirements, for the use case that might need to be addressed during design or implementation. These might include performance requirements or other quality attributes.
Assumptions	Any assumptions that were made in the analysis and writing of the use case description.

Comparing this list to our high-level user story we get a sense of the level of definition found in each method. Use cases are attempting to define requirements to such a level that developers can design and build from the text. (RUP does allow for iteration, but not to the extreme level found in XP). You can write requirements with use cases and still do XP. The question is why would you? In XP, we are not asking or expecting the customer to articulate exactly what they want. If you are well-versed in use cases you might be tempted to adopt this style in XP. On the whole this is not a good idea; remember we want the customer to write in his own words. If you're an avid use-case writer, you can adopt what is known as essential use cases. This refers to the distilling of the use case to the bare minimum.

Perhaps the biggest negative with use cases is the requirement that the customer conform to the developer's particular dialect. We are asking the customer to explain himself using our tribal language.

Converting Functional Specifications

A common scenario for XP development, especially in new implementations, is balancing Agile approaches with ingrained Waterfall ideologies. You might find a customer who is happy to allow the development team to do their own thing as long as corporate policy is followed with respect to milestones and deliverables. Even in this far-from-ideal situation you run with some XP practices. On the requirements side, you might be handed a functional specification; the customer won't see any value in converting this into user stories! In this case, the technical team might opt to translate the specification backward into user stories. Why bother with this? One reason is that estimation of technical tasks and subsequent iteration management will be so much easier. The functional specification does not aid the team in developing inside the iteration. At the end of the day, XP without user stories (generated from whatever means) will not be possible.

If you do convert into user stories, at least explain the reasoning and process to the customer. There's a good chance they will jettison the Waterfall approach in the future if they've had first-hand experience of how XP can work for them.

Prototyping with User Stories

Customers familiar with Staged Development, which includes prototypes, might not be comfortable proceeding without some kind of visual sign off. Eventually, you will hope that they will drop this approach as they learn and trust your XP process. In the meantime, you can extend use of cards to include a miniprototype. This is how this works:

- The customer writes a standard user story.
- With the customer, you develop a screen mock-up on the whiteboard.
- The screen is sketched on an interface guide card.
- After the meeting, a nonworking prototype screen is developed. This is screen-printed and fixed to the interface guide card (the image has to be sized down).

Figure 10.5 illustrates this and also shows how the customer writes a parallel acceptance test for the user story.

FIGURE 10.5
The UpdateCustomerProfile user story page.

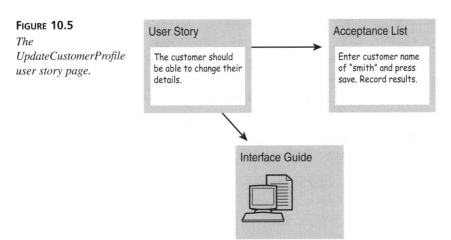

Don't get bogged down in devising a hundred and one uses for index cards! The point is that they are very flexible and you should feel freedom to leverage them anyway you can. Keep your XP value of simplicity in mind as you consider how to capture requirements. Take the simplest path possible.

Summary

User stories could be one of the hardest parts of XP to learn. They are deceptively simple and yet crucial to project success. The beauty of the story is that it returns the onus on specifying requirements back to the customer in a very nonthreatening way. Customers are drawn to the ability to express themselves in their own words, whereas developers delight in the lack of paperwork.

In the next hour you will learn how developers no longer go it alone, but they work in pairs. What does Pair Programming look like, and is it cost effective? Hour 11, "Software Development with Pair Programming," will make this clear, and you will be surprised at some of the answers!

Q&A

Q Is there a particular style of index card that should be used with user stories?

A No. Cards can be blank, lined, or specially printed with story name, description, and tasks. The size should be large enough to write on, but small enough to handle easily. No doubt you will need some experimentation to settle on the cards that work for you.

Q How many stories are in a typical release or iteration?

A The number of stories is a little hard to define one rule of thumb is one story/developer/month. A six-month project with six developers could have between 20 and 40 stories.

Q What happens to the stories after the release?

A Typically, they are discarded. It would seem that keeping track of historical task estimates would be useful for future estimation, but because of the dynamic nature of XP development, this might not be the case. The customer owns the cards, so hand them over to him!

Workshop

This workshop tests whether you understand all the concepts you learned in this hour. It is very helpful to know and understand the answers before starting the next hour's lesson.

Quiz

1. What are the key elements of a user story?

   a. Description and tasks.

   b. Actors, descriptions, and estimates.

   c. Depends on the tool used; word processors have more storage capability.

   d. Name and description.

2. What are the drawbacks to using a word processor with user stories?

    a. Sorting and sharing are difficult.

    b. Wiki Wiki is better; it has a browser interface.

    c. Hardware requirements are increased.

    d. Added cost to project.

3. How does the team develop software from a user story?

    a. By using interface guide cards for prototyping.

    b. User stories are more useful in planning not development.

    c. They breakdown the story into tasks and work on these.

    d. They work closely with the customer refining requirements.

4. Why is the testable benchmark important?

    a. Customers will have to write acceptance tests based on the story.

    b. This is less important than the accuracy of the story.

    c. Automation cannot be executed without it.

    d. If the user story is not testable there will be no way of knowing when the story is finished.

Answers

1. d.

2. a.

3. c., d.

4. a., d.

Activities

1. Buy some index cards. Using an old or current functional specification, convert features into user stories.

2. You have been commissioned to build an online store that sells, believe it or not, books! Take the role of customer and write user stories that describe the base functionality you will need. Become familiar with tearing up the cards and rewrites.

HOUR 11

Software Development with Pair Programming

In this hour you will learn how to use Pair Programming in writing your production code. This XP practice is integral to the way software is written by developers. In this hour you will learn

- What Pair Programming is
- How to arrange the physical environment of Pair Programming
- The costs and benefits of Pair Programming
- Some of the common objections raised about Pair Programming, and how XP answers them
- Keys to succeeding with Pair Programming

Getting into the Pair Programming Mindset

Pair Programming is where two developers share the same machine and work side-by-side to solve and produce code. We know both anecdotally and through research that collaboration in development produces better quality code. More than that, the experience of programming can be much more rewarding. Tackling a problem together is by no means revolutionary; we've all experienced the results that come from synergy. In XP, we take the practice of collaboration to the extreme. We'll turn the dial up to "10" by doing *all* development in pairs.

Later in this hour, evidence will be offered favoring the use of Pair Programming, and some of the common criticisms raised by naysayers will be addressed. For now, let's jump right into explaining what Pair Programming is and how it's used in XP.

Remember how I explained that XP practices work together, and that taking a practice by itself lessens the results we can achieve? Pair Programming is an excellent proof for this because it works together with collective ownership, coding standards, and refactoring.

How does Pair Programming work in reality? One developer types at the keyboard (drives) while their partner reviews, analyzes, talks, helps, prompts, and thinks. Think of it as two minds instead of one: One has a detailed view, whereas the other considers system-wide implications. In actuality, roles aren't quite as clear-cut, but it does illustrate one aspect of this way of working. Both roles are active and the partner (nontyper) remains very much engaged in the process of development. He isn't just looking over your shoulder as you do the real work.

The session begins with the question "may I drive?" The driver continues working at the keyboard until the natural turn of events, when the partner returns the question. The partner might be tempted to help or takeover while the driver fleshes out a line of reasoning. The driver might use the commonly accepted statement "trust me." Let the driver complete whatever code they need to demonstrate his thinking. Back and forth it goes until the task is finished.

Let's be honest, it is a little unnerving when you begin with Pair Programming. You're opening your thought process, not just your resulting code at code review time. Code review is no longer an event, with XP and Pair Programming you have *continuous* code review. Building in quality removes many of the errors that are typically uncovered at acceptance or system test time. If code reviews are good, why not review *all* the time! Nobody is keeping score here, and you won't be chastised for code quality at the end of development. In reality the entire team's quality begins to improve as developers switch pairs, and the tacit knowledge held by the experts is transferred among the team.

Quite soon into the project you will find that knowledge is being shared equally across the team, this is mainly because of pairing and switching developers. At the very least you will have two developers who will know a section of the code with the same depth of understanding. The problem of what to do when the database guy is away sick or on vacation is nullified with Pair Programming.

Another valuable benefit to Pair Programming is that the partner can take care of any logging or record keeping while the driver continues to work. In a single developer scenario there is a frequent break in the flow of programming as time is taken for logging. Some development shops forgo journaling because they feel the overhead is too high to justify. Even if the team believes personal record keeping is a worthy practice, the hassle of context switching back and forth soon becomes unbearable. Pairing frees up the driver to stay in the flow while the partner journals and logs as necessary.

Creating the Physical Space

Physical space is always important when it comes to development, and there are many forms to choose from including cubicles, offices, open-plan, or virtual. The classic cube-farm, where workers are figuratively and literally isolated from each other, remains the norm. The all-to-frequent meetings and the odd cooler conversation are the only moments when developers connect. Why is it that we create and solve more in one whiteboard session than in a whole day of solitary grind? To move away from the solo programming style to XP will necessitate some furniture rearrangement. You can make some simple and immediate changes to your physical layout.

Let's walk though some typical changes to layout. Figure 11.1 is the typical desk with a single developer, with the machine located somewhere along the horizontal edge of the desk. Sitting next to each other is difficult, and the best solution is to slide the machine to the end of the desk, creating closer proximity.

11

FIGURE 11.1

*Rearranging your desk
space to Pair Program.*

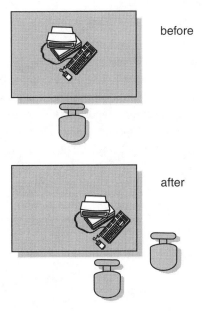

before

after

Figure 11.1 does offer some challenges with paper and other materials, but you can use creativity and your own space to solve this problem. Next, we have the L-shaped desk shown in Figure 11.2, clearly Pair Programming is hindered here.

FIGURE **11.2**

*Rearranging your
L-shaped desk for Pair
Programming.*

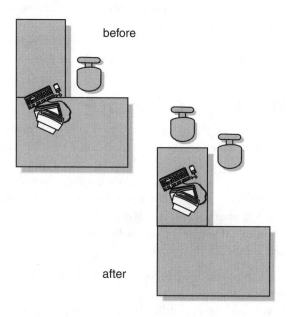

before

after

The only real solution is to either break away a section of the desk (if this is possible) or to relocate the machine to one end. Figure 11.3 is the last example, and a cubical or corner desk is in use. Again, moving the machine to one end, as has been illustrated, is the only real option.

It must be said that utilizing existing workspace is always going to result in some give and take. You will effectively loose the benefits attached to ergonomic desks that have special keyboard recesses to reduce occupational overuse. Another interesting side effect to Pair Programming is that some developers report back or neck tensions as they stretched to read the driver's screen. Pay special attention to how developers are sitting in your particular configuration because preventing repetitive strain or static muscle-tension problems is much simpler than curing them. One company using XP paid for the services of a registered masseuse to apply monthly neck and back rubs! On a serious note, the facilities aspect of Pair Programming must be resolved. Modern desktop environments have attempted to minimize side effects caused by *individuals* using computers.

FIGURE 11.3

Rearranging your cubicle for Pair Programming.

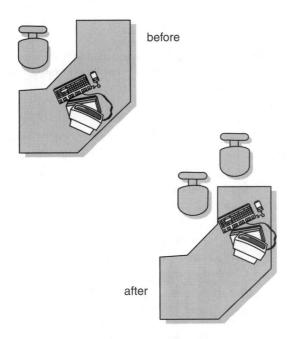

before

after

11

Real-time sharing of machines returns benefits from collaboration, but also raises the prospect of new, insidious problems. Be aware of these issues as you implement XP. The simplest way to keep on top of this is to poll developers from time to time about how they are feeling physically. Make whatever adjustments are necessary.

Pair Programming Costs and Benefits

We know that collaboration makes sense because it produces better quality work, higher morale, and increased creativity, but what about economics? Does having two developers share a machine improve the bottom line? Laurie Williams, from North Carolina State University, has conducted research into the costs and benefits of Pair Programming, and has arrived at some surprising conclusions. How much longer does development take when pairing? Her study found

- Development time with Pair Programming was around 15% longer than with individual programming

- Pair Programming yielded at least 15% less defects than individual programming

Visit `http://www.pairprogramming.com/` for more information and research on Pair Programming. Metrics and results for this section were developed, from "The Costs and Benefits of Pair Programming," by Alistair Cockburn and Laurie Williams.

In a University of Utah experiment with software engineering undergraduates, students were given four programs to complete. Program 1 results were affected by the overhead caused by the pair working together for the first time. Even with taking this into consideration, pairs were immediately writing code with fewer defects than individuals. Figure 11.4 illustrates how quality continued to improve over the experiment.

FIGURE **11.4**

Pair Programming improves quality.

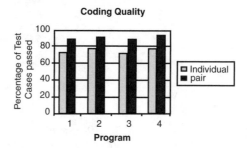

What do these results tell us? That costs are considerably lower over the complete project lifecycle with Pair Programming. Cast your mind back to Hour 3, "Overcoming Software Development Problems with XP," where it was explained how XP endeavors to flatten the cost of development. Usually, costs attached to development rise rapidly as the software moves from design through coding into test and release. Fixing errors in design are easy; nothing exists at that point! Let's walk though what the real costs of development are with Pair Programming, with some help from Laurie Williams's test results.

Let's compare the costs with a typical 50,000-line development project, using individual and pair developers. Figure 11.5 shows that with a speed of 50 lines of code (LOC) per hour it will take 1,000 hours to write the software. Using what we know about the 15% extra effort required with Pair Programming, this gives us 1,150 hours for the equivalent task.

FIGURE 11.5

Comparing development effort with individual and Pair Programmers.

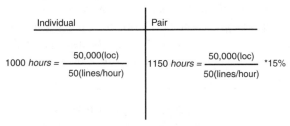

Upfront development time

Individual	Pair
$1000\ hours = \dfrac{50,000(loc)}{50(lines/hour)}$	$1150\ hours = \dfrac{50,000(loc)}{50(lines/hour)} \ ^{*}15\%$

Where:
LOC is Lines of Code

Let's look at the other end of the scale: What is the impact of lowering defect counts? Taking representative statistics from Watts Humphrey's *A Discipline for Software Engineering* we can assume that programmers have 100 defects per thousand lines of code. If we continue the assumptions and expect only 30% of defects to remain after some degree of software development rigor has occurred, we'll be left with 1,500 defects from our 50,000 LOC. Figure 11.6 demonstrates how reducing defect rates by 15% will considerably reduce the effort to remove outstanding issues.

FIGURE 11.6

Comparing total of development with individual and Pair Programming.

Defect fix time after development

Individual	Pair
15,000 hours =1500* 10 (hours/defect)	12,750 hours = (1500*85%) *10 (hours/defect)

We've taken the total time taken to capture, rectify, and test defects as being 10 hours per defect. Saving 2,250 hours at the end of the project has very real, bottom-line impacts. How often has development been called complete after the budget has been consumed only to find innumerable bugs reported by field or release testing? Pair Programming is a winner based on the reduction in defects alone.

Improving Developer Morale with Pair Programming

Pair Programming has some obvious, verifiable economic benefits, but what about the less tangible aspects? Do developers like it? In an online survey conducted by Laurie Williams, while at the University of Utah, found that over 90% of respondents would rather pair than work alone. Working in isolation, drawing demarcation lines between developers, testers, and managers is ultimately unmotivating. Collaboration in a safe, positive environment where "we" takes the place of "I" is simply more rewarding than the alternative of solo success or failure. To quote "Strengthening the Case For Pair Programming":

A natural correlation exists between these two measures [confidence of work and enjoyment] of satisfaction. That is, pairs enjoy their work more because they are more confident in their work. Someone is there to help if they are confused or unknowledgeable. They can bounce ideas off a friend. They leave each session with an exhilarated, we nailed-that-one feeling.

 The full text of this article is available in the July/August 2000 issue of IEEE Software. Online survey results are available at http://collaboration.csc.ncsu.edu/laurie/Papers/ieeeSoftware.PDF.

So, Pair Programming is good for the top and bottom line!

Testimonials from the Field

Over the last few pages you've learned how Pair Programming works in theory and the benefits that can be derived for its use. It's often interesting to listen and learn from real programmers. Does Pair Programming really work? The Wiki Wiki XP Web site has some interesting testimonials from Pair Programmers and includes this as a summary of the benefits:

1. Projects with high quality (attention to quality) have lower schedule pressure:
   - Products with the lowest defect counts have the shortest schedules (Jones 1991, *Applied Software Measurement*).
   - Poor quality is the most common reasons for schedule overruns (Jones 1994, *4000 Projects, Assessment and Control of Software Risks*).

2. Higher quality comes through culture/values/process, inspection, testing, early feedback, refactoring, and so forth.

3. Regarding inspection and quality and schedule, inspection is a powerful tool:
   - Inspections have been found to produce net schedule savings of 10 to 30 percent (Gilb and Graham 1993, *Software Inspection*).
   - Each hour spent on inspections avoided an average of 33 hours of maintenance (Russell 1991, *IEEE Software*).
   - Inspections were up to 20 times more efficient than testing (Russell 1991, *IEEE Software*).

4. Pair Programming, in part, is a way to do effective, real-time, responsive inspection, which supports higher quality, which supports reduced schedule pressure.

This list was taken from Wiki Wiki at http://www.c2.com/cgi/
wiki?PairProgramming on May 3, 2002.

Answering Pair Programming Objections

Pair Programming has been discussed over the past 30 years or so in software engineering circles, but its not until the advent of XP that we've seen its application so prevalent. It's easy enough to understand how Pair Programming works, yet it raises some common objections. Objections are likely to come from management and developers, whereas customers may be less concerned because they value the results from XP rather than the process. Let's tackle some of these objections and criticisms, as shown in Table 11.1.

TABLE 11.1 Common Objections to Pair Programming

Objection	Response
The cost of development will be too high	We covered this in the last section; to summarize, up-front costs are slightly higher (15%), but are more than offset by reduced defects (15%). Pair Programming could be justified solely on economic reasons.
I work better alone	More than likely this developer has never tried Pair Programming. Reducing defects in his own code will lessen his workload and increase personal satisfaction.
I don't need someone looking over my shoulder	Pair Programming is two minds working as one not one judging the other. What is the alternative to XP's real-time code review? The choice is formal QA inspections of completed source code. The mini-feedback created by Pair Programming removes defects and issues as you go, rather than after completion.
I'm so fast; my partner won't be able to keep up	It could be that your personal throughput is higher than average, which is all the more reason to share your skill and technique with the team. The project succeeds by the synergy of all the team members. Also, development efficiency is not measured purely by lines of code, and the extra defects in the solo developer's code add to the total time to complete.
I need my own personal space	XP recognizes the need for some personal space for emails, light documentation, or reading. Pair programming doesn't extend to reading email!

TABLE 11.1   continued

Objection	Response
I will lose my freedom	To a certain extent this is true when it comes to machine environment and setup. We all have our own preferences when it comes to fonts, colors, and IDE layout. This challenge is not insurmountable; settle on an agreed tool setup before you start pairing. The give and take with these seemingly important issues are well worth the results!

Two developers using the same machine opens interesting questions around network accounts and login. For example, who is logged into the machine? With tools that have integrated source control facilities, the logged-in user will be the checked out username. The resulting confusion around who worked on the code is reduced by XP's use of collective code ownership and Pair Programming itself.

In summary, from the developer's viewpoint, Pair Programming will require a degree of flexibility and openness. As a developer, you will lose some personal freedom with this environment, but this is outweighed by the knowledge sharing and improved code quality. It's more fun, too!

Making Pair Programming Work for You

When you've arranged the furniture and squared away objections from every quarter, what are some keys to making Pair Programming work for you? Table 11.2 lists some of the ingredients to Pair Programming success:

TABLE 11.2   Keys to Successful Pair Programming

Tip	Description
Take lots of breaks	Pair Programming exposes developers to a new level of communication. Pair Programmers report that eight hours of this intensity is all they can do. Don't underestimate the need for frequent breaks away from development. These can be similar to the micro-breaks that help reduce repetitive strain.

TABLE 11.2 continued

Tip	Description
Agree on tools upfront	The team should settle on an editor and development environment before works begins. In the past, developers have been able to use their editor of choice or window layout in IDEs. Settle on layout and preferences early; this seems like an unimportant issue, but developers can become quite passionate about their setup! The simplest, nonconfrontational approach is to leave the tools set at defaults where possible.
Don't major on the minors	Quibbling over issues such as tools, fonts, and desk layout should not be taken to extremes. Helping and supporting your pair partner will ensure the team's ultimate success not which color you use for your desktop!
Take time to listen and trust	Developing communication will take time; you'll evolve your own language and dialog. Resist the temptation to jump in and takeover; extend trust to your partner because she might be in midstream. A strange but true aspect of Pair Programming is that the partner can sometimes *see* more clearly than the driver. Learning the balance between speaking and holding your peace helps to maintain the flow. Remember, you'll be the driver soon enough!
Don't get distracted by the physical layout	Arranging the furniture and creating the space are enablers to successful Pair Programming, but they won't assure success alone. The interrelationship facets of pairing are certainly more significant than how the chairs are positioned. Quelling doubt and oiling interactions should be at the top of your list as you implement Pair Programming.
Switch the pairs	Make sure the team comprehends up-front that the pairs will change and that by the end of the project you will have paired with everybody. The coach should watch for interactions and switch as needed. This works well when the team is slightly more junior; the senior developers can both mentor and learn as they pair. This is a two-way street because less experienced developers can sometimes find thinking outside of the box to be more natural; after all they have less baggage!
Be gentle	As a leader you can opt to force developers into pairing, rejecting those that raise concerns or objections. Do this at your peril; "my way or the highway" is a power trip and the team members who remain will respect you less for it. Make a concerted effort to understand what the developer's issues really are, and if you part company do so in a way that leaves the door open (for both of you).
Don't over-promise	Pair Programming is certainly better than individual development, but it won't save the world. When communicating to managers and developers, drive home the point that XP practices work together and that it's vital that the whole project is led that way.

11

This list should help you steer your implementation of Pair Programming, enabling you to get it right the first time. In reality, you might only get one shot.

Summary

Over the last hour we've defined what Pair Programming is, its benefits, and the keys to success when implementing. The power of two minds focused together on the same task, one taking the tactical view, the other strategic, generates surprising results. We found that, contrary to what you'd expect, the effort is only slightly higher than with solo developers. The capability of Pair Programming to reduce the number of defects, while at the same time raising the level of morale in the team explains its popularity. The prospect of two developers sharing a machine elicits some puzzled expressions and questions, which can be answered with a growing body of solid research.

In the next hour you'll discover how you can continuously build your system, giving both you and your customer real feedback into the state of the system. From here we'll move from a process viewpoint on XP to work more hands-on with some of the common XP tools.

Q&A

Q   Where can I read more about Pair Programming?

A   The Internet is your best source for the latest information as more and more developers begin to use Pair Programming. Here are some of the best links:

- http://www.pairprogramming.com/
- http://collaboration.csc.ncsu.edu/laurie/
- http://www.c2.com/cgi/wiki?PairProgramming
- http://www.c2.com/cgi/wiki?PairProgrammingFacilities
- http://www.c2.com/cgi/wiki?PairProgrammingErgonomics
- http://www.xprogramming.com/Practices/PracPairs.html
- http://www.extremeprogramming.org/rules/pair.html
- http://discuss.fogcreek.com/joelonsoftware/default.asp?cmd=show&ixPost=2058
- A personal favorite is "All I Really Need to Know about Pair Programming I Learned in Kindergarten" by Laurie Williams and Robert Kessler at http://collaboration.csc.ncsu.edu/laurie/Papers/Kindergarten.PDF

Q Does pairing extend to other roles beyond developers?

A There is no direct research to support this, but it is a natural extension of collaboration. An example of this is when a developer and writer work together on online help.

Q How can I be fairly evaluated by my manager on my performance review if none of my work stands on its own?

A Some developers are unlucky enough to be working for companies that still measure productivity by lines of code (LOC)! It's reasonable to assume that such an industrial-age firm would not be using XP, anyway. The change is away from individual to group results. Your increased value or productivity is measured beyond just coding to leading, problem-solving, creativity, and the like.

Q Why not just do peer code review instead of peer programming?

A This goes back to the whole premise of XP; take best practices and make them extreme. Code reviews are good but can never be as good as real-time review. Also, code review is closer to Quality Control (QC) than QA; you're checking code that has already been written. Issues you uncover will have to be pretty major to warrant a code retrofit. With Pair Programming you'll catch most problems *as you go*.

Q Do Pair Programmers also "pair-write" the test units?

A Certainly! Pair Programming covers all the aspects of code construction. Writing unit tests is integral to the code development itself.

Workshop

This workshop tests whether you understand all the concepts you learned in this hour. It is very helpful to know and understand the answers before starting the next hour's lesson.

Quiz

1. If development time is greater with Pair Programming, how can it be cost effective?

    a. The prime benefits are softer, relating to morale and other team aspects.

    b. Defect counts are lowered and this affects the overall cost of development.

    c. The ratio of skilled to less-skilled developers is higher, lowering overheads.

    d. Hardware costs are halved.

2. What is the role of the programming partner?

    a. Constant code review.

    b. Monitoring development velocity.

    c. Actively engaged in helping, encouraging, analyzing and considering strategic design issues.

    d. Completing documentation in real time.

3. What does the partner say to indicate they would like the keyboard?

    a. "May, I drive?"

    b. "Can I have the keyboard?"

    c. "It's my turn."

    d. "It's not important."

4. Why are frequent breaks important when Pair Programming?

    a. Reduces the chance of repetitive strain.

    b. Allows the pair to share the driving role.

    c. Enables the pairs to be switched more easily.

    d. It's hard to maintain the extra level of communication that Pair Programming requires.

Answers

1. b.

2. a., c.

3. a.

4. d.

Activities

1. Try Pair Programming with a friend over a lunch break or after hours. Decide on a simple task, such as writing a function that calculates prime numbers from 1 to 1,000.

2. Investigate the claims of Pair Programmers on Wiki Wiki. You will be able to email them directly or pose your own questions.

PART IV

Using the XP Tools

Hour

Hour **12**

Building Software the XP Way

In this hour you will learn how XP takes the idea of building or integrating the software and accelerates the cycle. Continuous integration is more than a concept or theory because XP has tools and techniques that make it a reality. In this hour we will cover

- What integration is and why frequent integration is important
- Where the practice of daily builds came from and how it works
- What some of the obstacles to build automation are and how to avoid them
- How you can continuously build the system, giving the customer real feedback into the state of the system

The Integration Cycle

Integration is the process of assembling the team's individual components and building them into the software product. This sounds simple enough; everyone ensures his or her components pass unit tests, and then hands them over to the build master or system for final construction. In reality, the number of interactions and dependencies between modules can create a nightmare. The task of troubleshooting build errors can drive the mostly easygoing developer over the edge! This explains the "integration hell" tag! There's a chicken or egg problem here; integration is hard, so it's postponed until the last possible moment, but the greater the time between integrations the more grueling it becomes. Figure 12.1 shows how changes increase over time.

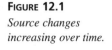

FIGURE 12.1

Source changes increasing over time.

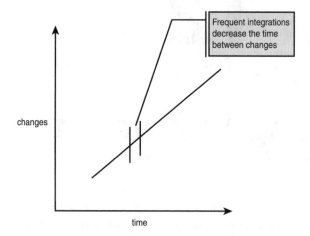

> Frequent integrations decrease the time between changes

changes

time

Changes to the source code that make up the software might not necessarily follow the linear growth we see in Figure 12.1. In some cases the project starts slowly while the basic infrastructure is built, and then source code, quickly grows in size as more components are added. All the more reason to start integrating as soon as possible.

XP places a premium on small releases where the customer sees his software grow in value over time. Small releases sounds like a laudable goal, but how can it be achieved? Waterfall projects, where there might be a single release after months of development, argue that time spent on build automation is wasted. But even with a monolithic release cycle project the team can benefit from frequent builds.

Continuous integration in XP is supported by the practices of Pair Programming, refactoring, collective ownership, testing, and coding standards. Figure 12.2 illustrates how small releases necessitate frequent builds, and this continuous integration is supported by other XP practices.

Figure 12.2
Continuous integration is supported by other XP practices.

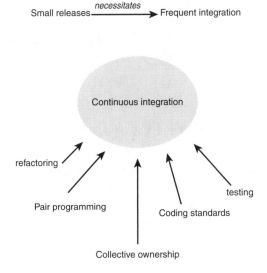

Over the next few sections we'll cover why building the software everyday is so crucial to the success of your project. You'll learn where the concept of the "daily build" came from, and how to define what a good build is.

Shipping the Product

Does it really matter how often the system is built? Software development is a means to an end that creates a product with business value for the customer. The foremost role of each team member is to ship the product. Jim McCarthy, former director of Microsoft's Visual C++ team, puts it this way in his book *Dynamics of Software Development*:

> If you build it, it will ship. You must get the product visible… The point of this rule is to engage the team in building the product frequently, regularly, throughout the development cycle, with the highest possible quality and in a public place where all team members can have access to it.

 From the *Dynamics of Software Development*, Jim McCarthy, Microsoft Press, 1995.

It's absolutely vital to the success of the project that the team stays focused on shipping the product; all else is secondary. Developers aren't simply writing and compiling code, but are integral to the customer's product release. The all-too-common alternative is that developers "go dark" while the heavy work of construction is underway. It's almost like the customer is pacing back and forth at the delivery room door. Will it be a boy or a girl? (I better not take this analogy too far!) In all seriousness though, XP holds to rapid feedback between technical and business. Developers listen a little, build a little, and then demonstrate to the customer.

Working software (or product) is the heartbeat the customer is interested in monitoring.

Building the Software Everyday

Microsoft is generally credited with inventing the concept of the daily build. Whether this is actually true is a moot point, and they certainly used it to good effect during their Windows NT development. A daily build is where automated scripts are run (usually nightly) to extract source from the version control system, compile, link, and then build. Normally, at the end of the build some kind of smoke test is run to check build status.

The daily build of the product is one of the most important diagnostic tools for the health of the software.

The term *smoke test* is derived from the electronics industry where people would plug in a circuit board or component, and then applied power to see what smoked.

These tests ensure the basic stability of the product by checking daily that nothing has been checked in that jeopardizes the basic product. If something is uncovered, it is repaired immediately. This provides a foundation for the new work to be added each day and ensures that the project doesn't stray too far from a stable working version.

Figure 12.3 illustrates how developers work by checking-out the source from the repository, and then use a dedicated build machine to run builds as required.

The importance of a regular build cannot be underestimated. A good way of thinking about it is to consider how much time it would take to recover from a fatal flaw in a check-in. If you build weekly, and someone checks in erroneous information on Monday that you don't find until you build on Friday, you might have to repair a week of work before health is restored. You've lost two weeks. If you built daily, you would lose only two days.

Building frequently is fundamentally about getting the project to a known state and ensuring that it stays there.

Figure 12.3

Developers using source control and a dedicated build machine.

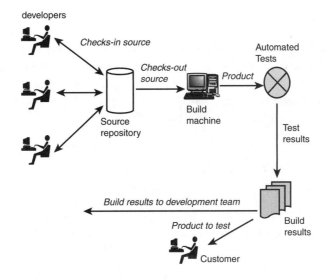

Defining a Good Build

Writing scripts that pull together the source and build the product is certainly the basis for rapid development, but what is a good build? If everyone's role is to ship the software, the ability to run a few scripts that attempt a build means nothing by itself. The build must pass a series of verification tests that enable the team to call the build good. Depending on your project, you might devise your own criteria for a successful build; here is an outline to start with:

- All working source files are checked into the source control repository.
- All source files are compiled (irrespective of date).
- Object or intermediate files are linked to create deployment binaries (such as executables, JAR files, and dynamic link libraries).
- The system is verified against a series of tests; this smoke test ensures the testability of the system.

The build can be called good or successful if the system passes to verification or smoke tests. It's ready for testing or review by the customer and team.

The team has two choices if the build breaks (fails tests):

- Fix problems immediately. If the build cycle is short, that is fewer changes between builds, problems will be easier to track down. Going home if your code broke the build is not just bad form, but it lets the whole team down. Collective ownership means collective responsibility. Fixing the broken build remains the top priority of the development team.

12

- Back out the changes. The team might decide to back out changes in a component if integration problems are traced to fundamental flaws or problems—for example, in the first time a third-party module is used in the build. Generally speaking, XP minimizes the risk of complicated integration problems by increasing the frequencies of builds. However, we should at least recognize the possibility of unknowns that threaten to sidetrack the team. The better decision is to rollback the change and perform more testing before integrating again.

Integration Hell—When Will We Ever Learn?

I had a couple of recent experiences that illustrate why frequent builds will save your skin and sanity. I watched as a project with 10 or so developers struggled time and time again to integrate every six to eight weeks. For some reason they never had the time to get their source and build house in order! Too much work, too much trouble. Each build weekend followed the same pattern of name-calling, finger-pointing, and raised voices. The common statement was "it works fine on my machine." Unfortunately, the customer was not running their global knowledge portal on the developer's PC! Here's an interesting insight into a developer mindset: They claimed the *integration* was fine, and the problems were caused by *deployment*. So, the build worked (compiled), but didn't work (pass any tests). The team stubbornly refused to learn the hard lessons and persisted in lack of source control and manual builds until the bitter end.

I was called in after a subsequent offshoot development began to flounder and mandated automated build. We took maybe two days to clean source control and write batch scripts. From this point onward the build took around 10 minutes from start to finish, including deployment to test servers.

I'll take automation anytime; I like my weekends.

Placing the Source into the Safe

The keystone of building, no matter how often, is that all source must reside on a source control repository. Your development tool will dictate, up to a point, which product you choose as its integration with the IDE could be a definite plus for developers. Source control is easiest to get under control at the start of the project. Tidying up in mid project is a headache for all concerned. Some teams like to plan out the structure of the source management system early in the project. You can take this approach or decide a high-level layout, leaving the remainder until required. Figure 12.4 demonstrates a possible structure for your source management system.

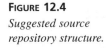

FIGURE **12.4**

Suggested source repository structure.

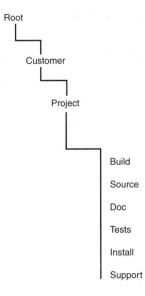

An interesting thing to note is that we have a build folder. In actuality, this is no more than a mirror or reflection of the underlying source folders. The reason for this technique is that it can simplify the build process by only requiring the build tool to get source from one tree. Most source systems enable users to replicate or shadow working folders to others in the repository. Otherwise, you'd need to check out or get (read-only copy of files), and then mask the folders that were not required (documentation, and so on). Applying a recursive "get" will usually result in a folder structure on the build machine that mimics the repository. Your job of writing a build script will be much more complicated!

Another frequently missed aspect of source control is that all supporting libraries and binaries should also be included. Keep in mind that your goal is to build the entire application from the source-management system, and failing to include your external components will stymie this. You should be able to point at a clean or pristine machine at the source database, run the base build script, and then watch as the system is built from scratch. This is not as hard as it sounds and requires dedication rather than technical brilliance.

At the risk of stating the obvious: Your source-management system should be backed up! Don't let one hard-drive failure ruin all your hard-won gains from source management.

Making a Start with Build Automation

You are ready to start build automation when you've managed to add all the source and supporting files into your repository. There are many approaches to build automation, starting with the simple batch file, right through to the use of a full-fledged build tool such as Ant or Nant.

 We'll cover Ant in detail during Hour 16, "Automating Your Software Development."

Any build script will follow this general outline:

- Connect to the source code repository
- Extract the latest versions of source
- Extract any supporting libraries or binaries
- Execute either a compile, or more likely, call the relevant make files for each project
- Create deployment packages, if required
- Call smoke tests
- Log results (this might include email notification of status or update on the project Web site)

The classic Make utility is well known and used; it enables developers to perform both incremental and clean builds. Make checks the date of target files (intermediate binaries or target) and executes compiles if the target date is older than the source. The capability to incrementally build certainly lowers build time, but can mask unusual component dependencies. For this reason, the developer will call a clean build or rebuild; this builds all files regardless of date.

For increased flexibility and power, XP developers tend to use Ant as their build tool of choice. Ant is an open-source tool that is driven or controlled by a build file, formatted in XML. Ant also offers some integration with Junit and can be used to run post-build smoke tests. Nant is a recent addition to the XP build tool family and is modeled closely on Ant. The difference is that Nant is written for the Microsoft .NET framework and as such does not require Java. Development shops that are working with .NET should consider this tool.

Extreme Building with Continuous Integration

The value of frequent integrations is self-evident. The capability to spread the risk and pain across the development life cycle far outweighs any up-front work required. The extra work required to increase integration cycles is more perception than reality if you've established good working structures. Let's walk through our development model and see how we can increase build frequencies.

Developers work in pairs to write product code; they start by writing unit tests in their test framework (junit, cppunit, VBUnit, nUnit, and so on). Then, they write just enough code for the test to pass. After the unit tests pass, they run the complete test suite for the system on their own machine. The pair continues to work on the component until it integrates with the system on their machine and passes smoke tests. At this stage they will migrate the source to the integration machine.

 Your ability to run system-wide tests might be hindered to some extent by the development environment. At the very least you should apply some kind of smoke test against the system.

Alternatively, the team may opt to use an automated monitoring tool such as CruiseControl. CruiseControl was initially developed by ThoughtWorks, Inc. but is now open source and freely downloadable from SourceForge.net. Cruise Control monitors the source repository status and triggers a build based on freshly checked-in source. Figure 12.5 illustrates this workflow.

Use of CruiseControl or similar homegrown build monitor will only work after the fully automated build is in place using a tool such as Ant, Nant, or simple make files.

The diagram shows a separate build machine, which is not mandatory in your quest for automating builds, but it does simplify setup somewhat. Also, moving to a separate physical machine underlines the symbolism of integrating. Even with increased build frequencies, the importance of adding completed code to the software shouldn't be underestimated by the team. With each integration the team is increasing the business value of the system, and the customer is inching closer to their goal.

12

Figure 12.5

Continuous integration in action.

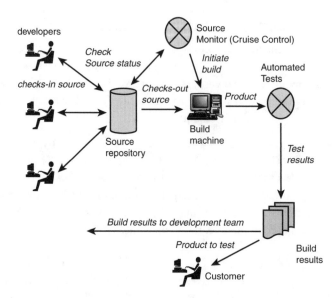

Reducing Your Integration Obstacles

Automating integration and starting the process early will clear roadblocks for you, but obstacles might still remain. Improving the communication between pairs can reduce integration conflicts. The popular practice of listening to music via headphones to increase focus and remove distraction has no place in the XP world. Of course, Pair Programming would be difficult if headphones were in use! Spare developers; that is, the unpaired developers who are working on build automation, research, documentation, or some other task, might miss vital verbal cues if they mask background sound with head-phones.

Developers can minimize any remaining communication problems by adding change comments into source or via the configuration management system. In the open space of the XP warroom there is still a place for solid, "just enough" change notes.

Basic development hygiene issues such as following code standards and keeping unit tests up to date will catch simple conflicts, as well.

There are some common problems that can trip up your build automation, some of which are listed for you in Table 12.1.

TABLE 12.1 Common Build Automation Problems

Problem	Solutions
Build times are too long	Break down the build into a number of parallel streams, using a master build file. Ensure you are using the fastest compiler, for example Jikes rather than javac for Java. Buy faster hardware! Use incremental builds during the day and complete builds after hours. Use profiling tools to measure where the build bottleneck is.
Distributed development stretches communication	Use master/child build files, allowing each site to run its own builds. Integrate the complete suite at a predetermined time. Use a single integration machine, offsite developers can use virtual clients such as VNC or Terminal Server. Ensure that teams have adequate network bandwidth. Manage source control from a central repository. Use collaboration tools such as NetMeeting or ICQ to keep communication lines open.
Too many source-code conflicts at integration time	Commit your changes more frequently, and therefore minimize the number of changes. Use a single-integration machine or token to ensure only one developer is integrating at one time.

12

So, we can reduce our integration obstacles by careful planning and good communication. The extra effort required to get your build automation up and running will be well worth it in the end!

Summary

XP promises the customers that they can guide the system as it's developed, and not only that, but they will also get rapid feedback on progress. Integrating more frequently, as each new piece of functionality is added will enable this to happen the team and customer to gain real feedback on the state of the software. There's no doubt that integration does offer some real challenges as the team builds the system, but XP practices reduce this pain. We've seen how a little up-front work can reap great rewards as the pace of change increases.

In the next hour you'll learn about which tools work best with XP, and how we can balance the simple with the practical.

Q&A

Q Where can I get CruiseControl, and what do I need to run it?

A You can download CruiseControl from `http://cruisecontrol.sourceforge.net/`. To run CruiseControl you will need Java, Ant, a Web server, and some kind of servlet engine, such as Tomcat.

Q Continuous integration sounds like a great idea, but it's a little daunting for me right now. Where can I start, today?

A Start using a source control repository such as CVS, PVCS, or Microsoft Visual SourceSafe. Add all your project source and supporting libraries to source control. Then, work at building from source control on a clean or build machine. It's only a small step from here to full-blown build automation.

Workshop

This workshop tests whether you understand all the concepts you learned in this hour. It is very helpful to know and understand the answers before starting the next hour's lesson.

Quiz

1. What is the main problem with integration?

    a. The number of components makes it difficult.

    b. There are no real tools to ease the pain.

    c. The task is mostly manual, which slows development down.

    d. Conflicts occur between components developed by team members.

2. What XP practices support integration?

    a. Pair Programming, refactoring, collective ownership, testing, and coding standards.

    b. Pair Programming, on-site customer, collective ownership, testing, and coding standards.

    c. Pair Programming, collective ownership, and testing.

    d. All other practices support it

3. How do we define a good build?

    a. Passes the customer's acceptance tests.

    b. Compiles and links without error.

    c. The build passes a verification or smoke test.

    d. Source code is checked in and passes unit tests.

4. Why is a build important?

    a. It's the heartbeat of development and is the best measure of the state of the system.

    b. Enables the customer to know work is being done

    c. Helps to keep the team focused on shipping the product.

    d. Assures the system quality by passing tests.

Answers

1. d.

2. a.

3. c.

4. a., c.

Activities

1. Write a build script that extracts the latest source from your repository and builds on a clean machine.

2. Download CruiseControl, install it, and begin to experiment with automating your build from Activity 1.

12

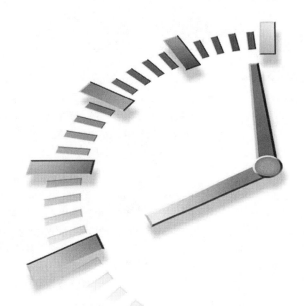

HOUR 13

Using XP Development Tools

In this hour you will discover the tools used in XP software development and where to get them. In this hour we will cover

- The kind of tools that are used in XP
- The importance of version control, and what tools supply these features
- An introduction to the xUnit testing framework
- How integrated development environments can be leveraged when using XP
- How the simple tools are often the best at enabling more efficient software development

Gathering Your XP Toolset

Over the last few hours you've learned that one of the underlying values of XP is simplicity. Simplicity extends not only through how we approach development and run our project, but also includes the kind of tools we use in development. You will find that most of the tools used in XP software development are either free or, at the very least, inexpensive. XP is used across multiple language and software platforms, but in this hour we'll direct our focus at two the of the leaders—Java and Microsoft .NET.

You will discover as you spend more time in the XP newsgroups and communities that Java is by far the most popular language used by XPers. The term Java, though originally used to describe the portable software development language created by Sun (http://www.sun.com/java), has since been extended to cover an entire platform: object model, message brokering, database connectivity, clients, and middleware. If you're new to using Java for development, you'll be pleasantly surprised to find a host of free tools available in the Java space.

Microsoft developers are arriving a little late to XP, but this is beginning to change with the advent of Microsoft's .NET platform. COM developers can still enjoy the benefits of XP, but expect new tools and enhancements to be targeted at .NET. .NET developers can work in any compliant language (over 20 at the time of writing), most will be using C# (pronounced C sharp) or Visual Basic .NET. (Microsoft is also working on a Java-like language compiler called J#, but it produces .NET not Java-compatible byte-code). Microsoft .NET languages are all termed *first-class* languages, meaning they offer equiv-alent functionality. In the past, developers were sometimes forced to select a certain lan-guage based on constraints inherent in each language. Developers are no longer penalized in either functionality or performance with .NET by using, say, Visual Basic. When we speak of .NET tools we are addressing any of the compliant languages: C#, Visual Basic .NET, JScript, and so on.

If you're interested in learning more about Microsoft .NET it will be covered in Hour 15 "Unit Testing with Microsoft Tools."

During the rest of this hour we will discuss both Java- and .NET-related tools. To start, Table 13.1 lists the common tools used in XP and some examples for each.

TABLE 13.1   Tools Listed by Type

Tool Type	Description	Examples
Defect Management	Defect tracking and recording. Used in XP around release and acceptance time.	Rational ClearCase, Visual Intercept, Compuware TrackRecord, BlipIt

TABLE 13.1 continued

Tool Type	Description	Examples
Collaboration	Tools that simplify the teams' interactions, ease restrictions imposed by distance, report on status, and aid in collaboration.	Wiki Wiki, Whiteboard, Paper, Project Web, NetMeeting, Rational ProjectConsole
Testing	Automated unit testing, acceptance test tools, and GUI testers.	JUnit, ComUnit, VBUnit, Nunit, httpUnit, Rational Visual Test
Quality Assurance	Code quality, conformance to standards and traceability.	DevPartner CodeReview
Performance	Component and system performance measuring tools.	Jmeter, jUnitPerf, PerfMon, TrueTime, RealTime, Microsoft Visual Studio Analyzer
Source Control	Source code configuration management, including versioning and change control.	CVS, Visual Source Safe, PVCS
Development Environments	Integrated development environments (IDE)that allow developers to edit, debug, compile, and build from a single tool.	IBM VisualAge, Microsoft Visual Studio. NET, JBuilder

An open source Web site called Source Forge is the home for most of the software development tools used by XPers. It can be found at `http://sourceforge.net/`.

Debates rage in XP circles around the need to use some of the tools listed in Table 13.1. For instance, when using Pair Programming, the requirement to run a software inspection tool, such as Compuware's DevPartner CodeReview, is greatly reduced. A QA tool such as CodeReview might still have value in XP when the team undergoes an external audit, for example. CodeReview can be easily run against the code base to produce metrics on naming conventions and code standard adherence. The difference in an XP project is the team is much less likely to be overwhelmed by a huge error count after they run their code checker.

13

Testing Your Software with the xUnit Testing Framework

Central to XP software development is the reversal of the test cycle—programmers write tests before they develop their source. Conceptually, we can understand how it makes sense to consider *what* we should test before we start programming the component. But how can you possibly write the test first? Kent Beck wrote a testing framework for

SmallTalk (SUnit) that was both simple to use and easy to extend. Later he and Erich Gamma ported the tool across to Java, and JUnit was born. As XP has caught on across the globe, more and more languages have been ported across to the xUnit model. We'll cover JUnit in detail during Hour 14, "Unit Testing with Java Tools," but for now we'll take a high-level look.

 NEW TERM The *xUnit* testing framework is a simple, easy-to-use unit testing tool. We refer to it as xUnit because there are many versions of the framework, depending on language; for example, JUnit for Java, VBUnit for Visual Basic, SUnit for SmallTalk, and so on.

With JUnit you write a subclass of the class `TestCase` for each object that you'll be testing. You will then add as many testing methods as you need to exercise the object. Usually you will begin each test with name Test, for example, `TestMaxFileSize`, `TestNoFile`, `TestMissingFile`, `TestBadFile`, and so on.

 Some xUnits actually *require* that the test case start with the word Test. Check the documentation on your particular unit-testing framework.

In most cases, the test runner tool will use reflection to ascertain test names at runtime. In the case of simpler scripting frameworks you might need to manually specify your test names. The test runner will then execute your tests, calling a setup method (where you can specify database connection strings, and so on) and a concluding teardown method. Most xUnits, such as JUnit, also come with a GUI tool that displays test details that developers will keep running in the background and execute tests as they continue working.

When running unit tests on the integration machine, the team will most likely call unit tests from the command prompt, reporting results to either Web page, console, or email. The beauty of the xUnit testing framework model is the simplicity it brings to the chore of testing. Expensive commercial tools could perform most of what JUnit does, but are overkill unless you want to run full-blown GUI testing.

GUI or interface testing is an area where xUnits struggle; they are testing at the code level not presentation. Tools such as Rational's Visual Test can be programmed to run UI testing by scripting, capturing display bitmaps, and then comparing to a golden or known good image. The overhead attached to maintaining these UI test scripts quickly outweighs their benefits. A perfectly acceptable alternative to automating UI testing is to employ a usability expert, who will evaluate the GUI based on user testing and industry standards.

Unit testing of presentation layers can be executed by calling the relevant windowing or abstraction layer methods. Using this approach might be satisfactory for simple interfaces or HTML-based presentation layers where the screen can be compared at the text rather than bitmap level.

In this section, we've focused attention on JUnit; if you use another software development language you are excused for thinking that you're on your own! This isn't the case, and the list of languages supported by xUnits is growing as developer's port across more and more languages to the framework. We've sifted through the unit-testing frameworks that are currently available, and Table 13.2 lists these for you. You will find some less popular ones, too! If you're language is not on our list, take up the challenge and write an xUnit!

TABLE 13.2   xUnit Testing Framework Download Resources

Language/ Platform	Web Site
.NET	http://nunit.sourceforge.net/
AppleScript	http://homepage.mac.com/a_a_converse/Menu3.html
C	http://check.sourceforge.net/
C++ Builder	http://groups.yahoo.com/group/extremeprogramming/files/ CppUnit17BCB30Pro.zip
C++	http://www.xprogramming.com/ftp/TestingFramework/CppUnit/ CppUnit15.zip
COM	http://comunit.sourceforge.net/
Delphi	http://dunit.sourceforge.net/
Eiffel	http://w3.one.net/~jweirich/software/eiffelunit/
GemStone	http://www.xprogramming.com/ftp/TestingFramework/GemStoneSmalltalk/ TestFrame.st
Haskell	http://hunit.sourceforge.net/
HTML	http://sourceforge.net/projects/htmlunit
HTTP	http://httpunit.sourceforge.net/

13

TABLE 13.2   continued

Language/ Platform	Web Site
Jade	http://www.xprogramming.com/ftp/TestingFramework/Jade/ TestFramework.zip
Java	http://www.junit.org/
JavaScript	http://www.jsunit.net/
Objective-C	http://oops.se/objcunit/
Oracle	http://oracle.oreilly.com/utplsql/
Palm	http://www.geocities.co.jp/SiliconValley-SanJose/7344/download-en.html
Perl	http://search.cpan.org/search?dist=Test-Unit
PhpUnit	http://sourceforge.net/projects/phpunit/
PowerBuilder	http://www.geocities.com/pbunit/
Python	http://www.xprogramming.com/ftp/TestingFramework/python/Cayte/ PyUnit.zip
Ruby	http://homepage1.nifty.com/markey/ruby/rubyunit/index_e.html
Smalltalk	http://ANSI-ST-tests.sourceforge.net/SUnit.html
TINI	http://tiniunit.sourceforge.net/
Visual Basic	http://www.vbunit.org/
Visual Objects	ftp://ftp.knowvo.com/pub/archive/vo-unit.zip
WebObjects	http://wounittest.sourceforge.net/
XSLT	http://xsltunit.org/

Some languages have multiple versions or incarnations of their testing framework. For example, at the time of writing, Visual Basic has been ported by at least three authors. You might want to experiment until you find the tool that best fits your need.

One final but important note on writing and running unit tests—they must execute quickly. Usually, this isn't a problem because you're writing tests that are operating at the object level. The problem is that your catalog of tests grows as the system grows, and there might come a point when invoking your tests begins to slow development. The point, after all, is that you want quick, verifiable feedback on the state of your system. Cases where you are interacting with a database backend or offline store are the worst offenders at killing your test speed. Setting up and tearing down database connections are notoriously expensive in terms of overhead and latency. One way around this is to limit your data sets to known good subsets of the main database. Run your complete, data load or test after hours. This way you'll capture any niggly object-creation problems, memory leaks, or database-locking errors.

Time spent enhancing the speed of your tests, is time well spent. If in doubt throw more hardware at the problem!

Tracking Defects with Tools

Even with XP, defects will occur in your code! Pair Programming and the strong unit-testing regime minimize program or logic errors (bugs), but customers might still find their new software behaves unexpectedly. In this case, you have a number of options available:

- Paper-based tracking, using Post-It notes, and so on
- Spreadsheet
- Homegrown defect database
- Open source or free tool
- Commercial defect management tool

You could get away with the paper-based approach in the case where your XP project is running in a single location. Defects can be separated into failures (observable problems with the software) and faults (underlying problems with the code). Any defect-tracking tool you choose should be able to support these two types. In reality, unexpected behavior often results in a dispute between customer and developer: Is it an error or poor specification? Defects can then result in changes or new functionality being requested, and the best place to keep these is in some kind of tool. Avoid the practice of keeping two systems, one for bugs and the other changes. As long as your tool can report on these separately you'll do fine with one central application.

Defect tracking applications can quickly become invasive because they are in the habit of including sophisticated work-flow solutions around the defect tracking and change cycle. Don't let the tool control you; be the master not the slave. Table 13.3 lists some of the commonly available defect-tracking tools used by XPers.

13

TABLE 13.3   Tools Listed by Type

Tool	Platform	Link
BugZilla	Perl	http://www.mozilla.org/projects/bugzilla/
BlueTail Ticket Tracker	Open source	http://btt.sourceforge.net/
elementool	Web-based	http://elementool.com/
Mantis	PHP/mySQL	http://mantisbt.sourceforge.net/
CodeTrack	PHP	http://www.openbugs.org/
Teamatic	Web-based	http://www.teamatic.com/index.jsp
BlipIt	ASP/SQL Server	http://www.greendoorservices.com/
Visual Intercept	Windows	http://www.elsitech.com/
ClearDDTS	Unix	http://www.rational.com/products/clear_ddts/
TestTrack	Windows, Linux, Solaris, Mac OS X	http://www.seapine.com/ttpro.html
TrackRecord	Windows	http://www.compuware.com/products/qacenter/ trackrecord/

These tools are generally on the lower end in terms of sophistication and features, but fit well with the keep it simple approach of XP. The exceptions to this are ClearDDTS, TrackRecord, and Visual Intercept, which are liable to dent your budget yet at the same time do offer some interesting integration and reporting features.

> Some XPers frown on the idea of using defect databases claiming it's a defeatist attitude. Only use one if the paper-based method begins to hinder the team.

One last comment about selecting defect trackers: Don't take too long! You could eat into some serious project time downloading and experimenting with these tools. Decide on your requirements up front and investigate a limited set of options. Reading Wiki Wiki or the XP newsgroups can help you limit research time.

Using Paper-Based Tools

You could invent or assemble an impressive array of electronic tools to manage and run your project, but why not try the simplest things that could possibly work? Any project manager who has tried to manage a fast-paced software development project by using

Gantt or PERT charts has by now discovered that they simply don't work. Programming is happening at a much lower level than is captured on a project plan; you definitely don't want to attempt and insert individual components on your plan! After reading about planning, tracking, and user stories, you already know what the tool of choice is for XP leaders—paper! Figure 13.1 depicts a typical XP team room wall with, in this case, user stories fixed to the wall.

FIGURE 13.1

XP project room show-ing user stories.

This XP project has taken to entering user stories via Microsoft Word, and then printing them out. The top line on our wall consists of the user stories; going across and under each story are the sheets displaying the relevant engineering tasks. It's common sense that if you're already capturing user stories on index cards or paper that you could easily display them in this manner. Would there be any real value in using a spreadsheet or the like to capture these stories?

Another must-have tool is the ubiquitous whiteboard, get as many as you can because you can never have too many. Whiteboards are by nature a holder of transient data and writing; "don't erase on pain of death," across the board is no guarantee that your work will be there in the morning. Another form of this collaboration tool is the flip chart or giant Post-It pad; use these to capture your semipermanent work. The great thing about using brown-paper flip charts is that you are truly portable.

13

Post-It notes are useful as always; one practice is when the customer's acceptance tester scribbles failed tests on Post-Its, and then attaches them to the offending pair's workstation (or on a central iteration planning wall).

The Tools Are the Means, Not the End

I've always been a firm believer in the value of building a project Web. It seemed so obvious that the team could benefit from a central starting point that would contain all they needed to know about the project. What made me realize that the project Web was the answer to all the team's needs was when Microsoft announced Web integration with Project. At last I could capture status, update the plan, and report on progress, all in a one-stop shop. (It took me a while to figure out that software development can't really be managed by Gantt charts; now I know better.)

Anyway, I galvanized the tools guy (the developer in charge of build and development tools) into action, and soon he was busy creating the project Web. After a few days I noticed that he was continually fiddling or enhancing the site; after all, there were so many neat features he could add. The function I wanted more than any other was integration with Microsoft Project's collaboration to enable the team to see status against plan. Initially, this seemed simple enough and was quickly working, allowing developers to enter in their time against tasks. The customer could then see progress. Sounds like a dream come true? Well, it was, but in the end it frustrated the team into working in the manner dictated by the tool and failed.

I realized that just because you can do something, technical and its got the "gee-whiz" factor doesn't mean your team should waste time with it. The focus on this one tool could have been better spent establishing the right open space.

The lesson for me was don't go overboard with collaboration tools, use the simplest thing that can work and change if needed. In my example, a large wall chart with Post-It notes would have worked best.

Finding Software Tools to Speed Up Your Code

Application performance is one area of software development that tools will definitely help you. The customers will normally explicitly define requirements for their system's response time and scalability. You should be wary of comments such as "the system should be really fast," and if the customer speaks in this kind of vague language be quick to convert into something measurable. Load testing and performance will be particularly useful when the site moves into the staging area.

A common and highly effective technique is to perform load or stress testing at the application level and drill-down to the method level when bottlenecks have been uncovered. In the Java space, JMeter (`http://jakarta.apache.org/jmeter/index.html`) is a powerful, fully Java-compliant http Web tester. JMeter enables the user to configure and run simulated load tests using a GUI interface. Microsoft supplies similar functionality in its (surprisingly, free!) Web Stress Tool (`http://webtool.rte.microsoft.com/download.asp`), which enables developers to record Web browser activity, and then replay a configurable number of users or connections.

After individual Web pages have been exposed as performance bottlenecks, the developer can zero in on the underlying objects.

> A good idea is to turn on your database profiler while you stress your Web site. You will find that most performance issues can be traced back to the database. Tune the database and you tune the application.

Most commercial software vendors supply varying degrees of performance analysis in their product suites. Products such as Microsoft's Visual Studio .NET integrates application and source-level performance tracing into the IDE. Compuware's TrueTime extends tracing capability to capturing metrics from the final binaries at runtime. In Figure 13.2, we have an example of TrueTime drilling into a single function call, displaying the constituent child calls.

FIGURE 13.2

TrueTime function call window showing the cost of individual child function calls.

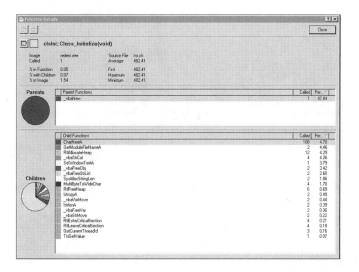

13

Your choice of performance monitoring tool will be directed, to a large extent, by your platform and IDE selections. If you follow your language's recognized coding approach (for example, acquiring objects late and releasing early), your performance issues should be confined to network and database.

Source Control Tools

It's absolutely vital that you store all your application source code into some kind of repository. This repository should be able to store any kind of file type used by your team and should support versioning of changes. There are two broad approaches to source control: Either lock files out to individual users or allow any developer to edit a file and handle changes by merge. Merging of changes is how the most popular open source control system (Concurrent Versions System) works. The capability to support multiple, simultaneous edits fits within the XP practice of collective code ownership. CVS is a command-line tool, but there are numerous GUI interfaces available for Windows, Linux, Mac OS X, and Unix. Increasingly, commercial tools such as Apple's Project Builder (Mac OS X) are integrating support for CVS repositories. Microsoft-centric developers tend to use Visual Source Safe for development because the integration with Visual Studio is hard to beat. Table 13.4 lists some of the commonly used source control systems:

TABLE 13.4   Version Control Systems

Tool	Platform	Link
CVS	Open	`http://www.cvshome.org/`
Visual Source Safe	Windows	`http://msdn.microsoft.com/ssafe/`
ClearCase	Windows, Unix, Linux	`http://www.rational.com/products/clearcase/index.jsp`
PVCS	Windows, Unix	`http://www.merant.com/pvcs/products/professional/index.html`

Your XP development team should follow some basic rules of thumb when it comes to version control:

- Check in or commit changes as often as possible to ensure the team has the latest working source.
- Only check in source code that works (that is, compiles and passes tests).
- Use a single repository for ALL project-related files, including documents, third-party tools, and test data.

- Integrate source control with your automated build process.
- Backup your repository!
- Build your system entirely from source control.
- Don't put intermediate files, such as .obj's, into the repository.

After you've established source and version control it will become fairly transparent—don't worry it will make your job easier!

Tools to Check Your Code Quality

Code quality review tools go back to the days of the C Lint utility, which reported on possible code quality violations. XP could claim to do away with the requirement for code quality or conformance testing tools; after all, with Pair Programming we have continual code reviews. As we mentioned earlier in this hour, the use of a code quality tool might be of interest to your customer. In the case of a "covert" XP project your customer might expect you to prove conformance to coding standards that they mandate. (A covert XP project is a project where you are using most of the XP practices internally, but are interfacing to your customer using their defined methods, for example, specifications and sign off.)

Please visit http://www.compuware.com/products/devpartner/ visualbasic/codereviewvb.htm for more information on CodeReview.

In the case where your customer or their external auditor requires verifiable proof of standards adherence you could use a tool such as Compuware's DevPartner. DevPartner is available for C++, Java, and Visual Basic. The product consists of a number of useful development tools, but the one we are interested is CodeReview. CodeReview operates with Visual Basic .NET analyzing your code, comparing to language-specific best practices, naming conventions and reporting on complexity. (Complexity is important because it is an indicator of how hard the code will be to maintain and the probability of defects.) In the example displayed in Figure 13.3 we have a CodeReview report of a Visual Basic project, which has around 5,000 lines of source code.

13

We can select which rules CodeReview runs, suppressing any less important errors (such as missing procedure help definitions). The end result lists of over 3,000 errors, which can then be sorted by priority. Figure 13.4 illustrates how the tool separates problems into types and also supplies help on how to resolve the issue.

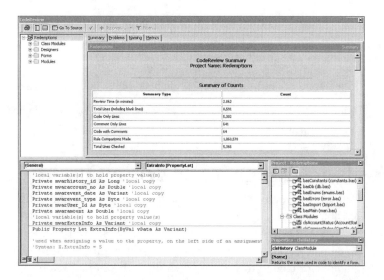

FIGURE 13.3
CodeReview reporting source code issues.

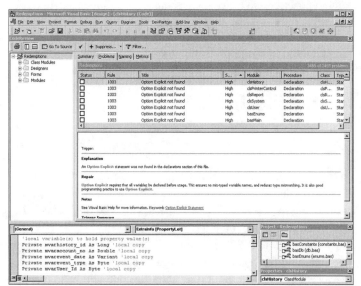

FIGURE 13.4
CodeReview highlighting a source code error and supplying resolution.

A tool such as CodeReview is useful not just in highlighting conformance errors, but also pointing out possible performance bottlenecks. Finally, in Figure 13.5 we've listed methods by complexity and we clearly have some work to do!

FIGURE 13.5
CodeReview listing methods by complexity.

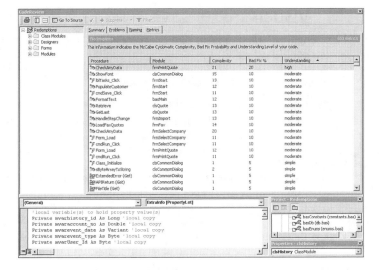

As you can see using a tool such as Compuware's CodeReview can still be very helpful, even when using XP. Used in a Pair Programming situation, developers might run the review on an ad hoc basis.

Leveraging Integrated Development Environments

You learned earlier that no particular software vender owns XP; therefore, developers aren't required to purchase any kind of special tool. However, most developers are now using some form of IDE, such as IBM's VisualAge for Java or Microsoft's Visual Studio .NET for their software development. Historically, these tools were often high end and expensive, but increasingly we're seeing a new move toward free or open source IDEs. Simple tools such as text editors or formatters were commonplace, but using them meant developers lost productivity gains available from IDEs. The good news for the modern developer is that free tools are approaching the functionality of the more expensive commercial products. (Often the commercial product sets have grown over the years from successive feature bloats and now boast a host of features that might have been implemented for marketing reasons alone! More is not always better!) Let's spend a few moments looking at these IDE's, investigating how they might be used in XP.

13

IBM's VisualAge for Java

IBM's VisualAge for Java is an IDE for professional Java developers. VisualAge for Java comes in three versions:

- Professional—basic, single-user version

- Enterprise—team version (allowing multiple developers to share a common repository) plus numerous other features and wizards that IBM deemed "enterprise" level, such as EJB and legacy system access wizards

- Professional or Enterprise Entry—the same as Professional/Enterprise versions, but are limited to 750 classes. Professional and Entry Editions are downloadable from the IBM VisualAge for Java home page at `http://www-3.ibm.com/software/ad/vajava`.

You should definitely review VAJ Entry Enterprise Edition if you're developing Java applications, and you expect less than 750 classes. (You can always upgrade if required later.) VisualAge has a very rich interface, supporting the full software development cycle. Figure 13.6 illustrates VisualAge's source window.

FIGURE 13.6

VisualAge for Java in the source window.

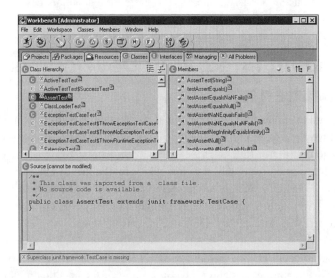

VisualAge for Java Enterprise Edition can provide source control through a shared team repository. The repository contains all versions of the project source, allowing the team to manage code and to track source code changes.

There are two XP practices that you can enhance by using VAJ: collective code owner-ship and coding standards. VAJ provides built-in support for code formatting that auto-matically reformats source code in a consistent manner. At project startup the team can set their source settings to follow the team's coding standards. Figure 13.7 illustrates how the formatter function enables the user to define spacing rules. You gain access to these preferences from the Window, Options menu selection.

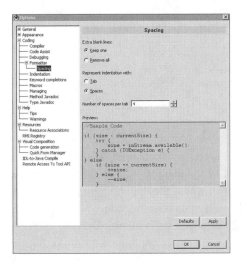

FIGURE 13.7
VisualAge for Java's formatting configura-tion screen.

Perhaps one of the most powerful features of VAJ from an XP developer's viewpoint is the capability of the IDE to support method-level source control and collective owner-ship of code. To enable collective ownership in VAJ we will need to use a single user-name for all source repository access. (You could continue with your individual username approach, but this will limit your ability to truly allow shared ownership.) In reality, on an XP project you will need two users: the repository administrator and the shared developer. When you've created your VisualAge project you will need to add your shared username. Do this by opening the Repository Explorer and selecting the Window, Repository Explorer, Admin, Users menu option. Figure 13.8 illustrates how we add the single user to our project.

Setting up your project with a single user is your first step toward collective ownership. You will still need to manage and think through integrations.

13

FIGURE **13.8**

Adding a single user in VisualAge for Java.

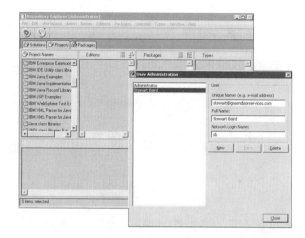

Let's consider how development occurs in XP, and how it relates to VAJ. Work starts with a programming pair replacing the current project edition in their workspace with the latest version available from the team repository. They then create open editions of the project and any packages in which they intend to work. The programming pair proceeds to create or modify unit tests and program code, after open editions of the project and packages are created. The component is not released until unit tests have successfully passed testing, at this stage the programming pair will version and release the code.

Now and again, multiple pairs of programmers might be working on the same piece of code. When this happens, the version numbers assigned by VAJ will begin to branch. For example, if com.ibm.myTestClass was at version 3.7 before a pair began programming, it will increment to version 3.8 when they version it. Things get a little tricky with our collective ownership strategy; consider the case where another pair was working on com.ibm.myTestClass at the same time as the first pair. In this case, the version would increment to 3.7.1 for the first pair and to 3.7.2 for the second pair. The two pairs of programmers should notice this branching and they would need to investigate how to integrate their work. In line with XP thinking, we take the stance that these integration conflicts will be less common and we'll deal with issues swiftly when they arise. Problems with duplication and integration breakage are reduced by the frequency at which the team builds.

You might decide that assigning a build master or integration coordinator is required if conflicts begin to slow the team. The role of this team member is to monitor code development and help guide continuous integration. The role could fall to the resident VAJ expert, who will direct her efforts at training the team in the use of VAJ's source-management features. Continual integration conflicts might indicate root causes, and the team can take the opportunity to refactor the offending class or module.

We've seen that VAJ can be trained to work well in the XP environment. Let's take a look at the Microsoft IDE offering.

Microsoft's Visual Studio .NET

Visual Basic has long been the poor cousin in the software development community. The lack of object-oriented language features and deployment challenges with component registration being two of the main reasons. With the release of Microsoft Visual Basic .NET developers have access to a language that has its roots in the easy-to-learn roots of BASIC, but with the power of a fully .NET compliant language. The primary development tool or .NET is the Visual Studio .NET product family. With this IDE, Microsoft has delivered a single tool that supports all their .NET languages: C++, C#, Visual Basic, and now J#.

Visual Studio .NET has one thing in common with VAJ—learning it isn't for the faint of heart! Figure 13.9 illustrates Visual Studio .NET, showing the source window.

FIGURE 13.9

Visual Studio .NET in the source window.

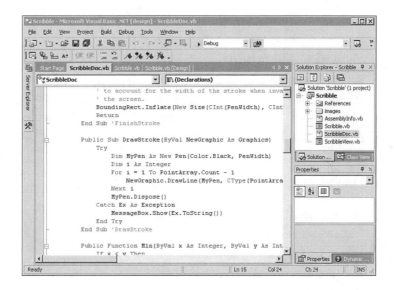

Visual Studio .NET comes in three versions

- Enterprise Architect
- Enterprise Developer
- Professional

XP developers will find that either of the Enterprise options will work the best as the Professional version lacks source management integration. You could use an external source repository such as CVS, which would remove that limitation. To help you clarify what each version has to offer we have provided a feature breakdown in Table 13.5.

TABLE 13.5   Visual Studio .NET Version Types

Product/Feature	Enterprise Architect	Enterprise Developer	Professional
XML Web services	X	X	X
Windows Forms	X	X	X
Web Forms	X	X	X
Mobile Web Forms	X	X	X
Pocket PC and Windows CE .NET-based applications	X	X	X
.NET Framework and the common language runtime	X	X	X
Console Applications	X	X	X
Class Libraries	X	X	X
Windows Control Libraries	X	X	X
Web Control Libraries	X	X	X
Windows Services	X	X	X
Visual Studio .NET Debugger	X	X	X
Remote Debugging	X	X	X
Dynamic Help	X	X	X
Task List	X	X	X
HTML Designer	X	X	X
Microsoft SQL Server 2000	X	X	
Microsoft Visio-based database modeling	X		
Microsoft Visual SourceSafe	X	X	
Application Center Test	X	X	
Visio-based UML application modeling	X		
Enterprise templates and frameworks	X	X	
Visual Studio Analyzer	X	X	

Unlike IBM, Microsoft does not offer a free or light version of their IDE, but you will be able to order a trial version of Visual Studio .NET Professional from
`http://msdn.microsoft.com/vstudio/`.

Contrary to popular belief you don't need to buy Visual Studio .NET to
develop .NET applications. The .NET Framework is a free download from
`http://msdn.microsoft.com/library/default.asp?url=/nhp/default.asp?`
`contentid=28000519` and includes both the Visual Basic and C# compilers.
You can use Notepad or similar text editor to then write source code and
compile from the command prompt.

Visual Studio .NET will reformat source code as you type; therefore, there's no need to
invoke a formatter function. You can establish standards for each file type of your project, including SQL, HTML, and XML. The Enterprise Architect ships with a template
facility that enables the development shop to push out predefined templates to the team.
These templates are of most use in the XP project to kick-start some of the tedious work
of development. Defining your formatting and source completion rules is done through
the Tools, Options menu and then by selecting the appropriate development language.
Figure 13.10 depicts the setting of C# formatting rules.

FIGURE 13.10

*Setting formatting
rules in Visual Studio
.NET.*

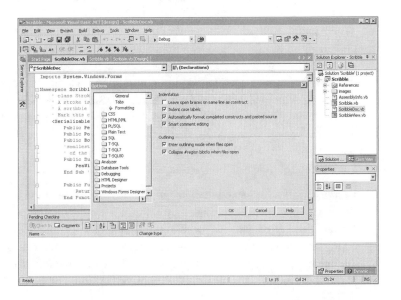

13

The IDE also includes completion functions that fill out object properties and methods
as the user types. One timesaving feature is real-time syntax checking, which operates
silently in the background alerting the developer to errors with a subtle blue squiggly
line under the offending code. Figure 13.11 shows how by hovering over the code caus-
ing the error we get a ToolTip that describes the error.

Figure **13.11**

Real-time error detection in Visual Studio .NET.

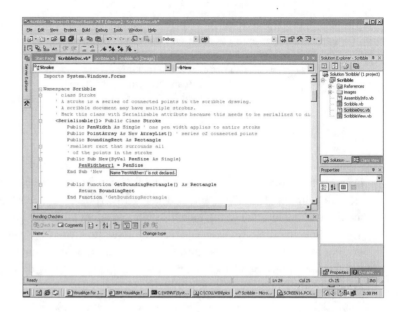

Visual Studio .NET suffers in the area of source control or configuration management with only file-level control offered by Visual Source Safe. This is by no means a showstopper to using Visual Studio .NET in an XP project, but it does mean the team should minimize the size of its classes. Developers should also accept that the shared ownership of code wouldn't extend to real-time at the method level. Shared code base is treated differently in Visual Studio .NET than in VAJ, with each developer or workstation login having individual source control logins. Access to the source repository is through the IDE; integration is seamless. To add your Visual Studio .NET solution to the repository simply select File, Source Control, Add Solution to Source Control. See Figure 13.12 for an example of this.

Each pair will have locked their subproject or component at the file level; therefore, integration clashes will be caused by external dependencies rather than source changes. Visual Studio .NET will still need to refresh the pair's local environment with any dependent source or binary files before they begin work. Integration conflicts will be at the interface level, not the method level as in VAJ. On the one hand Visual Studio .NET is weaker than VAJ at source management, but this does mean that integration is a little easier.

FIGURE **13.12**

Adding a project to Source Safe in Visual Studio .NET.

Other Integrated Development Environments

Visual Studio .NET and VAJ could be classed as the "heavyweights" of the software development tool world with a list of features as long as your arm. But what about the XP team on a budget or with an aversion to proprietary tools? You'll be glad to learn of a couple of IDEs that buck the trend toward feature bloat. An IBM subsidiary company, Object Technology International, has released the new Eclipse Java IDE. The IDE is extensible through its plug-in architecture, and no longer locks the user into a particular JDK version. As an XP developer you will be interested in Eclipse's built-in refactoring support, formatting, and source control integration. Unlike VAJ, which uses IBM's default propriety version control, Eclipse can be configured to use popular packages such as CVS or Rational's ClearCase.

Sun has released a free edition of their Java IDE, Sun ONE Studio, (this was formerly known as Forte), which can be downloaded from http://www.sun.com/java. Sun ONE has support for refactoring through the RefactorIT plug-in (http://www.refactorit.com/). One advantage that Sun ONE has over, say VAJ, is its wider support of non-Windows–based platforms. If you're a developer working in these environments you might consider taking Sun ONE for a spin.

Borland's JBuilder is one of few IDE's to deliver integration with the Ant automated build framework, and with version 7 they've included a number of new refactorings. A trial version can be downloaded from http://www.borland.com/jbuilder/.

13

As with many software tool types, there is no perfect IDE and you should select yours based on platform, features, support XP practices (such as refactoring), extensibility, and, perhaps lastly, price. Table 13.6 lists most of the popular IDEs available today and is a great place to start exploring your own best tool.

TABLE 13.6 Integrated Development Environments

Tool	Platform	Vendor	Link	Free?
Visual Studio .NET	.NET (Windows)	Microsoft	`http://msdn.microsoft.com/vstudio/`	No
VisualAge for Java	Java (Windows IDE)	IBM	`http://www-3.ibm.com/software/ad/vajava`	Yes (Entry only)
Eclipse	Java (Windows IDE)	IBM	`http://www.eclipse.org`	Yes
Sun ONE Studio	Java	Sun	`http://wwws.sun.com/software/sunone/index.html`	No
JBuilder	Java	Borland	`http://www.borland.com/jbuilder/`	No
JDeveloper	Java	Oracle	`http://www.oracle.com/ip/develop/ids/index.html`	No
ControlCenter	Java	TogetherSoft	`http://www.togethersoft.com/products/controlcenter`	No
IDEA	Java	IntelliJ	`http://www.intellij.com/`	No
WebObjects	Java, Objective-C	Apple	`http://www.apple.com/webobjects/`	No
C++Builder	C++ (Windows)	Borland	`http://www.borland.com/cbuilder/`	No
CodeWarrior	Java, C++, C	Metrowerks	`http://www.metrowerks.com/`	No

Summary

The main thing to take away from this hour is to find the simplest tool for your task and don't get sidetracked by features. The JUnit Java testing framework is a perfect example of how the XP software development community leverages a simple, but powerful tool. There are integrated development environments that support some of our core XP practices, such as collective code ownership and refactoring. The growing directory of open source or free XP tools lowers any economic barrier to entry into the world of XP. This should help you sell the concept to your boss.

In the next hour you will learn how to use the JUnit Java-based, unit-testing framework. Time to roll up those programming sleeves.

Q&A

Q If I don't use the Java programming language, will I be a second-class citizen in XP?

A No, not at all. In fact XP has its roots in SmallTalk, not Java. If you attended any of the XP conferences, such as XP Universe, you might find that the technical training sessions are biased toward Java. The important thing is that there is an xUnit testing tool for your language, and you have source control.

Q It looks like XP favors the use of open source libraries and development tools. Does this mean they lack robustness?

A No. The standard of main open source projects, such as JUnit, is very high. These tools are developed by people who have both passion and commitment to excellence. When was the last time your commercial tool crashed?

Workshop

This workshop tests whether you understand all the concepts you learned in this hour. It is very helpful to know and understand the answers before starting the next hour's lesson.

13

Quiz

1. What is the main advantage of CVS over Visual Source Safe?

    a. Integration of VisualAge for Java.

    b. Higher performance.

    c. Capability to handle multiple project types.

    d. Supports multiple file edits and doesn't require file locking.

2. What XP practices does VisualAge for Java support?

    a. Refactoring, collective code ownership, coding standards.

    b. Integration and testing.

    c. Testing, coding, and version management.

    d. Depends on which version.

3. What is the biggest weakness with JUnit?

    a. Poor support for GUI testing.

    b. It's tied to specific JDK version.

    c. Limitation in number of tests.

    d. Supports multiple file edits and doesn't require file locking.

4. There is one important issue with testing. What is it?

    a. XP projects mandate the use the relevant xUnit.

    b. Tests must run quickly.

    c The testing framework should be integrated with the build.

    d The xUnit should me integrated with the IDE.

5. What is the most important tool in the XPer's toolbox?

    a. Fast machine.

    b. Integrated development suite that supports xUnit.

    c. Web-based collaboration tool.

    d. Paper.

Answers

1. d.

2. b.

3. a.

4. b.

5. d.

Activities

1. Based on your existing development language, download the relevant xUnit and begin to experiment with the supplied examples.

2. Define a short list of defect-tracking requirements for your team. Evaluate the best defect-tracking option from our list.

Hour **14**

Unit Testing with Java Tools

Over the next hour, you will learn how you can use JUnit to test your Java programs. The content of this hour is aimed more at developers than at project managers or other team members. You will still gain value from understanding how JUnit works if you're not a developer; you may even write some code! Let's get started then with JUnit. This hour covers

- Why test-first programming is important
- What JUnit is and how to use it
- How to install and test JUnit
- How to write your first JUnit test case
- What some of the limitations and constraints of unit testing are

Revisiting Test-first Programming

In Hour 6, "XP Practices in Action," you learned that in XP you write a test *before* you write the code you are testing. Customers write acceptance tests based on their user stories, whereas developers write unit tests that relate to the *tasks* on the story. There are exceptions to this rule but on the whole it is quite accurate. (The exceptions could be items that relate to tasks that have no code attached, such as equipment requisition and the like.)

Most developers cringe at the prospect of "boring" testing and put it off for as long as possible. Sometimes this means foregoing the pleasure entirely! XP relies on the creation of tests, written in the projects software development language. So, testing is really coding. Testing and coding are so tightly coupled in XP that they form one programming element. This explains why a developer's task estimates include testing and coding. Writing program logic without a supporting set of tests makes no sense in the context of XP.

When is the best time to start testing? As soon as possible. Tests and the results that come from them tell developers that they are on the right track in both understanding requirements and actual logic. The time to start testing then is before you begin the main work of development with your task. The testing approach adopted by XP is very simple; write a few tests for each new class or component and then write just enough code for the test to pass. After the tests pass, go back to your component and continue to add code. The interesting thing about your first test run is that it will fail; in fact, you want it to fail because it verifies your test logic is correct.

Writing tests first means we think of the test cases in terms of what's required, thinking from the outside-in and basing our assumptions on specifications. Testing first is also easier from an emotional angle as well; developer's egos are less likely to be bruised by a test failure when there's no or little code there! The converse is spending hours or days working on a component, pouring your very life into and then finding that *your* work failed.

I'll start discussing unit testing with XP by explaining the Java-based testing tool: JUnit.

Overview Of JUnit

JUnit is an open-source unit testing framework for use with the Java programming language. Hour 13, "Using XP Development Tools," discusses the use of unit testing frameworks and explains how the xUnit testing approach could be applied across multiple languages. JUnit was ported from Kent Beck's original SmallTalk testing framework (SUnit) and enabled the vast number of Java programmers to easily test their components. Figure 14.1 illustrates the layout of the JUnit testing framework.

FIGURE 14.1

The architecture of JUnit.

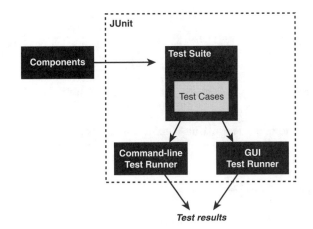

As you can see from Figure 14.1, developers write components and then test them with the JUnit framework. Each class has tests that *test everything that could possibly break*. At the very least there will be one `TestCase` class for each of your classes. Tests are prefixed with the word `test` and are grouped together into a `TestSuite` class to enable multiple tests to be run at one time.

The purpose of this hour is to explain JUnit, not teach the Java programming language. The book *Sams Teach Yourself Java in 24 Hours* is an excellent resource for learning how to program in Java. You can download the latest version of Java from Sun at `http://www.sun.com/java`.

After your test is written, you can then run your test suite from either a command-line interface or via the supplied GUI tool. The output from either test runner is the same—test results that verify whether tests have passed or failed. The underlying approach to JUnit, and indeed all xUnit frameworks, is very simple: You run a test and then compare the result to an expected good result. If the comparison fails, the test framework displays the programmer-defined error message.

A common approach to tackling unit testing is to write print statements to the console (`System.out.println()` in Java) and then, either manually or through file difference tools, compare the results. JUnit takes away the need to use this unreliable method.

14

Each test case follows this basic cycle:

```
Loop through the test methods
{
    setUp();  // execute any initialization logic
    doTests(); // execute each test method
    tearDown();       // execute clean logic at end of test
}
```

The best way to really learn JUnit is to download it and try it out for yourself. In the next section you'll do just that!

Installing JUnit

So where do you get JUnit? Actually it's available on quite a few sites but the real home of JUnit is `http://www.JUnit.org/`. Go ahead and click the "Download" menu option to copy the framework to your local machine. The download is a respectable size of around 400KB. For the purposes of this tutorial, unzip the JUnit3.7.zip file into the root of your C drive (`c:\`). This creates a folder called `c:\junit3.7`. Your version of JUnit may be different if a new version is released after the time of writing. To keep the tutorial simple, go ahead and rename the `c:\Junitx.x` folder to `c:\junit`.

> JUnit can be run on any Java-compatible platform. The example uses a Windows machine, but the tests themselves work equally on Unix, Linux, or Mac. If you're using a non-Windows PC follow your own platform-specific extraction and configuration options.

Opening a command window in Windows and listing the contents of `c:\JUnit` should result in the listing shown in Figure 14.2.

FIGURE 14.2

JUnit installed on your local hard drive.

Now that you've extracted JUnit, you need to add `Junit.jar` to your class path. This enables the Java compiler to resolve where and what JUnit is. To do this, from inside your command window, type

SET CLASSPATH

This tells you your current CLASSPATH setting. If your CLASSPATH is undefined, you will get an error message stating "environment variable not found"; this is fine. All this means is you haven't had an application before that would have created a CLASSPATH for you.

To append `JUnit.jar` to CLASSPATH, enter this at the command prompt inside your window:

SET CLASSPATH=%CLASSPATH%;C:\JUNIT\JUNIT.JAR

Obviously, adding JUnit to your class path like this will get old pretty fast! So, add it to your system so that it's always available. The best place to do this is either in your `autoexec.bat` file for Windows 95 and Windows 98 machines or through My Computer in Windows 2000 and Windows XP.

In Windows 2000 or XP you can use the environment variables window to enter CLASSPATH information. Go into Control Panel, choose System, click the Advanced tab, and then choose the Environment Variables button. Select the command-button to display a list of variables and their values. Figure 14.3 shows how you can double-click CLASSPATH and then enter the new value.

If you already have a setting in your CLASSPATH, make sure that you *append* the `junit` path by separating the new path with a semicolon. Try adding the JUnit folder to your CLASSPATH if you get a "class not defined" error when running JUnit.

That's it! All that remains now is to test your installation. You can do this by running either the command-line or the GUI tools.

CLASSPATH is not case-sensitive.

14

FIGURE **14.3**

Setting your
CLASSPATH *in Win-*
dows 2000 or XP.

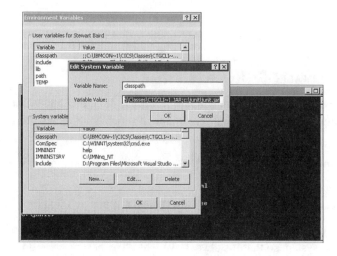

Important: Don't install the JUnit.jar file into the extension directory of your JDK installation. If you do so, the test class on the files system will not be found.

To test your JUnit installation from the command-line, enter this at the prompt:

```
java junit.textui.TestRunner junit.samples.AllTests
```

You should see the TestRunner processing through the sample tests and finish by passing 90 tests. Figure 14.4 illustrates the display you should see.

FIGURE **14.4**

Running JUnit in the
command-window.

Any errors while attempting to run the samples with the TestRunner indicate either a Java or a JUnit setup problem. You can check whether Java is installed correctly by entering the following at the command prompt:

```
java -version
```

This command reports on the version of your Java runtime. You should expect to see some version 1.3 or greater. Figure 14.5 shows the version number of Java.

FIGURE 14.5

Checking your Java version number.

Make sure you install the full Java Development Kit (JDK), not simply the Java Runtime Environment (JRE). The JRE does not include the Java compiler (javac.exe) you will need while you develop in Java.

If you run the version checker on Mac OS X, you will find that you have some variant of Java version 1.3; this is fine because Apple has yet to support version 1.4. (Apple has slated an expected release date for 1.4 from some time in Fall 2002; check http://www.apple.com/java for the latest news on this.)

After you have Java up and running, your problems with JUnit should go away.

Running JUnit from the command line is useful when you automate the entire integration and testing process. If you're developing your components locally before integrating, a better option is to use the graphical interface tool. There are two versions of this GUI TestRunner: One is the basic AWT version and the other runs using the newer Swing libraries from Sun. To run sample tests, enter the following commands at the prompt, as shown in Table 14.1.

14

TABLE 14.1   Commands to Run the GUI JUnit TestRunner

GUI TestRunner	Command-line
AWT	`java junit.awtui.TestRunner junit.samples.AllTests`
Swing	`java junit.swingui.TestRunner junit.samples.AllTests`

The command has three parts, as explained in Table 14.2.

TABLE 14.2   Syntax of TestRunner

Part	Description
`java`	Java runtime executable
`junit.swingui.TestRunner`	Class name for the Junit you want to run
`junit.samples.AllTests`	The name of the class or classes you want to test

The Swing version of the interface extends the JUnit runner by allowing the user to run individual tests and to browse for the class library from the application. If you run the Swing version you should see the display illustrated in Figure 14.6.

FIGURE 14.6

Running the JUnit Swing GUI application.

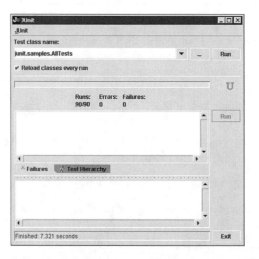

Extreme programmers often talk about getting a green bar on unit tests; if this book were in color you'd see that the solid progress bar next to the "JU" is a happy green color! By now you've verified that your JUnit is installed correctly and that you're able to run each of the TestRunners. The next step is to write your first unit test!

Before you do that, run a test that you know will fail and watch out for that red bar! As part of the JUnit samples, you have a test class named SimpleTest.class. There are some errors in this class that you'll now expose using JUnit. Run either the command-line or GUI TestRunners and you should get three failures. In case you've forgotten the command line to enter, it's provided in Table 14.3.

TABLE 14.3   Commands to Run JUnit TestRunners

JUnit TestRunner version	Command-line
Console	`java junit.textui.TestRunner junit.samples.SimpleTest`
AWT	`java junit.awtui.TestRunner junit.samples.SimpleTest`
Swing	`java junit.swingui.TestRunner junit.samples.SimpleTest`

Remember that Java is case sensitive. Make sure you enter in your class names with the correct case.

Having run SimpleTest with the Swing TestRunner, your result should resemble Figure 14.7.

FIGURE 14.7

JUnit displaying test failures.

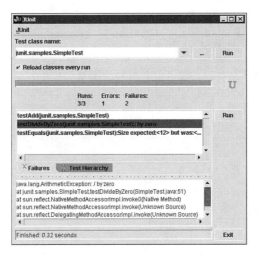

You will notice in the result window that JUnit differentiates between failures and errors. A failure is anticipated and checked for with assertions. Errors are unanticipated problems, such as an `ArrayIndexOutOfBoundsException`.

14

Writing Your First JUnit Test

Now you're ready to write your first unit test with JUnit, The best place to start is to walk through one of the samples that comes with your JUnit installation. Each unit test should follow these steps:

1. Subclass `junit.framework.TestCase`.

2. Add any setup code into the `setUp()` method.

3. Define your tests. Each should return void (that is, it has no return value) and its name should start with `test`—for example, `testMaxSize()`, `testConvertAmount()`, and `testAdd()`.

4. Release any resources that were consumed during your `setUp()` method by overriding the `tearDown()` method.

5. Define a suite of tests if you need to collect tests together.

You will find `SimpleTest.java` in your `junit\samples` directory. Open this up in your text editor and you should see the source code provided in Listing 14.1.

Comments have been removed from the source code in Listing 14.1.

If you're new to the Java language you may want to get a copy of SAMS *Teach Yourself Java in 24 Hours*.

LISTING 14.1   SimpleTest JUnit Test Listing

```
1 package junit.samples;
2 import junit.framework.*;
3 public class SimpleTest extends TestCase {
4     protected int fValue1;
5     protected int fValue2;
6     public SimpleTest(String name) {
7         super(name);
8     }
9     protected void setUp() {
10         fValue1= 2;
11         fValue2= 3;
12     }
13
14     public static Test suite() {
15         return new TestSuite(SimpleTest.class);
```

LISTING 14.1 continued

```
16    }
17    public void testAdd() {
18        double result= fValue1 + fValue2;
19        // forced failure result == 5
20        assertTrue(result == 6);
21    }
22    public void testDivideByZero() {
23        int zero= 0;
24        int result= 8/zero;
8/zero;
25    }
26    public void testEquals() {
27        assertEquals(12, 12);
28        assertEquals(12L, 12L);
29        assertEquals(new Long(12), new Long(12));
30        assertEquals("Size", 12, 13);
31        assertEquals("Capacity", 12.0, 11.99, 0.0);
32    }
33 }
```

The following is taking place in `SimpleTest.java`:

- Line 1: You create a new package for the sample test class.
- Line 2: You reference the JUnit testing framework library. (For .NET readers, this is analogous to `namespace` in those environments.)
- Line 3: You name the test class, subclassing the base `TestCase` class.
- Lines 9–12: You override the base `setUp()` method and set the initial values for your test variables.
- Lines 14–16: You override the base test suite and return a new instance of the test case.
- Lines 17–21: Your test class implements the "adding numbers" test, `testAdd()`, which simply adds two numbers together. Line 20 raises an assert message if the addition fails. Don't worry, we can add! The sample forces an error for demonstration purposes only. Ordinarily, you would provide a string message for the first parameter. Using the simple form of `assertTrue()` does not return a useful message to the TestRunner.
- Lines 22–25: Here, you force an exception by attempting to divide by zero in the `testDivideByZero()` method. This raises an *error* as opposed to test *failure*.
- Lines 26–32: The `testEquals()` method tests various equalities and, in the case of lines 30 and 31, causes a failure message to appear in the `TestRunner()`.

14

That's it! Seems too easy to be true? Well, that's the beauty of the JUnit framework and explains why its use is catching on through the Java community.

Test-first Saves Your Sanity

Why go to all the bother of writing tests anyway? Has that thought crossed your mind yet? Intellectually, test-first programming makes a whole lot of sense but I never realized it until it saved me from extra work.

In my case I started well along the test-first road; after creating my stub method, I switched back to the unit testing framework and wrote my test series. My programming partner and I considered what we'd have to test to verify our component. Pretty soon we had a handful of tests to write. I drove the keyboard while my partner helped.

After some time back and forth between code and test, we had a working test suite that passed 100%. The code was complete.

Not long after that, we had the "never" happen; we thought the database structure would *never* change, but of course it did. We ran our unit tests again and, as we dreaded, they all failed. Here's the catch: We knew our tests were good and that the components had passed before, and so all we had to do now was recode some of our underlying components.

Having a test suite already in place meant that we had a solid basis to build on. We were confident that our new code was good. The alternative would have been to spend hours walking through the code in the debugger, comparing print statements or file stream output.

Tests gave us courage to work!

Testing Challenges

In a few areas, unit testing with a tool like JUnit is either ineffective or at the least challenging. With careful planning, thought, and correct tools, most of these issues can be resolved.

User Interfaces

As I explained in Hour 13, some vendors such as Rational supply tools that allow full automated testing of user interfaces. These typically work with the test developer capturing both user input and an exact bitmap image of the screen for each action. These bitmap "photographs" are then used for comparisons while the test runs. Although this does work, the slightest change to the interface will break your test. The need to match video output goes down to the level of the display card itself; these often must match on both developer and test workstation. In no time at all automated testing becomes some unlucky person's full-time job!

Applying the JUnit approach to user interface testing means both capturing events and calling window-level methods. It is possible to hook into the user interface at the code level, but the results will never match the comparison method used by a product like Rational's Visual Test. Accepting the limitations of JUnit is not as bad as it sounds in the case of user interfaces because modern systems have moved business logic back into a middle-tier layer. The interface code is quite light in comparison to database and business layers. This means your business logic unit tests are exercising most of the code anyway so your coverage is good.

Web-Based Systems

Web interfaces and Web-based systems offer similar challenges to user interface testing. Problems are compounded, though, by the wide variation in platform and browsers available. Using the Visual Test bitmap model quickly becomes tiresome. Your pain is lessened somewhat by tools such as ASPUnit (for Microsoft ASP applications) and HttpUnit. The idea with these tools is to capture the HTTP traffic stream and then perform textual comparisons. Your success with these types of tools may be quite high depending on the site's complexity. Another way to improve the chore of testing Web applications is to maintain good, sound design by separating presentation, business, and data layers. Approach writing applications in JSP or ASP carefully; with these development platforms, falling into the trap of mixing business and presentation code is easy.

Database or Slow Test

Your tests must run quickly. Database components that work with large data sets and slow response times will be a challenge with automation. Although the idea with JUnit is to run your test frequently as your code develops, this is impractical if each test takes 10 minutes! Not all is lost, however; you can get around this in a couple of ways:

1. Use test or sample data sets that mimic your full load.
2. Use "mock" objects that sit between your database layer and database. These objects act as if they were connected to the database but return predefined data sets.

With both of these workarounds you can still run your full-load tests after hours, reporting on results for the next day.

We must recognize that some code will be too hard or time-consuming to test with automated tools like JUnit. Measuring how much effort is involved in creating and maintaining these automated tools will enable you to make the right call. It may be more effective to supplement your automation with limited manual intervention.

14

Summary

The XP value of courage is enabled for the developer by the use of automated testing frameworks, such as JUnit. JUnit is a Java-based testing framework that is both easy and flexible to use. You learned how to install and configure this powerful tool. The stiffest challenge for developers is not using and understanding JUnit but the change in mindset that test-first programming brings.

In the next hour, you discover how to write unit tests with Microsoft .NET. What you've learned this hour will give you a head start even though it's the "other side of the force!"

Q&A

Q Do I really test everything that could break?

A Almost! There is no real absolute with what to test; let your conscience be your guide. Write tests for everything that you can think of anyway. Testing of the system functions after aliens have abducted the user may not be that useful!

Q What if my system has already been written without tests?

A Sounds like real life! Start by writing tests as you work on code; writing unit tests after the event is hard to sell to both management and customer. The customer may wonder why you didn't do it before or they might not care if their system works anyway. Writing tests is not an end in itself; the software in the hands of the customer is.

Workshop

This workshop tests whether you understand all the concepts you learned in this hour. It is very helpful to know and understand the answers before starting the next lesson.

Quiz

1. What JUnit class must you subclass to write a test?

    a. You write your own

    b. `TestSuite()` or `Tests()`

    c. `TestCase()`

    d. `TestRunner()`

2. Why would you use the command-line `TestRunner`?

    a. The test runs much faster.

    b. Your IDE lacked support of the GUI version.

    c. Personal choice.

    d. Results can be easily captured and reported in an automated scenario.

3. What would you do in the `setUp()` class of your `TestCase`?

    a. Set database connection.

    b. Perform primary subclassing.

    c. Create or consume any resources you will need during the test.

    d. Call your test suite.

4. Why is database testing difficult in JUnit?

    a. Java has poor database support.

    b. Tests must execute quickly in JUnit and database back-ends can slow the cycle.

    c. JUnit is for testing of classes not databases.

    d. Mock objects are too difficult to use in this context.

Answers

1. c.

2. d.

3. c.

4. b.

Activities

1. Extend the money class from the JUnit samples so that it supports currency conversion from U.S. dollars to a currency of your choice. Create a test case for this new method.

2. Investigate `AllTests.java` from the JUnit samples and add your new test cases to the suite.

14

HOUR 15

Unit Testing with Microsoft Tools

In Hour 14, "Unit Testing with Java Tools," you learned how to use JUnit to test Java-based software. We will continue in a similar vein over the course of this hour by introducing the Microsoft .NET unit-testing tool: NUnit. You will learn

- The difference between Microsoft COM and .NET
- How to get and install the .NET framework
- How to install and test NUnit
- How to create your first NUnit test using a tutorial example

Reviewing Microsoft COM and .NET

As you read and learn more about Extreme Programming you will get the definite sense that Java is the prominent development language of choice for XPers. Developers working in the Microsoft world of COM and Windows have been slow to join the XP wave. In this book I've tried to remain unbiased in the Java versus Microsoft debate. A narrowing of the gap between the two camps has begun to come about with the arrival of Web Services and other XML-based initiatives.

The purpose of this book is to learn XP, not get drawn into "holy wars" between Sun and Microsoft. So, we'll continue our discussion this hour by addressing unit testing on the Microsoft platform. It can be said that Microsoft has *two* platforms at the moment: the legacy COM world and .NET. We'll direct our focus at .NET rather than COM because this is the new platform. Before we delve into NUnit it will be helpful to get a quick refresher on .NET versus the COM platform.

Microsoft COM

In 1992, Microsoft introduced the Component Object Model (COM) as way to build reusable components and applications. At one time, COM was primarily described as a method of embedding one document inside another, and then it was extended into a technology for distributing self-contained applications. Most recently COM has been the platform for building middle-tier business logic.

In the 90s Microsoft released easy-to-use development tools, such as, Visual Basic and Visual FoxPro that enabled developers to quickly build COM applications. During the 1990s COM-based applications grew in complexity and prominence in the enterprise. The downsides of the tightly coupled binary approach, with the use of registry keys and GUIDs gave rise to the now infamous "DLL Hell." Components worked fine on the developer's workstation, but failed when deployed to production. The use of shared resources worsened this nightmare as applications that appeared quite separate to the user (such as email and Web clients) were often inexplicably linked. Installing the latest version of a seemingly innocuous piece of software could have disastrous results!

Microsoft .NET

In July 2000, Microsoft announced a new platform—.NET. Some degree of confusion surrounded what exactly ".NET" meant—was it just some new marketing trick or another rebranding of COM? We can answer this in two words: the Internet. Where in the past Internet and Web technologies had been tacked on to Windows; now the vision was to integrate Web-based services into the very heart of Windows. Standards-based technologies such as XML, SOAP, and UDDI formed the basis for this new platform.

Microsoft .NET can be described as the idea that the Internet itself will be a new kind of operating system. From a user's point of view, .NET is important because it makes his information accessible across all devices. .NET enables this software integration through the use of XML Web services, which are small, building-block applications that connect to each other via the Internet.

See http://www.xmethods.net for a list of various Web Services available on different platforms.

15

With the arrival of .NET, Microsoft is talking in a new language: industry standards and platform independence. The intention is that by opening up applications using XML, the traditional barriers between systems can be broken down once and for all. XML becomes the common language by which all systems can communicate. Esperanto for computers!

Microsoft .NET covers a lot of ground from vision and marketing right down to a common language runtime that separates applications from the underlying operating system. We're concerned about the tools that are used to develop .NET applications and how to test them in an XP world. Figure 15.1 illustrates the building blocks of .NET.

FIGURE 15.1

An overview of the .NET architecture showing how tools and standards fit together.

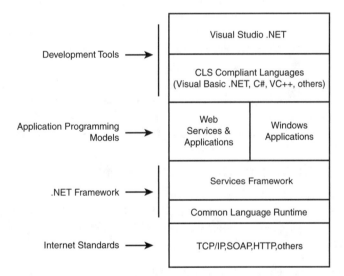

.NET applications or services run inside a common language runtime (CLR) that translates .NET byte-code (known as intermediate code) into native Intel X86 instructions. This enables Microsoft to expose a rich-services layer for developers while running compiled applications at native speeds. Another interesting facet of .NET is the ability of developers to write code in a multitude of languages—as long as they support the Common Language Specification (CLS).

The multilanguage capability of .NET explains why we only need a single unit-testing framework for all .NET compliant languages.

One development language was conspicuous by its absence at the launch of
.NET—Java. It would appear the reasons for the lack of a Java compiler for
.NET were more legal than technical. Microsoft has since announced a Java-
like compiler called J# (pronounced J-sharp). Visit http://msdn.microsoft.com/
visualj/ for the latest on this product.

Let's make a start at unit testing with NUnit.

Establishing Your .NET Environment

To use NUnit you will need to configure both .NET and the NUnit testing framework
itself. At the time of this writing, .NET is a separate download that does not ship with
Windows. The plan is to include .NET on the Windows XP server, as it stands .NET can
run on either Windows 98, NT, 2000, or XP.

From time-to-time Microsoft releases service packs for the .NET Framework.
Check http://msdn.microsoft.com/netframework/ for the latest downloads.
It's important to apply any service packs before you begin any development
work.

Downloading and Installing .NET

Before you can begin development in Microsoft .NET you'll need the software development
kit (SDK). You can either order the SDK on CD or simply download it from the Microsoft
site. The URL is http://msdn.microsoft.com/netframework/. The download size is a
hefty 130MB, so either borrow a friend's broadband connection or be prepared to wait!

When you've downloaded the SDK, double-click your install file and follow the instructions.

You don't need the Microsoft Visual Studio .NET product suite to write and
build .NET applications; the SDK comes with the C# and Visual Basic .NET
compilers. Visual Studio .NET will definitely be worthwhile if you plan to
start serious .NET development. See http://msdn.microsoft.com/vstudio/
for more information on Visual Studio .NET.

If you have already installed Visual Studio .NET, you won't need to download the SDK because it comes with the product.

Setting Up and Running the .NET Testing Framework

You can download the latest version of NUnit from `http://nunit.sourceforge.net/`.
Unlike the monster download size of the .NET framework you'll be presently surprised
by how small NUnit is! Installing NUnit is simplified by the fact that it is supplied in a
Windows Installer file. Double-click the `nunit.msi` file to install NUnit on your local
machine.

> The MSI file extension denotes a Microsoft Windows Installer file. If the
> installer fails to run when you double-click the `nunit.msi` file, you'll need to
> download Windows Installer from `http://www.microsoft.com/downloads/`.

You should have no problem setting up NUnit, assuming you installed .NET first. Before
you start your test example, you'd better check that NUnit is up and running. To do this
start the NUnitGUI application (you will find this under your Program Files, NUnit
folder), and then select the Browse button to the load `SampleAll.dll` (this will be under
the samples folder) .NET library. Click Run and you should see the resulting screen
we've depicted in Figure 15.2.

FIGURE 15.2

*NUnitGUI application
showing results from
the test run on*
`SampleAll.dll`.

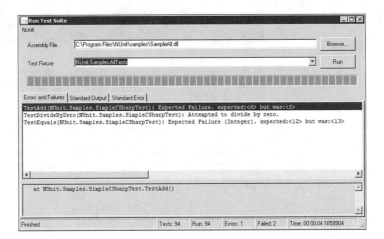

Notice we have three errors in the failure window—don't panic! If you check the sample
code for this DLL you will note that they were generated on purpose (the sample source
code is in the `src` folder under `samples`).

NUnit is now installed and is ready to test your .NET components.

Writing Your First NUnit Test

In Hour 14, we explained how JUnit works by walking through one of the JUnit samples. NUnit comes with almost exactly the same sample files as JUnit, so rather than revisit the Money test, let's look at a fresh test case.

We are using Visual Basic .NET in our sample test and application. NUnit works exactly the same way for any other .NET-compliant language. Visual Basic is a good common denominator for our tutorial purposes because most developers have some knowledge of it.

The Sample User Story for the NUnit Test

Our fictitious customer has just drawn up the first user story for his new interactive Rugby Web site. Clearly, our customer is unabashedly ethnocentric in his outlook, and is only interested in New Zealand's rugby history. The requirements seem pretty straight-forward except for the probability calculator; we'll cross that bridge when we come to it. Figure 15.3 displays our user story.

FIGURE 15.3
Rugby Calculator sample user story.

New Zealand Rugby Calculator

The system should return key information about New Zealand rugby teams versus other rugby playing nations. In particular we need to know:
  1. Number of times played against
  2. Number of times beat NZ
  3. Number of times NZ beat them
  4. Probable outcome of the next match

At the outset we would like reports for; USA, Scotland, England and South Africa.

Note: www.rugbyrugby.com will be able to help you with data

To refresh your memory, you will need to take the following steps to test and code our user story:

- Write a class that has the public methods we need
- Write our NUnit test case
- Run our tests; they should fail
- Go back to the class and write just enough code for our test to pass
- Rerun our NUnit test

Creating the Sample Application

We will start by creating a new project in Visual Studio .NET. Select a new Class Library project and call it Rugby. Do this by going to the File, New, Project menu. (We're saving our files in the c:\TYSXP folder; the location is unimportant.) Figure 15.4 demonstrates how we add the new project.

FIGURE 15.4

Creating the new Rugby *sample project in Visual Studio .NET.*

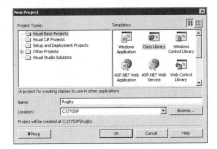

You will now have a Class Library with a single class file (class.vb). Right-click it and rename it rugby.vb. Now add the stub methods, as follows in Listing 15.1:

LISTING 15.1   Shell Rugby Class

```
Public Class Rugby
    Private _Team As String
    Public Sub New()
    End Sub
    Public Property Team() As String
        Get
End Get
        Set(ByVal Value As String)
        End Set
    End Property

    Public Function GamesPlayed() As Integer
    End Function

    Public Function Play() As String
End Function

    Public Function NumberOfTimesBeatNZ() As Integer
    End Function
    Public Function NumberOfTimesBeat() As Integer
    End Function
End Class
```

That's all we need for in our class module.

Creating the Unit Test for Rugby Class

We now have an outline, or stub class library, that has public methods. Our next step is to add a new project to our existing Rugby solution (rugby.sln). Go ahead add a new Class Library project using the same procedure we used when creating our sample Rugby project. Call this new project RugbyTests. After adding the new project you should have both projects under the same solution, as illustrated in Figure 15.5

FIGURE 15.5

The Rugby sample solution showing both test and application.

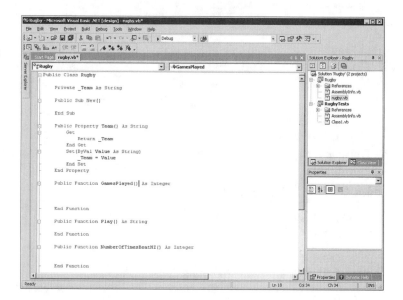

We're getting closer to being able to write our unit tests using NUnit; the last remaining step is to add a reference to the core NUnit library. Do this by right-clicking the RugbyTests project and selecting Add Reference. Use the Browse button to locate and select your NUnitCore.dll; you will find this in the bin folder of your installed directory. As you can see in Figure 15.6, in our configuration, we installed NUnit in the default location of c:\Program Files\NUnit.

We now have a reference to NUnit; it would be a good idea to add some code! With the aim of keeping it simple, we'll start by writing one test, executing it with NUnit, and then checking the result. Before you go any further, rename your default class file (class.vb) as RugbyTests.vb. Listing 15.2 is our shell or outline code for the RugbyTests class.

FIGURE 15.6

Adding a project reference to the NUnit testing framework.

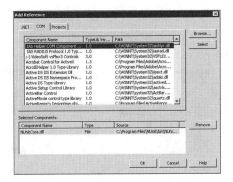

15

LISTING 15.2 Shell RugbyTests Class

```
1 Imports System
2 Imports NUnit.Framework
3 Public Class RugbyTests
4     Inherits TestCase
5     Private objRugby As Rugby.Rugby
6     Public Sub New(ByVal name As String)
7         MyBase.New(name)
8     End Sub
9     Protected Overrides Sub SetUp()
10  objRugby = New Rugby.Rugby()
11     End Sub
12     Shared ReadOnly Property Suite() As ITest
13         Get
14             Suite = New TestSuite(GetType(RugbyTests))
15         End Get
16     End Property
17     Public Sub TestSetUSCountry()
18  objRugby.Team = "USA"
19         Assert("Failed to set USA as country!", objRugby.Team = "USA")
20     End Sub
21 End Class
```

The following is taking place in `RugbyTests.class`:

- Lines 1 and 2: We import, or make a reference to, the base System library and NUnit itself.

- Line 3: The public method name for our test class: `RugbyTests`.

- Line 4: We inherit the base test case class from the NUnit framework.

- Line 5: We create a private variable to hold the instance of our `Rugby` class. (We could have done this in each test, but we've opted to instantiate the object once to the lower overhead associated with object creation.)

- Line 6–8: Standard method constructor for the `RugbyTests` class. (The method constructor is called when the object is created.)
- Line 9–11: We override the base setup method with our own and create an instance of the Rugby object. Setup is also a great place to add database connections and the like.
- Line 12–16: We expose a suite property that returns the underlying test class (NUnit will use this to create the `RugbyTests` object).
- Line 17–20: Our actual test! In `TestSetUSCountry()` we are testing to see if the Rugby class correctly sets the country to USA. In line 18 we set the country name to USA, and then in 19 we raise an assert if the property has not been set.

Perhaps the most interesting line in our sample is line 19 where we call the Assert method. Assert comes in a number of overloaded types; we are using the version that takes two parameters:

- Message string—The message to be displayed if the test fails.
- Boolean test—If the test returns False the assert method will display our message and flag a failure.

Let's run the test! Before we do that we better build both the `Rugby` and `RugbyTests` projects. Figure 15.7 shows us right-clicking the `RugbyTests` project and selecting build.

FIGURE 15.7
Building the
`RugbyTests` *class.*

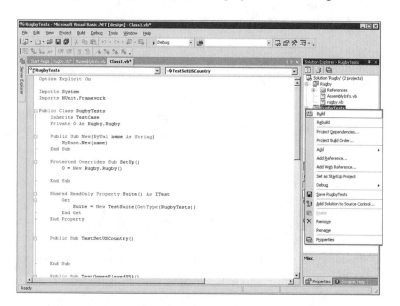

Assuming there are no build errors with our projects; we're ready to start testing.

Compile-time errors are reduced in Visual Studio .NET by the background compiler. The friendly blue squiggly-line is the gentle reminder that your code is broken!

To run our NUnit tests we're going to use the GUI TestRunner. Run `NUnitGUI` from your Start menu, and then browse over to `RugbyTests.dll` in your `RugbyTests` bin folder. Figure 15.8 shows `RugbyTests.dll` selected from the `NUnitGUI` Browse window.

FIGURE 15.8

Selecting the `RugbyTests.dll` *in* `NUnitGUI`.

All that remains is to press run and watch our test run. Not surprisingly our test has failed. This could be because we have no code in our `Rugby` class! Actually, running NUnit in this way and getting a red bar the first time the test is run is exactly what we want. We now know that our test—simple as it is—works and we can now start to add some code into the `Rugby` class. Figure 15.9 displays our failure message.

FIGURE 15.9

`NUnitGUI` *failing our first test.*

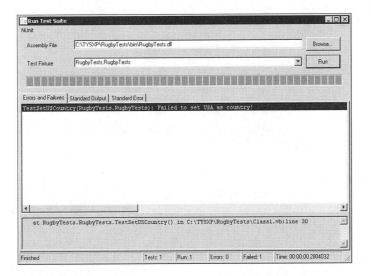

We'd better take a moment to finish our tests before we are tempted to go back to our Rugby class to add the working code. Listing 15.3 is our complete source code for the finished RugbyTests class:

LISTING 15.3   The Completed RugbyTests Class

```
Imports System
Imports NUnit.Framework
Public Class RugbyTests
    Inherits TestCase
    Private objRugby As Rugby.Rugby
    Public Sub New(ByVal name As String)
        MyBase.New(name)
    End Sub
    Protected Overrides Sub SetUp()
        objRugby = New Rugby.Rugby()
    End Sub
    Shared ReadOnly Property Suite() As ITest
        Get
            Suite = New TestSuite(GetType(RugbyTests))
        End Get
    End Property
    Public Sub TestSetUSCountry()
        objRugby.Team = "USA"
        Assert("Failed to set USA as country!", objRugby.Team = "USA")
    End Sub
    Public Sub TestGamesPlayedUSA()
        objRugby.Team = "USA"
        AssertEquals("Failed TestGamesPlayedUSA()", 2, objRugby.GamesPlayed())
    End Sub
    Public Sub TestTimesBeatEngland()
        objRugby.Team = "England"
        AssertEquals("Failed TestTimesBeatEngland()", 18,
➥objRugby.NumberOfTimesBeat())
    End Sub
    Public Sub TestTimesEnglandBeatNZ()
        objRugby.Team = "England"
        AssertEquals("Failed TestTimesEnglandBeatNZ()", 4,
➥objRugby.NumberOfTimesBeatNZ())
    End Sub
    Public Sub TestTimesScotlandBeatNZ()
        System.Console.Write("Running TestTimesScotlandBeatNZ()")
        objRugby.Team = "Scotland"
        AssertEquals("Failed TestTimesScotlandBeatNZ()", 0,
➥objRugby.NumberOfTimesBeatNZ())
    End Sub
    Public Sub TestPlayUSA()
        objRugby.Team = "USA"
        AssertEquals("Failed TestPlayUSA()", "No chance!", objRugby.Play())
    End Sub
End Class
```

15

The completed class follows the same approach as our shell example in Listing 15.2. We do have some more tests that reflect the customer's user story in Figure 15.3 and a couple of new methods. The new methods are described in Table 15.1.

TABLE 15.1 New Methods Used in `RugbyTests` Test Library

Method	Description
`AssertEquals()`	`AssertEquals` is similar to `Assert` except it takes two test parameters: the expected result and the actual result. Our message will be raised if the two fail to match.
`System.Console.Write()`	This is one of the base .NET system methods, which is typically used to write text messages out to the console or command window. In NUnit the message will appear in our Standard Output window.

For completeness we'll list our `RugbyTests` tests in Table 15.2.

TABLE 15.2 New Methods Used in `RugbyTests` Test Library

Test Method	Description
`TestSetUSCountry()`	Tests that `Rugby` class sets and gets a country of USA.
`TestGamesPlayedUSA()`	Tests if the `Rugby` class returns the total number of times New Zealand has played the USA in rugby.
`TestTimesBeatEngland()`	Tests if the `Rugby` class returns the total number of times New Zealand has beaten England in rugby.
`TestTimesEnglandBeatNZ()`	Tests if the `Rugby` class returns the total number of times England has beaten New Zealand in rugby.
`TestTimesScotlandBeatNZ()`	Tests if the `Rugby` class returns the total number of times Scotland has beaten New Zealand in rugby.
`TestPlayUSA()`	Tests if the `Rugby` class returns the correct (probable) result of a game played between New Zealand and the USA in rugby.

We've used real data in our test cases; visit `http://www.rugbyrugby.com/` for the latest statistics. Yes, New Zealand and the USA have only played twice!

Rebuild your `RugbyTests` project once more and rerun your `NUnitGUI` tests.

You can leave NUnitGUI running while you add code to your test class.

The bad news is that our tests are still failing, but the good news is NUnit is running our new test. Figure 15.10 shows our new NUnitGUI display with all four tests failing.

FIGURE 15.10

NUnitGUI *failing our full test.*

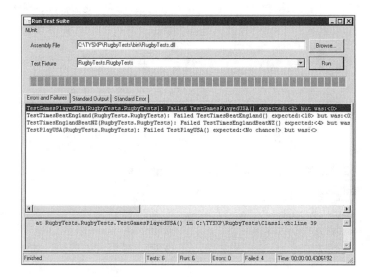

This is a good point to recap and take a breather. By now we have

- Analyzed the customer's user story
- Built an initial shell Class Library that contains all our methods, but no program logic
- Created a new NUnit test harness by adding a new Class Library project and referencing the core NUnit library
- Added all the necessary test code to verify that Rugby class is working
- Run our unit tests and received our expected failures

We don't want to get too comfortable with those failures, so let's add the rest of our code to Rugby class until they pass. Listing 15.4 is our complete Rugby class that should now pass the tests.

LISTING 15.4   The Completed Rugby Class

```
Public Class Rugby
    Private _Team As String
    Public Sub New()
    End Sub
    Public Property Team() As String
        Get
            Return _Team
        End Get
        Set(ByVal Value As String)
            _Team = Value
        End Set
    End Property
    Public Function GamesPlayed() As Integer
        Select Case _Team
            Case "USA" : Return 2
            Case "England" : Return 18
            Case "Scotland" : Return 24
        End Select
    End Function
    Public Function Play() As String
        Select Case _Team
            Case "USA" : Return "No chance!"
            Case "England" : Return "Almost always!"
            Case "Scotland" : Return "Not in 24 attempts!"
            Case "South Africa" : Return "Too close to call!"
        End Select
    End Function
    Public Function NumberOfTimesBeatNZ() As Integer
        Select Case _Team
            Case "USA" : Return 0
            Case "England" : Return 4
            Case "Scotland" : Return 0
            Case "South Africa" : Return 26
        End Select
    End Function
    Public Function NumberOfTimesBeat() As Integer
        Select Case _Team
            Case "USA" : Return 2
            Case "England" : Return 18
            Case "Scotland" : Return 22
            Case "South Africa" : Return 29
        End Select
    End Function
End Class
```

We've completed Rugby class! Make sure you rebuild your project to get the latest changes. With the exception of the highly dubious Play() method, the class is pretty straightforward. Your NUnitGUI should still be running from our last test run, so go ahead and rerun the RugbyTests class. The pleasant sight of a green bar, indicating our tests have passed should greet you, if all is well. Figure 15.11 shows our passed tests and the message we wrote with System.Console.Write().

FIGURE 15.11

NUnitGUI *passing the completed test sample.*

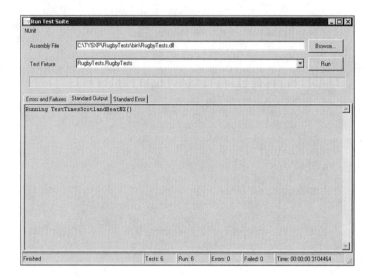

Debugging with NUnit

It's reasonable to expect that you'd want to debug your NUnit tests while developing. Doing this is very simple; all you need to do is configure Visual Studio .NET to start the NUnitGUI while debugging. Follow these steps:

1. Right-click the RugbyTest's NUnit test project and select Properties.

2. Select Debugging under the Configuration Properties group.

3. Enter NUnitGUI.exe in Start external program.

Figure 15.12 illustrates setting the debug properties for your project.

Your startup project must be set to RugbyTests for debugging with NUnit to work.

FIGURE 15.12

Setting Visual Studio .NET to run NUnitGUI *while debugging.*

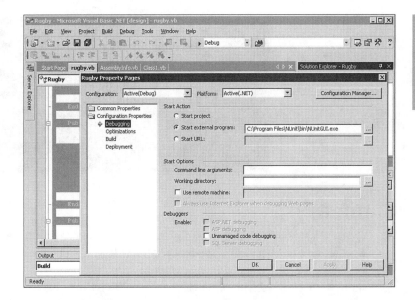

15

You can now set breakpoints and watches as you would normally. Pressing F5 (Run) will launch NUnitGUI and break your program on either error or breakpoint.

Running NUnit from the Command Line

You'll find that the GUI TestRunner is convenient when performing local unit testing, but moving to the command-line tool makes sense for automation purposes. Running the console application, NUnitConsole.exe, couldn't be easier. All you need to supply is the name of the test suite to run and the library name. The syntax is

```
NUnitConsole [/wait] TestCaseClass
```

The NUnit.Runner class expects the name of a TestCase class as argument. If this class defines a static Suite property it will be invoked and the returned test is run. Otherwise, all the methods starting with Test having no arguments are run. When the wait command-line argument is given, Runner waits until the users press the Return key. Runner prints a trace as the tests are executed followed by a summary at the end. Figure 15.13 shows the results of running NUintConsole over our RugbyTests library.

The console application runs tests much faster than the GUI tool, therefore, you might want to consider if your test suites grow in size.

FIGURE **15.13**

*Running NUnit tests
from the command
line.*

Summary

Over the last hour we've successfully managed to avoid any heated arguments about whether Java or Microsoft is the best platform! Instead, we've learned how the XP practice of testing can be applied while working with the Microsoft .NET platform. General skills you've learned with JUnit can be applied to NUnit. One nice aspect of using the xUnit tools is that each version operates in pretty much the same way—less to learn!

With NUnit you've learned how to first create a shell class, and then build the tests and finally code our class until the tests pass. Along the way, you've become acquainted with some interesting rugby facts!

In the next hour, we'll tie unit testing together with the complete build process and introduce a new tool: Ant.

Q&A

Q Can I use NUnit to test ASP.NET applications?

A Yes, if you have classes in your Web project that have public methods. Testing of your code-behind pages is not possible because they contain private methods for events and logic. There is a rumor in the XP community that a project is under way to produce a true ASP.NET test tool, so check `www.sourceforge.com` from time to time. You might get lucky!

Q What programming languages does the .NET Framework support?

A The .NET Framework is language-neutral; virtually any language can target the .NET Framework. Currently, you can build .NET programs in a number of languages, including C++, Visual Basic .NET, JScript, and C#. A large number of third-party languages are also available for building .NET Framework applications. These languages include COBOL, Eiffel, Perl, Python, Smalltalk, and others. For a complete list see `http://www.gotdotnet.com`.

15

Q How much does .NET cost?

A It's free. However, the Visual Studio .NET development suite is not! Strictly speaking you don't need Visual Studio .NET to write .NET applications, but it will make your life easier.

Q Is there a cross-platform version of the .NET runtime?

A No, not at this time. However, there is a version of the .NET Framework called the .NET Compact Framework, which enables .NET applications to run on small devices, such as mobile phones. Rumors abound in the press about possible ports to Linux or Unix. Microsoft argues that basing .NET on XML and Web services removes the need to run .NET on multiple operating systems. Cynics would counter this by pointing out that .NET is another away for Microsoft to sell server or enterprise software.

Q Is it absolutely necessary to build a stub class first before you start your test class?

A No. You begin with the unit tests right away, but this would mean that your editor features, such as Intellisense and method completion, would be nullified. Also, your compile would fail anyway until you defined your objects. Do some research on Reflection in .NET if you're still interested in trying this.

Workshop

This workshop tests whether you understand all the concepts you learned in this hour. It is very helpful to know and understand the answers before starting the next lesson.

Quiz

1. Which languages can be used with NUnit?

   a. Any CLS compliant language.

   b. Visual Basic .NET.

   c. Any language, except for Java.

   d. Microsoft languages such as C#, Visual C++, and Visual Basic .NET.

2. What does Assert("Hello", Test()) do?

   a. Executes the test method `Test()` and compares to the string `"hello"`.

   b. Writes `"hello"` to standard output window.

   c. Writes `"hello"` to the standard error window.

   d. Writes `"hello"` to the failure window if `Test()` returns a `False`.

3. Does it matter what names you use for your test methods?

   a. No.

   b. No, but they should be declared as Friend.

   c. Yes, they must start with "test".

   d. Yes, they should be prefixed with the base class name.

4. How do you debug your test cases in Visual Studio .NET using NUnit?

   a. Include the test case classes in your project.

   b. Using a separate debugging tool.

   c. By setting NUnitGUI.exe to start when debugging is launched.

   d. Add the source code of NUnit to your base project.

5. Which rugby team holds the record for the most points scored in a game?

   a. Australia.

   b. New Zealand.

   c. England.

   d. This has nothing to do with XP!

Answers

1. a.

2. d.

3. c.

4. c.

5. b., d.

Activities

1. Complete our Rugby and RugbyTests classes by adding the missing test cases. Include some new methods such as total points scored against. If you want the facts visit http://www.rugbyrugby.com/, otherwise make them up!

2. Investigate the use of Reflection to enable true test first in .NET. Use http://msdn.Microsoft.com/ as your starting point.

HOUR **16**

Automating Your Software Development

In this hour you will learn how to use the automated build tool, Ant, to enable continuous or frequent integration. Ant is one of the key tools in the XP developer's toolbox and understanding it's use will be very valuable to you. Over the next hour we will cover

- What Ant is, and how you can use it to automate your development
- How to install and configure Ant
- The configuration and layout of the Ant build file
- How to use Ant to build a sample application
- How you can use Ant with Microsoft-based development

Implementing Automated Builds with Ant

In Hour 12, "Building Software the XP Way," you learned how XP development teams integrate and test their software as frequently as possible. Ant is a tool that can help you achieve continuous integration. Ant is a Java-based automated build tool that is part of the Apache Foundation's Jakarta project. The purpose of the Jakarta Project is to provide commercial-quality server solutions based on the Java Platform. These solutions are to be developed in an open and cooperative fashion. The Jakarta Project consists of a number of subprojects including the Apache Tomcat servlet engine and the build tool Jakarta Ant.

You can download the latest version of Ant from
http://Jakarta.apache.org/ant/. You only need to download your platform related compressed file, for example jakarta-ant-1.5-bin.zip for
Windows Zip.

Historically, developers have used tools such as the make utility to build applications. make relies on system or shell-specific commands that vary from operating system to operating system. Ant, on the other hand, is written in Java and is driven by an XML for-mat build file. Ant's cross-platform nature and its extensibility make it a key weapon in the XPer's arsenal.

Ant can be used to build or deploy on any platform that supports the Java
runtime. For example, you can use Ant to build Visual C++ applications on
the Microsoft Windows platform.

Extending Ant can be done by either modifying the underlying source code or by writing custom tasks in various scripting languages such as JavaScript and Python. As a last resort you can still call operating system commands using the built-in shell task. Go ahead and install Ant, and let's start to discover what makes Ant tick.

Installing Ant

Before you attempt to install Ant, make sure that you have installed the Sun JDK, version 1.2 or higher. You'll already have this installed if you've been using JUnit.

> To use Ant, you must have a JAXP-compliant XML parser installed and available on your classpath. If you have installed the binary download version of Ant you will already have the Crimson XML parser from Apache.

The binary or executable download of Ant consists of three directories: bin, docs, and lib (only the bin and lib directories are required to run Ant). To install Ant, choose a directory and copy the download file there. This directory will be known as ANT_HOME.

> On Windows 95/98 systems, the script used to launch Ant will have problems if ANT_HOME is a long filename. This is because of limitations in Window's handling of the for batch-file statement. The best option on these platforms is to install Ant in a short path, such as c:\Ant.

Before you can run Ant there is some additional setup you are required to do:

- Add the bin directory to your path environment variable.
- Create a new environment variable called ANT_HOME and set it to the directory where you installed Ant. On some operating systems the Ant wrapper scripts can guess ANT_HOME (Unix dialects and Windows NT/2000), but it is better to not rely on this behavior.
- Set the JAVA_HOME environment variable. This should be set to the directory where your JDK is installed.

Setting the Windows Environment

Assuming Ant is installed in c:\ant\. The following Listing 16.1 will set up your environment:

LISTING 16.1   Windows Setup Commands for Ant

```
set ANT_HOME=c:\ant
set JAVA_HOME=c:\jdk1.4.1
set PATH=%PATH%;%ANT_HOME%\bin
```

In Hour 14, "Unit Testing with Java Tools," you learned how Windows 2000/XP users can set their environments by using the My Computer advanced properties dialog box. You can use the same method here to set your ANT_HOME and JAVA_HOME paths.

16

Setting the Unix Environment

Assuming Ant is installed in /usr/local/ant, Listing 16.2 will set up your environment:

LISTING 16.2   Unix Setup Commands for Ant

```
export ANT_HOME=/usr/local/ant
export JAVA_HOME=/usr/local/jdk-1.4.1
export PATH=${PATH}:${ANT_HOME}/bin
```

> Don't install Ant's ant.jar file into the lib/ext directory of the JDK/JRE. Ant is an application, whereas the extension directory is intended for JDK extensions.

Checking Your Ant Installation

After you have unpacked your download file and have finished configuring your environment; you're ready to run Ant. Before we delve further into how Ant works, let's double-check that we have a working installation by verifying the current version of Ant. To do this, go to your command window and execute the Ant version command as listed in Listing 16.3.

LISTING 16.3   The Ant Version Command

```
ant -version
```

You should see the result illustrated in Figure 16.1.

FIGURE 16.1

Checking your Ant version.

```
C:\WINNT\System32\cmd.exe

C:\ant>dir
 Volume in drive C is CDRIVE
 Volume Serial Number is 14CF-B96D

 Directory of C:\ant

07/01/2002  09:22p    <DIR>          .
07/01/2002  09:22p    <DIR>          ..
07/01/2002  07:07p    <DIR>          bin
07/01/2002  07:07p    <DIR>          docs
10/12/2001  02:58a             3,324 KEYS
07/01/2002  07:07p    <DIR>          lib
10/12/2001  02:58a             2,754 LICENSE
10/12/2001  02:58a             2,776 README
10/12/2001  02:58a            24,955 WHATSNEW
               4 File(s)         33,809 bytes
               5 Dir(s)     513,755,136 bytes free

C:\ant>ant -version
Ant version 1.4.1 compiled on October 11 2001
C:\ant>
```

A list with the complete Ant command-line reference follows. Use this to experiment with Ant on your own.

Ant Command-Line Reference

To invoke Ant from the command line use the following syntax:

```
ant option... target...
```

Table 16.1 lists each Ant command-line option and describes its use.

TABLE 16.1 Ant Command-Line Options

Option	Description
help	Displays help information describing the Ant command and its options.
projecthelp	Displays any user-written help documentation included in the build file. This is text from the description attribute of any <target>, along with any text contained within a <description> element. Targets with description attributes are listed as "Main targets," those without are listed as "Subtargets."
version	Causes Ant to display its version information and exit.
quiet	Suppresses most messages not originated by an echo task in the build file.
verbose	Displays detailed messages for every operation during a build. This option is exclusive to -debug.
debug	Displays messages that Ant and task developers have flagged as debugging messages. This option is exclusive to -verbose.
emacs	Formats logging messages so that they're easily parsed by the Emac shell mode; that is, it prints the task events without preceding them with an indentation and a [taskname].
logfile filename	Redirects logging output to the specified file.
logger classname	Specifies a class to handle Ant logging. The class specified must implement the org.apache.tools.ant.BuildLogger interface.
listener classname	Declares a listening class for Ant to add to its list of listeners. This option is useful when integrating Ant with IDEs or other Java programs.
buildfile filename	Specifies the build file on which Ant should operate. The default build file is build.xml.
D<property>=value	Defines a property name-value pair on the command line.
find filename	Specifies the build file on which Ant should operate. Unlike the -buildfile option, -find causes Ant to search for the specified file in the parent directory if it is not found in the current directory. This searching continues through ancestor directories until the root of the file system is reached, at which time the build fails if the file is not found.

16

> The Ant project adds new properties and features with each release; check your particular version for extra or new features. Table 16.1 is correct for version 1.4.

The Ant Build File

Ant is driven by a build file that describes the projects, dependencies, and tasks required to build your application. The build file is written in XML and, as such, is in a human-readable format. The Ant build file normally resides in the project's base build directory or folder. By default, Ant looks for a file called `build.xml` in the current directory, reads, parses, and then executes the contents. Most builds follow a similar pattern as we've outlined in Figure 16.2:

FIGURE 16.2

The Ant build process.

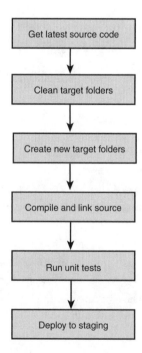

Ant will access the source control repository to extract the latest source code, clean or prepare the target folders, compile, and then deploy to some kind of staging area for functional tests. In our example, a step to run a suite of automated unit tests is also included, the output of which we could report via XML to the project Web site.

The build file has many XML elements, but the most important are the project, target, and task elements. Each build will have one project element that, in turn, has many possible targets such as debug, release, and test builds. The target is created by a series of tasks that describe the actions to take. The task, then, is where the actual work takes place. Examples of tasks are operating system–level commands such as make directory or delete file. Perhaps the easiest way to learn about the structure of the build file is by looking at an example file. Listing 16.4 shows the basic layout of the build file:

LISTING 16.4 The Ant Build File Layout

```
<project name="test" default="all">
    <property name="a.property" value="a value"/>

    <target name="all">
        <javac srcdir=".">
        </javac>
    </target>
</project>
```

The build file example will compile all the Java source files in the current directory (as denoted by .). All build files require one `<project>` element and at least one `<target>` element. Our project is called test, and the default target is all.

Remember that XML tags are case-sensitive and, therefore, `<project></Project>` will cause an error when you run Ant.

You can use Microsoft Internet Explorer to check your XML for you! Load your XML into the browser by using the File, Open command. IE will also automatically allow you to expand and collapse sections of your XML.

You'll find further descriptions of the configuration options and settings available in the build file in the following sections.

Projects

The project tag is the top-level attribute in the build file and describes the project itself. The project tag has three attributes: name, default, and basedir, see Table 16.2.

TABLE 16.2   Project Tag Attributes

Attribute	Description
name	The name of the project.
default	The default target to use when no target is supplied.
basedir	The base directory from which all path calculations are done. This attribute might be overridden by setting the basedir property beforehand. When this is done, it must be omitted in the project tag. If neither the attribute nor the property has been set, the parent directory of the build file will be used.

Targets

The target tag defines a collection of Ant tasks and can depend on other targets. You might have a target for compiling, for example, and a target for creating a distributable. You can only build a distributable when you have compiled first, so the distribute target depends on the compile target. Ant resolves these dependencies.

It should be noted that Ant's depends attribute only specifies the order in which targets should be executed. Ant tries to execute the targets in the depends attribute in the order they appear (from left to right). A target gets executed only once, even when more than one target depends on it.

A target also has the capability to perform its execution if (or unless) a property has been set. This allows, for example, better control on the building process depending on the state of the system (Java version, operating system, command-line property defines, and so on). To make a target aware of this property, you should add the if (or unless) attribute with the name of the property that the target should react to. For example:

```
<target name="build-module-A" if="module-A-present"/>
<target name="build-own-fake-module-A" unless="module-A-present"/>
```

The target will always be executed, if no if or unless attribute is present. The optional description attribute can be used to provide a one-line description of this target, which is printed by the -projecthelp command-line option.

It is a good practice to place your tstamp (timestamp) tasks in a so-called initialization target on which all other targets depend. Make sure that target is always the first one in the depends list of the other targets. Table 16.3 lists the target attribute for us.

TABLE 16.3   Target Tag Attributes

Attribute	Description
name	The name of the target.
depends	A comma-separated list of names of targets on which this target depends.
if	The name of the property that must be set for this target to execute.
unless	The name of the property that must not be set for this target to execute.
description	A short description of this target's function.

Tasks

A task is a piece of code that can be executed. A task can have multiple attributes or arguments. The value of an attribute might contain references to a property. These references will be resolved before the task is executed.

Tasks have a common structure:

```
<name attribute1="value1" attribute2="value2" ... />
```

Where name is the identifier of the task, and where the attribute (as many as you like from 1–N) are paired with a value (from 1–N). As in the previous example, attribute1 is the name of the attribute and value1 is the value associated with attribute1; similarly for attribute2. There is a set of built-in tasks, along with a number of optional tasks; it's also very easy to write your own. All tasks share a task name attribute, and Ant will use the value for the logging of any messages generated by the build.

Tasks can be assigned an id attribute, as well:

```
<taskname id="taskID" ... />
```

Where taskname is the name of the task, and taskID is a unique name for this task. You can refer to the corresponding task object in scripts or other tasks via this name.

Properties

A project can have a set of properties. These might be set in the build file by the property task, or might be set outside Ant. A property has a name and a value. Properties can be used in the value of task attributes. This is done by placing the property name between "${" and "}" in the attribute value. For example, if there is a builddir property with the value build, this could be used in an attribute like this: ${builddir}/classes. This is resolved as build/classes.

Ant provides access to all system properties as if they had been defined using a
<property> task. For example, ${os.name} expands to the name of the operating system.
In addition to the user-defined or system properties, Ant has some built-in properties,
which are listed in Table 16.4:

TABLE 16.4   Project Tag Attributes

Property	Description
basedir	The absolute path of the project's basedir (as set with the basedir attribute of <project>).
ant.file	The absolute path of the build file.
ant.version	The version of Ant.
ant.project.name	The name of the project that is currently executing; it is set in the name attribute of <project>.
ant.java.version	The JVM version Ant detected; currently it can hold the values 1.1, 1.2, 1.3, and 1.4.

Now you should have a good understanding about how to run Ant and the structure of
the build file. We'll put it all together in the next section and complete a simple sample
build.

Building HelloWorld with Ant

The best way to learn Ant is to build a very simple Java class using our build file. We'll
need two files for our example: the Java source class and our build.xml file. Open your
favorite text editor and enter the code in Listings 16.5 and 16.6. Save your Java file as
HelloWord.java, and your Ant file as build.xml.

LISTING 16.5   HelloWorld Sample Class

```
public class HelloWorld{
    public static void main(String []args){
        System.out.println("Hello World!");
    }
}
```

LISTING 16.6   HelloWorld Ant Build File (`build.xml`)

```
1 <project name="HelloWorld" default="compile" >
2     <property name="build.dir" value="output"/>
3     <target name="init" description="Clean and setup  directory">
4         <delete dir="${build.dir}"/>
5         <mkdir dir="${build.dir}"/>
6     </target>
7     <target name="compile" depends="init" description="Compile source">
8         <javac srcdir="." destdir="${build.dir}"/>
9     </target>
10 </project>
```

Let's take a line-by-line look at our build file:

- Line 1: We set the name of our project and the default target.

- Line 2: We use a user-defined property to store our build output directory name (`output` in our case).

- Line 3: We define the first of our two targets. The `init` target initializes or prepares the output directory.

- Line 4: We perform a recursive delete on our output directory.

- Line 5: We create the output directory using our `build.dir` property. Ant will replace `${"build.dir"}` with the value of the `build.dir` property.

- Line 7: We define our main target and include a dependency on the `init` target. This means that the target `compile` will execute `init` before it begins its own tasks.

- Line 8: We use the `javac` task to call the Java compiler on any `.java` files located in the current folder. The `destdir` attribute holds the value of our `output` directory.

> The jikes compiler from IBM is usually much faster than javac; it also does dependency checking and has generally better error messages. You can get jikes (a free download including source code) from http://www-124.ibm.com/developerworks/oss/jikes/. To use jikes, set `build.compiler` to jikes in your build file.

All that remains now is to run Ant across our build file. We're using the default filename (`build.xml`), so there is no need to specify the build file when we invoke Ant. Open a command window and navigate to the folder you saved your sample files in. We've used `c:\ant` as our source folder, but usually your build root will exist under your main source or project directory. To build HelloWorld, simply type **Ant <enter>** at the command prompt. You should see output we have displayed in Figure 16.3.

FIGURE 16.3

Building HelloWorld with Ant.

Congratulations, you've built your first application with Ant! You'll find the result of the build, `Helloworld.class`, in the output directory. We caused Ant to execute the default target (compiler) by not specifying any startup parameters. It's likely that you'll want to call particular targets, such as a release or debug build. In our case, we'll call the `init` target to clear out the results of our sample build. To do this, we run Ant with

```
Ant init
```

Figure 16.4 shows Ant running out `init` target, clearing out the directory structure.

FIGURE 16.4

Calling the `init` target with Ant.

Finally, we can get a listing that describes the build file by calling Ant with the `projecthelp` switch. To run this enter the following at the command prompt:

```
Ant -projecthelp
```

The `projecthelp` switch causes Ant to parse through your build file and print out the description attributes it finds. Figure 16.5 illustrates the results of executing Ant with `projecthelp` on our sample build file.

FIGURE 16.5

Displaying build file descriptions with Ant.

Most of this hour has been slanted toward Java development, but we don't want to leave Microsoft readers in the cold! With this in mind, we'll end with some tips to using Ant with Microsoft .NET.

Automated Builds on the Microsoft Platform

It was mentioned at the start of this hour that Ant could be used for non-Java solutions. Microsoft software development projects have a number of options when approaching automated builds:

- Use Visual Studio .NET's command-line interface in conjunction with make or Ant.
- Use Ant with the optional tasks for C# and Visual Source Safe.
- Use the native .NET build tool, Nant, in place of Ant.

Nant is, more or less, a direct port from Ant into Microsoft's C# language. The command-line interface, use of build files, and its general approach is almost exactly the same as Ant. Why use Nant rather than Ant? The main reason is that Microsoft software development projects may not run a Java Virtual Machine on their build or deployment targets. A pure .NET project would be an ideal place to use Nant.

You can download Nant from http://nant.sourceforge.net/. You'll need the Microsoft .NET framework to run Nant. One slightly annoying difference between Nant and Ant is that Nant uses a .build rather than build.xml as the default file.

There's no reason why you can't stay with Ant if you're working in a mixed environment. You might consider the consequences; overhead attached to maintaining two tools
is too high.

Ant supports Microsoft development by either command-line (or exec) tasks, or by the
use of optional tasks. To use these optional tasks, you'll need to copy optional.jar
from the source build folder into the Ant lib folder. We're interested in two sets of tasks:
the .NET and Visual Source Safe tasks. From Ant you can execute a standard C# compile
with the csc task:

> Future versions of Ant might include optional.jar in the lib folder.

```
<csc
        optimize="true"
        debug="false"
        docFile="documentation.xml"
        warnLevel="4"
        unsafe="false"
        targetType="exe "
        incremental="false"
        definitions="RELEASE"
        excludes="src/unicode_class.cs"
        mainClass = "MainApp"
        outputFile="NetApp.exe "
        />
```

> Make sure that you have csc.exe in the path environment variable (this is
> not the default after .NET has been installed). Check this by opening a com-
> mand window and executing csc from the prompt. The location of your C#
> compiler depends on your exact version of .NET. It will be located under
> your Windows system folder.

At the time of this writing there is no support for Visual Basic .NET or any of the other
.NET languages. You'll be forced to run these compilers from exec tasks in the build file.
Nant can run Visual Basic natively and, therefore, offers some benefits for Visual
Basic–heavy projects.

So, you can execute your C# builds from Ant, but what about Source Safe? You'll be
happy to hear (if you use Source Safe!) that Ant can access the repository directly. Ant
1.4 ships with the following Source Safe tasks (see Table 16.5).

TABLE 16.5   Visual Source Safe Ant Tasks

Task	Description
vssget	Retrieves a copy of the specified VSS file(s).
vsslabel	Assigns a label to the specified version or current version of a file or project.
vsshistory	Shows the history of a file or project in VSS.
vsscheckin	Updates VSS with changes made to a checked out file, and unlocks the VSS master copy.
vsscheckout	Copies a file from the current project to the current folder, for the purpose of editing.

16

Make sure you've added the Source Safe command-line tool (ss.exe) to your path environment variable and that the environment variable SSDIR points to your Source Safe root folder. You might need to create an SSDIR environment variable if it is missing from your installation.

As we go to press, Ant version 1.5 has been released. This new version extends Source Safe task support beyond we've listed in Table 16.5. To call a Source Safe get in Ant, all you need do is add the following task:

```
<vssget localPath="C:\tysxp\rugby"
        recursive="true"
        label="debug"
        login="sb,mypassword"
        vsspath="/Rugby"
        writable="true"/>
```

This task will perform a recursive get from $/rugby using the username sb and the password mypassword. It will get the files, which are labeled debug and write them to the local directory c:\tysxp\rugby. The local files will be writable.

So, you can use Ant to build Microsoft projects!

Summary

Ant is a very powerful tool that will aid you in integrating and developing faster. Your team will save time by investing some time up-front with build automation. Using a Java-based tool, such as Ant, has very real benefits as more software development cross system boundaries. Microsoft developers can choose to either leverage Ant as-is or run the .NET port, Nant, instead.

The next hour we'll build on your what you've learned about Ant; you'll be amazed at what you can do with this powerful tool!

Q&A

Q Do I have to use Ant to do XP correctly?

A No, not all. There are other commercial build tools available, and the old-faithful batch file might be all you need. Take an XP approach to your build tool; use the simplest thing that works. Ant is really quite simple to use and is worth the effort to learn.

Q How do I pass parameters from the command line to my build file?

A Using Ant `-Dname=value` enables you to define values for properties on the Ant command line. These properties can then be used within your build file as any normal property: `${name}` will put in value.

Workshop

This workshop tests whether you understand all the concepts you learned today. It is very helpful to know and understand the answers before starting tomorrow's lesson.

Quiz

1. What is the main difference between `make` and Ant?

    a. `make` runs on Unix

    b. `make` uses operating-specific instructions, whereas Ant uses a human-readable build file.

    c. Ant is open source.

    d. Ant is Java-based and, therefore, more modern.

2. What does invoking Ant with this syntax ant `debug` do?

    a. Runs Ant in debug mode.

    b. Builds the project called `debug`.

    c. Builds the target called `debug`.

    d. This is not a valid option for Ant.

3. What two environment variables should I set before I run Ant?

    a. PATH and CLASSPATH

    b. CLASSPATH and ANT_HOME

    c. JAVA_HOME and ANT_PATH

    d. ANT_HOME and JAVA_HOME

4. If I want to get a description of the build file, what do I do?

    a. Format and display the XML file with XSLT for browser viewing.

    b. Run Ant with the `-projecthelp` switch.

    c. The advantage of the build file is that it can be read in any text editor.

    d. Run Ant with the `-help` switch.

16

Answers

1. b.

2. c.

3. d.

4. b.

Activities

1. Write a `build.xml` for our Rugby project used in Hour 15. To do this you'll need to investigate the supporting libraries `Rugby` class needs. Consult the `vbc.exe` compiler for help on command-line switches you might need.

2. Familiarize yourself with the Ant reference manual, focus on language features that would be most applicable to you.

HOUR **17**

Making the Most of Ant to Automate Your XP Project

Over the next hour we'll dig deeper into Ant, uncovering how we can use the tool to ease the burden of end-to-end development. Building your software is only half the story; testing is where the true quality of the team's work is exposed. Ant can reduce the overhead required to manage this testing process. You'll find this hour particularly useful as you discover how Ant can also be used to build Microsoft .NET applications. Ant is much more than a simple build tool! In this hour we will cover

- How Ant can be used to establish your database
- How Ant can be used to run your unit tests
- How you can automate the delivery of unit test reports to the team
- How Microsoft development teams can benefit from a build tool designed specifically for the .NET platform
- A demonstration of a complete, end-to-end build from source control

Using Ant to Automate Unit Tests

During Hour 14, "Unit Testing with Java Tools," we learned that we could use JUnit to develop and run unit tests. JUnit's open-source foundation and wide acceptance make it the unit-testing tool of choice for Java-based XP developers. This section will show how you can integrate JUnit with Ant, which will enable you to both build and test your software. We discussed in Hour 16, "Automating Your Software Development," how Ant is driven by an XML build file that describes the targets and tasks to perform on your project. Figure 17.1 illustrates how Ant can be used to both build and test.

FIGURE 17.1

Integrating unit tests and build with Ant.

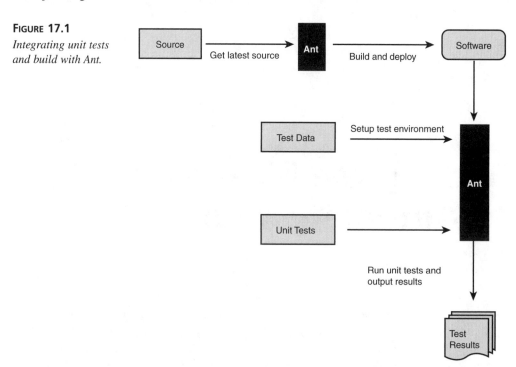

Figure 17.1 shows how to use Ant to establish the test environment before we execute our unit tests. We'll need to set a baseline of good data in our database if our unit tests are to have any meaning.

Your test data set might be a subset of the complete database. Limiting the size of the test data is a good idea where data volumes are high because this reduces test time. One approach is during the day to run automated tests using the small dataset, and then after hours run it again with the complete data.

Before we run our JUnit tests across the sample test cases, let's discover how to load test data into our database.

Setting Up the Database with Ant

Ant can be used to directly execute SQL commands onto any database that supports ODBC (via the JDBC bridge). We'll use the Rugby example from Hour 15, "Unit Testing with Microsoft Tools," as the basis for this tutorial. For a quick refresher, our customer has a requirement to build a Web-based solution that will enable users to query Rugby sports results by country. In Figure 17.2, we have our physical data model for the Rugby Web site. We've used Microsoft SQL Server as our modeling tool and database.

FIGURE 17.2

Rugby example data model.

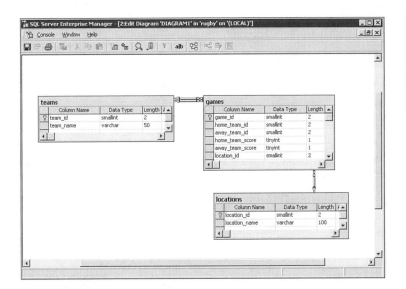

17

There are three tables in our model:

- Teams—A list of all the main Rugby playing nations.
- Games—The results of each game with date, teams, location, and scores.
- Locations—A list of all valid playing locations.

> In most cases you'd use a database-modeling tool, such as ERWin or PowerDesigner, to create your physical data model. In the case of SQL Server you can create your model from the tools provided with the product, and then generate the SQL script. Then, it's just a simple matter of copying and pasting your SQL script into the Ant build file.

Now we need to write an Ant build file that does the following:

- Establishes a connection to our target database.
- Drops (deletes) any existing tables.
- Creates new tables, including constraints, keys, and default values.
- Creates any database views or stored procedures required.
- Loads default test data into the database.

Listing 17.1 is our complete Ant build file.

LISTING 17.1 Ant Build File to Create Our SQL Database

```
1  <project name="Databasesetup" default="all">
2     <property name="driver" value="sun.jdbc.odbc.JdbcOdbcDriver" />
3     <property name="url" value="jdbc:odbc:rugby" />
4     <property name="username" value="sa" />
5     <property name="password" value="" />
6
7     <target name="all" depends="build,createviews,populate">
8     </target>
9
10    <target name="build" description="Create Database Tables" depends="drop">
11        <sql driver="${driver}" url="${url}" userid="${username}"
➥ password="${password}">
12
13        CREATE TABLE games (
14            game_id smallint IDENTITY (1, 1) NOT NULL ,
15            home_team_id smallint NULL ,
16            away_team_id smallint NULL ,
17            home_team_score tinyint NULL ,
18            away_team_score tinyint NULL ,
19            location_id smallint NULL ,
20            date_played smalldatetime NULL
21        )
22
23        CREATE TABLE locations (
24            location_id smallint NOT NULL ,
25            location_name varchar (100)
26        )
27
28        CREATE TABLE teams (
29            team_id smallint NOT NULL ,
30            team_name varchar (50)
31        )
32
33        ALTER TABLE games WITH NOCHECK ADD
34            CONSTRAINT DF_games_home_team_score DEFAULT (0) FOR home_team_score,
35            CONSTRAINT DF_games_away_team_score DEFAULT (0) FOR away_team_score,
```

LISTING 17.1 continued

```
36          CONSTRAINT PK_games PRIMARY KEY   CLUSTERED
37          (
38              game_id
39          )
40
41      ALTER TABLE locations WITH NOCHECK ADD
42          CONSTRAINT PK_locations PRIMARY KEY   CLUSTERED
43          (
44              location_id
45          )
46
47      ALTER TABLE teams WITH NOCHECK ADD
48          CONSTRAINT PK_teams PRIMARY KEY   CLUSTERED
49          (
50              team_id
51          )
52
53      ALTER TABLE games ADD
54          CONSTRAINT FK_games_locations FOREIGN KEY
55          (
56              location_id
57          ) REFERENCES locations (
58              location_id
59          ),
60          CONSTRAINT FK_games_teams FOREIGN KEY
61          (
62              home_team_id
63          ) REFERENCES teams (
64              team_id
65          ),
66          CONSTRAINT FK_games_teams1 FOREIGN KEY
67          (
68              away_team_id
69          ) REFERENCES teams (
70              team_id
71          )
72          </sql>
73      </target>
74      <target name="createviews" description="Create Database Views"
➥ depends="build">
75          <sql driver="${driver}" url="${url}" userid="${username}"
➥ password="${password}">
76
77      CREATE VIEW dbo.vw_Team_Results
78      AS
79      SELECT      dbo.teams.team_name AS home_team, teams_1.team_name
➥ AS away_team, dbo.locations.location_name,
80                      CAST(dbo.games.home_team_score AS char(3)) + ' - ' +
➥CAST(dbo.games.away_team_score AS char(3)) AS Score, dbo.games.date_played
81      FROM        dbo.games INNER JOIN
```

LISTING 17.1   continued

```
82 dbo.locations ON dbo.games.location_id = dbo.locations.location_id INNER JOIN
83   dbo.teams ON dbo.games.home_team_id = dbo.teams.team_id INNER JOIN
84   dbo.teams teams_1 ON dbo.games.away_team_id = teams_1.team_id
85         </sql>
86       </target>
87       <target name="drop" description="Drops Database Tables">
88         <sql driver="${driver}" url="${url}" userid="${username}"
➥ password="${password}">
89         if exists (select * from dbo.sysobjects where id =
➥ object_id(N'FK_games_locations') and OBJECTPROPERTY(id, N'IsForeignKey') = 1)
90         ALTER TABLE games DROP CONSTRAINT FK_games_locations
91
92         if exists (select * from dbo.sysobjects where id =
➥ object_id(N'FK_games_teams') and OBJECTPROPERTY(id, N'IsForeignKey') = 1)
93         ALTER TABLE games DROP CONSTRAINT FK_games_teams
94
95         if exists (select * from dbo.sysobjects where id =
➥ object_id(N'FK_games_teams1') and OBJECTPROPERTY(id, N'IsForeignKey') = 1)
96         ALTER TABLE games DROP CONSTRAINT FK_games_teams1
97
98         if exists (select * from dbo.sysobjects where id =
➥ object_id(N'games') and OBJECTPROPERTY(id, N'IsUserTable') = 1)
99         drop table games
100
101        if exists (select * from dbo.sysobjects where id =
➥ object_id(N'locations') and OBJECTPROPERTY(id, N'IsUserTable') = 1)
102         drop table locations
103
104        if exists (select * from dbo.sysobjects where id =
➥ object_id(N'teams') and OBJECTPROPERTY(id, N'IsUserTable') = 1)
105        drop table teams
106
107            if exists (select * from dbo.sysobjects where id =
➥ object_id(N'vw_Team_Results') and OBJECTPROPERTY(id, N'IsView') = 1)
108                    drop view vw_Team_Results
109        </sql>
110      </target>
111      <target name="populate" description="Populate Database Tables"
➥ depends="build">
112        <sql driver="${driver}" url="${url}" userid="${username}"
➥ password="${password}">
113
114    insert into locations values(1,'Wellington')
115    insert into locations values(2,'London')
116    insert into locations values(3,'Auckland')
117    insert into locations values(4,'Cardiff')
118    insert into locations values(5,'Christchurch')
119    insert into locations values(6,'Dunedin')
120    insert into locations values(7,'Inverleith')
121    insert into locations values(8,'Pretoria')
```

LISTING 17.1   continued

```
122      insert into locations values(9,'Edinburgh')
123
124      Insert into teams values(1,'New Zealand')
125      Insert into teams values(2,'Australia')
126      Insert into teams values(3,'England')
127      Insert into teams values(4,'France')
128      Insert into teams values(5,'Ireland')
129      Insert into teams values(6,'Lions')
130      Insert into teams values(7,'South Africa')
131      Insert into teams values(8,'Scotland')
132      Insert into teams values(9,'Wales')
133      Insert into teams values(10,'Argentina')
134      Insert into teams values(11,'Canada')
135      Insert into teams values(12,'Fiji')
136      Insert into teams values(13,'Italy')
137      Insert into teams values(14,'Japan')
138      Insert into teams values(15,'Tonga')
139      Insert into teams values(16,'USA')
140      Insert into teams values(17,'Samoa')
141
142      Insert into games(home_team_id, away_team_id, home_team_score,
    ➥ away_team_score, location_id, date_played)
143          Values(1,8,37,6,3,'2001-11-24')
144
145      Insert into games(home_team_id, away_team_id, home_team_score,
    ➥ away_team_score, location_id, date_played)
146          Values(1,8,48,14,3,   '2000-07-01')
147      Insert into games(home_team_id, away_team_id, home_team_score,
    ➥ away_team_score, location_id, date_played)
148          Values(1,8,69,20,6,   '2000-06-24')
149      Insert into games(home_team_id, away_team_id, home_team_score,
    ➥ away_team_score, location_id, date_played)
150          Values(1,8,30,18,9,   '1999-10-24')
151      Insert into games(home_team_id, away_team_id, home_team_score,
    ➥ away_team_score, location_id, date_played)
152          Values(1,8,36,12,3,   '1996-06-22')
153      Insert into games(home_team_id, away_team_id, home_team_score,
    ➥ away_team_score, location_id, date_played)
154          Values(1,8,62,31,6,   '1996-06-15')
155      Insert into games(home_team_id, away_team_id, home_team_score,
    ➥ away_team_score, location_id, date_played)
156          Values(1,8,48,30,8,   '1995-06-11')
157      Insert into games(home_team_id, away_team_id, home_team_score,
    ➥ away_team_score, location_id, date_played)
158          Values(1,8,51,15,9,   '1993-11-20')
159      Insert into games(home_team_id, away_team_id, home_team_score,
    ➥ away_team_score, location_id, date_played)
160          Values(1,8,13,6,4,'1991-10-30')
161      Insert into games(home_team_id, away_team_id, home_team_score,
    ➥ away_team_score, location_id, date_played)
```

17

LISTING 17.1   continued

```
162          Values(1,8,21,    18,3,     '1990-06-23')
163      Insert into games(home_team_id, away_team_id, home_team_score,
➡ away_team_score, location_id, date_played)
164          Values(1,8,31,16,6,    '1990-06-16')
165      Insert into games(home_team_id, away_team_id, home_team_score,
➡ away_team_score, location_id, date_played)
166          Values(1,8,30,3,5,'1987-06-06')
167      Insert into games(home_team_id, away_team_id, home_team_score,
➡ away_team_score, location_id, date_played)
168          Values(1,8,25,    25,9,     '1983-11-12')
169      Insert into games(home_team_id, away_team_id, home_team_score,
➡ away_team_score, location_id, date_played)
170          Values(1,8,40,    15,3,     '1981-06-20')
171      Insert into games(home_team_id, away_team_id, home_team_score,
➡ away_team_score, location_id, date_played)
172          Values(1,8,11,4,6,'1981-06-13')
173      Insert into games(home_team_id, away_team_id, home_team_score,
➡ away_team_score, location_id, date_played)
174          Values(1,8,20,6,9,'1979-11-10')
175      Insert into games(home_team_id, away_team_id, home_team_score,
➡ away_team_score, location_id, date_played)
176          Values(1,8,18,9,9,'1978-12-09')
177      Insert into games(home_team_id, away_team_id, home_team_score,
➡ away_team_score, location_id, date_played)
178          Values(1,8,24,0,3,'1975-06-14')
179      Insert into games(home_team_id, away_team_id, home_team_score,
➡ away_team_score, location_id, date_played)
180          Values(1,8,14,9,9,'1972-12-16')
181      Insert into games(home_team_id, away_team_id, home_team_score,
➡ away_team_score, location_id, date_played)
182          Values(1,8,14,3,9,'1967-12-02')
183      Insert into games(home_team_id, away_team_id, home_team_score,
➡ away_team_score, location_id, date_played)
184          Values(1,8,0,0,9,'1964-01-18')
185      Insert into games(home_team_id, away_team_id, home_team_score,
➡ away_team_score, location_id, date_played)
186          Values(1,8,3,0,9,'1954-02-13')
187      Insert into games(home_team_id, away_team_id, home_team_score,
➡ away_team_score, location_id, date_played)
188          Values(1,8,18,8,9,'1935-11-23')
189      Insert into games(home_team_id, away_team_id, home_team_score,
➡ away_team_score, location_id, date_played)
190          Values(1,8,12,7,7,'1905-11-18')
191
192      </sql>
193    </target>
194 </project>
```

Let's now investigate our build file, highlighting the key lines:

- Line 1: We set the name of our project and the default target.

- Line 2: A user-defined property that sets the database driver name, in our case the Sun JDBC-ODBC bridge driver. We'll use this setting in the SQL tasks that appear in our build file.

- Line 3: A user-defined property that sets the database connection path.

- Line 4: A user-defined property that sets the database username.

- Line 5: A user-defined property that sets the database password.

- Line 7: Our default target (all) that calls build, createviews, and populate targets in order, left to right.

- Line 10–73: Build target tasks and SQL for the database creation section. Notice that this target depends on drop; this means that drop database tables will run before this task starts.

- Line 11: SQL task including connection, driver, username, and password, which was defined in our properties section.

- Line 13–71: SQL to execute on our database. We've included SQL to add keys, constraints, and defaults.

- Line 74: Ant target used to create our view (only one at this point!). Note that this target depends on the build (that is, tables must exist first).

- Line 74–86: Create view target tasks and SQL.

- Line 77–84: SQL used to create our view.

- Line 87–110: Drop database tables target.

- Line 89–108: SQL commands used to delete our tables if they exit in the database.

- Line 111–193: Populate database tables target tasks and SQL. Notice that this target depends on the success of build.

> Our SQL Ant build file assumes that the database and ODBC connection exist before the script is executed. Our sample script is targeted at Microsoft SQL Server, so you can use the Enterprise Manager application to create your database. The ODBC connection can be added through the Windows Control Panel. Make sure you name your connection rugby.

Let's go ahead and run Ant over our SQL build file. Figure 17.3 shows Ant calling the targets in the order we'd expect.

FIGURE **17.3**

Using Ant to execute SQL commands.

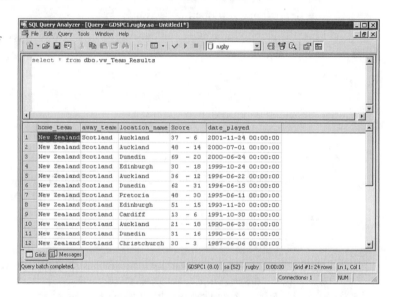

We can verify that the load worked as we expected by running a simple select query on our SQL view. We should see a list of games played by New Zealand and Scotland. Figure 17.4 displays the output from the Microsoft SQL Analyzer.

FIGURE **17.4**

Viewing the contents of the sample database built by Ant.

The SQL commands are embedded directly in the build.xml file, in reality it's better to load the SQL from an external source file. The src attribute on the SQL task is where you can assign an external load filename. This enables you to separate the build, database, and load functions even further. Your database SQL can be stored in the source repository, and then extracted at build time.

Table 17.1 ends this section with a list of attributes available with the SQL task.

TABLE 17.1   Ant SQL Task Attributes

Attribute	Description
driver	Class name of the jdbc driver
url	Database connection url
userid	Database username
password	Database password
src	File containing SQL statements
delimiter	String that separates SQL statements
autocommit	Autocommit flag for database connection (default false)
print	Print result sets from the statements (default false)
showheaders	Print headers for result sets from the statements (default true)
output	Output file for result sets (defaults to System.out)
classpath	Classpath used to load driver
onerror	Action to perform when statement fails: continue, stop, abort
rdbms	Execute the task only if the database server type is equal to the value in rdbms
version	Execute task only if rdbms version match

The rdbms attribute will be useful to you if you're deploying to multiple databases. Database vendors tend to differ on their interpretation of SQL syntax; your build script can reflect this, as demonstrated in Listing 17.2

LISTING 17.2   Verifying Database Server Type Ant SQL Task

```
1 <sql
2     driver="sun.jdbc.odbc.jdbcDriver"
3     url="jdbc:odbc:rugby"
4     userid="sa"
5     password="pwd"
6 rdbms="sqlserver"
7     version="7.0."
8     >
9         CREATE TABLE games (
10            game_id smallint IDENTITY (1, 1) NOT NULL ,
11            home_team_id smallint NULL ,
12            away_team_id smallint NULL ,
13            home_team_score tinyint NULL ,
14            away_team_score tinyint NULL ,
15            location_id smallint NULL ,
16            date_played smalldatetime NULL
17        )
18 </sql>
```

Running JUnit Test from Ant

Now that we have a way of establishing and configuring our database, we're ready to discuss how to run JUnit tests from Ant. A good place to start is to revisit our sample tests from Hour 14. Hour 14 explained how to install JUnit using the sample tests that come with the JUnit package. Automating these JUnit tests couldn't be easier. Listing 17.3 illustrates the build file we can use to test automation:

LISTING 17.3   Simple Ant Test Build File to Automate JUnit Tests

```
1 <project name="JUnit Tester" default="test">
2     <target name="test" description="Runs sample unit tests">
3         <junit printsummary="true">
4             <test name="junit.samples.VectorTest" />
5             <test name="junit.samples.AllTests" />
6         </junit>
7         </target>
8 </project>
```

Enter the text from Listing 17.3 into your favorite text editor and save as `alltests.xml`. For simplicity's sake we've saved our `allests.xml` into the JUnit default directory (`c:\junit` on a Windows machine). Let's look at each line of the build file:

- Line 1: We set the name of our project and the default target.

- Line 2: Our default target `test`.

- Line 3: The `junit` task tag, `printsummary` attribute, will cause Ant to write a summary after each test suite that displays number of test runs, failures, and errors.

- Lines 4 and 5: The two test suites Ant will call.

Run your Ant script using the buildfile option to specify the build file. You should see the output displayed in Figure 17.5.

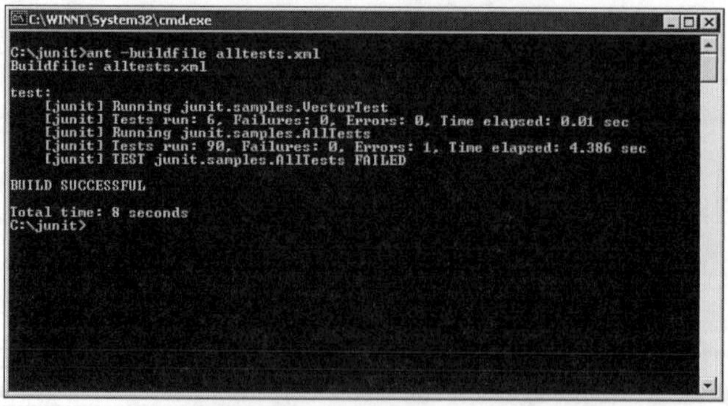

FIGURE 17.5

Running the simple automated test file.

The output is a little terse to say the least! For a little more detail we can use the formatter attribute. This will write the output to either file or console. Listing 17.4 illustrates the use of the formatter:

LISTING 17.4   Ant Build File Using the JUnit Formatter

```
1 <project name="JUnit Tester" default="test">
2     <property name="reports.dir" value=".\reports" />
3         <target name="setup">
4             <mkdir dir="${reports.dir}" />
5         </target>
6         <target name="test" description="Runs sample unit tests"
depends="setup">
7             <junit printsummary="true">
8             <formatter type="plain" usefile="false" />
9             <test name="junit.samples.VectorTest" />
10             <test name="junit.samples.AllTests" />
11             </junit>
12         </target>
13 </project>
```

Running our new build file shows that we've gone from the sublime to the ridiculous! Certainly, we now have much more information; the trouble with using a plain formatter is that the resulting output is hard to read or digest. Figure 17.6 shows the output of the plain formatter.

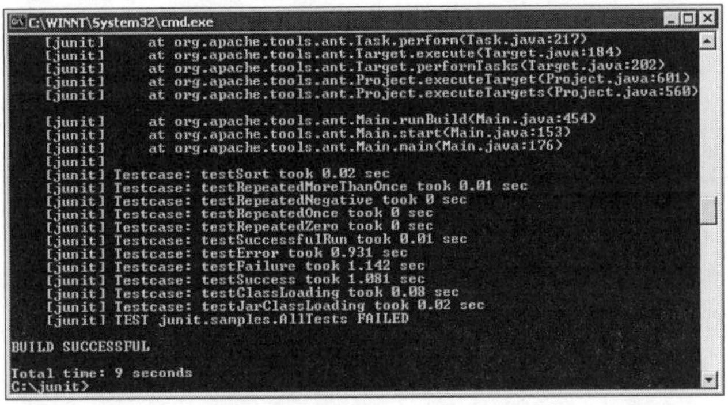

FIGURE 17.6

Running the simple automated test file with the formatter.

The answer to our formatting needs is XML! Ant comes with an optional task called junitreport, which will take the XML output of the formatter and render it into HTML. Go ahead and create a new build file called alltests3.xml and enter the text from Listing 17.5.

junitreport requires the Xalan XSLT parser, which can be downloaded from
http://xml.apache.org/xalan-j/. Put the JAR files from the Xalan download into your Ant lib folder. New versions of Ant might not require the
Xalan parser; check the help files that come with your version.

LISTING 17.5   Ant Build File Using the junitreport Class

```
 1 <project name="JUnit Tester" default="test">
 2     <property name="reports.dir" value=".\reports"/>
 3     <target name="setup">
 4         <mkdir dir="${reports.dir}" />
 5     </target>
 6     <target name="test" description="Runs sample unit tests" depends="setup">
 7         <junit printsummary="true">
 8             <formatter type="xml" usefile="true"/>
 9             <test name="junit.samples.VectorTest" />
10             <test name="junit.samples.AllTests" />
11         </junit>
12         <junitreport todir="${reports.dir}">
13             <fileset dir=".">
14                 <include name="TEST-*.xml"/>
15             </fileset>
16             <report format="frames" todir="${reports.dir}\html"/>
17         </junitreport>
18     </target>
19 </project>
```

Some new items were introduced in Listing 17.5:

- Line 8: We set the formatter attribute to write summary output to an XML file.
- Line 13: We create a new fileset in the current directory (.).
- Line 14: The name of our output file mask.
- Line 16: The format or style of our report and the target directory.

Run Ant with your new build file, and you should see the screen in Figure 17.7.

Assuming you've installed the Xalan XLST parser required by junitreport, you should
see the transform message displayed on Figure 17.7. All that remains is to view the
HTML in your Web browser. We specified that the output files be written to
reports\html; the resulting folder structure is displayed in Figure 17.8:

17

Figure 17.7

Running Ant with the junitreport *class.*

Figure 17.8

The folder output folder structure after running with junitreport.

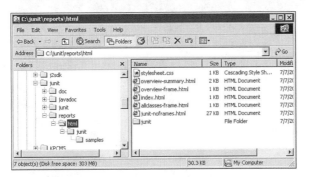

We instructed the junitreport class to generate our HTML as a frame view. If you click on "AllTests" you should see output we have illustrated in Figure 17.9:

Figure 17.9

The HTML output from Ant with the s *class.*

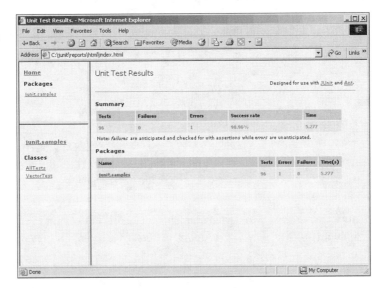

We've come a long way from the simple JUnit console application we covered in Hour 14! Over the last few pages we've demonstrated how to automate JUnit tests with Ant, providing a readable HTML view that can be integrated with your Project Web site and the like. The show isn't over yet, there's one more neat trick to show! Before that let's cover the attributes and facilities available from JUnit and `junitreport` class. Attributes for JUnit and `junitreport` are listed in Table 17.2 and Table 17.3, respectively.

TABLE 17.2   Ant JUnit Class Attributes

Attribute	Description
printsummary	Prints one line statistics for each test case. Can take the values on, off, and withOutAndErr. withOutAndErr is the same as on, but also includes the test output (written to System.out and System.err).
fork	Runs tests in a separate Java Virtual Machine (VM).
haltonerror	Stops the build process if an error occurs during the test run.
errorProperty	The name of a property to set in the event of an error.
haltonfailure	Stops the build process if a test fails (errors are considered failures as well).
failureProperty	The name of a property to set in the event of a failure (errors are considered failures as well).
timeout	Cancels the individual tests if they don't finish in the given time (measured in milliseconds). Ignored if fork is disabled.
maxmemory	Max amount of memory allocated to the forked VM (ignored if fork is disabled).
Jvm	The command used to invoke the Java Virtual Machine; default is java. The command is resolved by java.lang.Runtime.exec(), and is ignored if fork is disabled.
Dir	The directory to invoke the VM in (ignored if fork is disabled).

TABLE 17.3   Ant `junitreport` Class Attributes

Attribute	Description
file	The name of the XML file that will aggregate all individual XML test suites previously generated by the JUnit task.
todir	The directory where the XML output file will be written.

`junitreport` has two nested elements: `fileset` and `report`. `fileset` is the list of the individual XML files `junitreport` collects. These are generated by the JUnit task using the nested `<FileSet>` element.

The report element describes the document created by junitreport. Its attributes are listed in Table 17.4:

TABLE 17.4   Ant junitreport Report Element Attributes

Attribute	Description
Format	The format of the generated report. Must be noframes or frames.
Styledir	The directory where the stylesheets are defined. They must conform to the following conventions: • frames format: The stylesheet must be named junit-frames.xsl. • noframes format: The stylesheet must be named junit-noframes.xsl.
Todir	The directory where the files resulting from the transformation should be written to.

Using Ant to Email Test Reports

The final aspect of automated testing we have to cover before leaving JUnit is email. Producing a nice, easy-to-read HTML report is all well and good, but what about door-to-door delivery? You'll be pleased to learn that we can email our reports upon completion of the test run. Ant comes with a built-in task (mail), which enables plain-text emails to be sent by Ant. The more versatile email solution, however, is the MimeMail optional task.

With MimeMail we can collect our XML results and send a rich, HTML email to any recipient. We've taken our alltests3.xml file and created a new file called alltests4.xml, which will email our test results. (Make sure you change the email address before you attempt the sample!) Listing 17.6 is our new build file.

> To use MimeMail you'll need to download and install both the Java Activation Framework (JAF) and JavaMail. You can find these at http://java.sun.com/products/javabeans/glasgow/jaf.html and http://java.sun.com/products/javamail/index.html. Put the JAR files from these downloads into your Ant lib folder.

LISTING 17.6   Ant Build File for Sending Test Reports via Email

```
1 <project name="JUnit Tester" default="test">
2     <property name="reports.dir" value=".\reports"/>
3
```

LISTING 17.6   continued

```
 4      <target name="setup">
 5          <mkdir dir="${reports.dir}" />
 6      </target>
 7      <target name="test" description="Runs sample unit tests" depends="setup">
 8          <junit printsummary="true">
 9              <formatter type="xml" usefile="true"/>
10              <test name="junit.samples.VectorTest" />
11              <test name="junit.samples.AllTests" />
12          </junit>
13
14          <junitreport todir="${reports.dir}">
15              <fileset dir=".">
16                  <include name="TEST-*.xml"/>
17              </fileset>
18              <report format="frames" todir="${reports.dir}\html" />
19          </junitreport>
20      </target>
21
22      <target name="mail" depends="test">
23          <taskdef name="mimemail"
➥classname="org.apache.tools.ant.taskdefs.optional.mail.MimeMail"/>
24          <tstamp/>
25          <mimemail messageMimeType="text/html"
26          messageFile="${reports.dir}\html\overview-summary.html"
27          tolist="stewart@greendoorservices.com"
28          mailhost="mail.xtra.co.nz"
29          subject="JUnit Test Results: ${TODAY}"
30          from="sxbaird@xtra.co.nz">
31              <fileset dir=".">
32                  <include name="${reports.dir}\TESTS-*.xml"/>
33              </fileset>
34          </mimemail>
35      </target>
36 </project>
```

Let's look at the lines we've added to our build file:

- Line 22: We set a new target group, mail, that depends on our test target.

- Line 23: We define our new optional task and reference it by the name mimemail.

- Line 25: Our mimemail task, which will send an HTML formatted message (overview-summary.html), to stewart@greendoorservices.com.

- Line 32: Attach all XML files that start with TEST- from the reports directory.

Running Ant across alltests4.xml should produce the display shown in Figure 17.10.

FIGURE **17.10**

Running Ant with the Mimemail *class.*

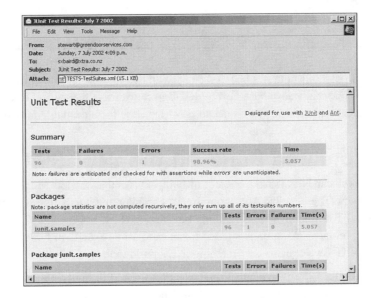

So, the email has been sent, but did it arrive? The message did arrive, consisting of an HTML body and test suite results in XML format. You can now get build messages from the comfort of your own armchair! Figure 17.11 is proof that our test email did actually reach its destination.

FIGURE **17.11**

Email client showing message from the Ant build.

MimeMail will prove to be a very useful addition to your automated test and build script. In XP, we do favor visible charts that hang on the wall for all to see; the Ant build email is still a great way to communicate to the wider team.

You can choose to use the results of these automated tests for future metric or profiling purposes. To rounding out the tutorial on MimeMail, Table 17.5 lists the attribute settings.

TABLE 17.5 Ant MimeMail Attributes

Attribute	Description
message	The message body.
messageFile	A filename to read and use as the message body.
messageMimeType	MIME type to use for message or messageFile when attached.
tolist	Comma-separated list of To: recipients.
cclist	Comma-separated list of CC: recipients.
bcclist	Comma-separated list of BCC: recipients.
mailhost	Host name of the mail server.
subject	Email subject line.
from	Email address of sender.
failonerror	Stop the build process if an error occurs sending the email.

Most of this hour has been taken up with delving further into what you can do with Ant, using mainly Java-based examples. Before we leave the subject of automated development will take a few minutes to investigate the tools available for Microsoft developers.

Automated Build on the .NET Platform

As it stands, Ant has a handful of built-in tasks that support Microsoft .NET development. These enable Ant to run the C# compiler and interaction with Visual SourceSafe. .NET development can certainly be automated by Ant, though Visual Basic .NET, and J# developers are still relegated to using exec calls to run their builds. A better option for .NET developers is the emerging .NET build tool, Nant.

As you can gather by the name, Nant is closely modeled on Ant and indeed the core help files relate to both. Obviously, there are differences in implementation. For example, when using Ant, the fork attribute starts the task in another JVM, whereas Nant uses the tag to run the task in another application domain.

Download Nant from http://nant.sourceforge.net/. Be sure and select the latest stable release.

Nant is open source, so you'll have the freedom to enhance or modify the tool if necessary. Installing Nant is a simple matter of unzipping the archive and then adding the `bin` directory to your Windows path. Nant is not as mature as Ant, which is reflected in the runtime and build file options. It also differs from Ant in that it expects the build file to be named `filename.build`. When you run Nant from the prompt it will search for the Ant file with a build extension and then assume this is your build file. (Multiple `.build` files will cause an error to be raised.) As with Ant, you can specify a build file with the `-buildfile` directive. By now build files are old hat for you, so we'll jump right in with a .NET example using Nant.

Building the .NET Windows Forms Example

Remember our Rugby example? Earlier in this hour we demonstrated how to use Ant to create and populate our test database. We're going to use the `rugby` database as the basis for our C# Windows Forms example. Our miniapplication connects to our local instance of SQL Server, presents a list of countries, and then displays the results for that country versus New Zealand in Rugby.

17

 By the way, these results are accurate; we apologize in advance to any Scottish readers! Yes, it's true they have never beaten New Zealand in rugby.

Listing 17.7 is our Nant build file listing for our sample Windows Forms application.

LISTING 17.7   Microsoft .NET Windows Forms Nant Build File

```
1  <?xml version="1.0"?>
2  <project name="RugbyWin" default="run" basedir=".">
3
4      <property name="basename" value="RugbyWin"/>
5      <property name="debug" value="true"/>
6      <property name="build.dir" value="build"/>
7
8      <target name="clean" description="cleans build directory">
9          <delete dir="${build.dir}" verbose="true" failonerror="false"/>
10     </target>
11
12     <target name="debug" depends="clean">
13         <property name="debug" value="true"/>
14     </target>
15
16     <target name="release" depends="clean">
17         <property name="debug" value="false"/>
18     </target>
```

LISTING 17.7　continued

```
19
20      <target name="build" depends="clean,vss">
21          <mkdir dir="${build.dir}"/>
22          <csc target="exe " output="${build.dir}\${basename}.exe "
23
imports="System,System.Data,System.Drawing,System.Windows.Forms,System.XML"
24              >
25              <sources>
26                  <includes name="*.cs"/>
27              </sources>
28              <references>
29                  <absolute file="System.dll"/>
30                  <absolute file="System.Data.dll"/>
31                  <absolute file="System.Drawing.dll"/>
32                  <absolute file="System.Windows.Forms.dll"/>
33                  <absolute file="System.XML.dll"/>
34              </references>
35          </csc>
36      </target>
37
38      <target name="vss">
39          <vssget localpath="c:\tysxp\rugbywin"
➥  dbpath="C:\Program Files\Microsoft Visual Studio\Common\VSS\srcsafe.ini"
40          user="sb" password="password" path="$/RugbyWin" recursive="true" />
41      </target>
42
43      <target name="run" depends="build">
44          <exec program="${build.dir}/${basename}.exe "
basedir="${build.dir}"/>
45      </target>
46 </project>
```

A quick read through the build file confirms that the Nant format is very close to what we've come to expect from Ant XML files. There are some Nant-specific variations though:

- Line 22: The csc, C# compiler task (which in our case is specified by an exe target), and a list of .NET libraries to import. (This is analogous to the using statement in C#.)

- Line 25–27: Directs Nant to compile all C# source files in our current directory.

- Line 28–34: A list of the external assembly references required to resolve dependencies.

- Line 38–41: The Visual SourceSafe extract target. We're using the vssget task to get a read-only copy of all files in the $/RugbyWin SourceSafe project. The output will be written to our local build directory.

- Line 44: Because we're too lazy to type; we automatically run `RugbyWin.exe` if the build succeeds.

> Developers familiar with the Ant Visual SourceSafe task will notice subtle differences between Ant and Nant syntax. For example, with Nant you must specify the complete path name to your SourceSafe database (that is the `srcsafe.ini` file). Also, the $ is required to indicate the root folder.

Run Ant with your new build file, and you should see the screen presented in Figure 17.12.

FIGURE 17.12

Building and running the sample .NET application.

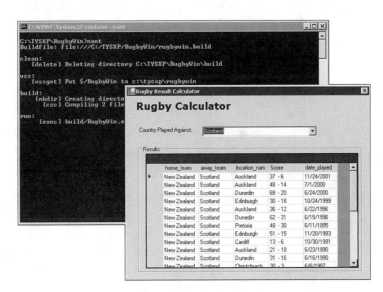

You can see in our example that Nant ran from the prompt, cleaned the target folder, extracted the latest source from SourceSafe, compiled our source, and, finally, ran our application. It works too!

Nant is still a work in progress, but has grown in leaps and bounds since its first release. At the time of writing it lacks the full-feature set of Ant, but its capability to run on a pure .NET platform is a definite plus to Microsoft shops. Consider using Nant if your target platform is Java free.

Summary

Over the last hour we've discovered that Ant can do much more than simple build automation. You can use Ant to tie together your complete development cycle, constructing an end-to-end process that solves the challenge of continuous integration. Even though Ant is ostensibly a Java-based tool, we've seen that it can be used and extended across platforms. Nant is a new, up-and-coming Microsoft .NET build tool that meets the needs of pure-.NET development shops. You'll find a wealth of support and information from the open-source community no matter which tool you select for your own software development project.

The next hour we'll change direction as we study how to implement XP in your organization.

Q&A

Q Does Nant ship with a SQL task?

A No, not at the time of this writing. You use the exec task as a workaround, by shelling-out to the command line to run SQL, or something similar.

Q Can Nant produce formatted emails like Ant?

A Yes, Nant has both a formatter and mail tasks built in.

Q Looks like build files get complex fast. How should I organize my build file?

A First, make sure that your build files are under source control! The best solution to complex builds is to separate out targets as nested build files that you then call from your master `build.xml` file. Embedding SQL in your SQL task, as we did in our example, is not a good idea for more than the simplest batches. Instead reference an external SQL file using the `src` attribute.

Workshop

This workshop tests whether you understand all the concepts you learned in this hour. It is very helpful to know and understand the answers before starting the next lesson.

Quiz

1. What is the main difference between Ant and Nant?

    a. Nant isn't completed yet.

    b. Ant offers greater functionality.

   c. Ant supports the SQL task.

   d. Ant requires the Java runtime, whereas Nant needs the Microsoft .NET
       framework.

2. Why would you want to execute SQL in your build file?

   a. Central management of information.

   b. This is not a good idea because version control is difficult.

   c. To establish the test or working database environment.

   d. To run SQL-based tests.

3. What does the `junitreport` task do?

   a. Calls JUnit and generates a report.

   b. Creates a formatted HTML based on JUnit tests.

   c. Generates a report and emails the results.

   d. Summarizes JUnit tests in either plan or XML formats.

4. What Nant task would you use to extract the latest source from Source Safe?

   a. `vsscheckout`

   b. `vssget`

   c. `ssget`

   d. `get`

Answers

   1. d.

   2. c.

   3. b.

   4. b.

Activities

1. Microsoft .NET developers: Download Nant and investigate how you can generate
   formatted reports based on your NUnit tests.

2. Java developers: Experiment with the source control tasks (use the one that fits
   your environment) and integrate into your build file.

PART V

Rolling Out XP in Your Organization

Hour

HOUR 18

Implementing XP in Your Organization

In this hour you will learn how to begin using XP in your project or organization. You might have already begun to use some aspects of XP as your confidence and knowledge has grown since the start of the book. This lesson will offer some guidance on how to implement XP practices and will cover

- How XP relates to the Technology Adoption Lifecycle
- How you can start to implement XP
- How you can retrofit XP into your current project
- What your physical environment should be like
- What some of the pitfalls are and how to avoid them
- How you can measure the success of your XP implementation

Understanding the Technology Adoption Curve

XP is a new, some would say, radical way of developing software, and this sense of "bleeding edge" can make its adoption challenging. It's helpful to understand how new technologies and ideas gain market acceptance. Geoffrey Moore, in his book *Crossing the Chasm: Marketing and Selling High-Tech Products to Mainstream Customers*, explains the lifecycle of a new product by using the classic, Technology Adoption Lifecycle. This curve is displayed in Figure 18.1.

 For more on technology adoption please refer to *Crossing the Chasm: Marketing and Selling High-Tech Products to Mainstream Customers*, by Geoffrey A. Moore, Regis McKenna, 1999, Harper Business.

FIGURE 18.1
The Technology Adoption Lifecycle.

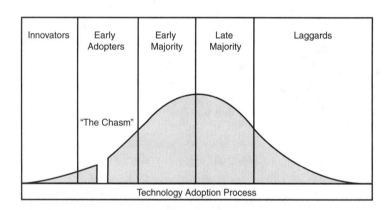

Broadly speaking the curve tells us that new ideas are slow to gain market share, but grow quickly after critical mass has been achieved. During the life of the idea or technology, five distinct groups of individuals interact with the fresh idea and Table 18.1 lists these.

TABLE 18.1 Technology Adopters

Group	Description
Innovators	They look for new technology or ideas; technology plays a central interest in their life. They love gadgets and readily try untested or beta products. Innovators often shape the emerging idea itself and are heavily involved in online groups and so on.

TABLE 18.1   continued

Group	Description
Early Adopters	They quickly buy into the idea when the possibility of real benefits has been established. They look for ways that the new idea, though still immature, can give them some kind of edge. They don't require any reference sites when it comes to the decision to adopt. At the end of the day, they are concerned with finding a strong match between their needs and the expected benefits.
Early Majority	They still relate to new ideas in much the same way as the Early Adopters, but are not swayed by the mere promise of results. They look for reference sites that demonstrate routine delivery of benefits. Their practicality outweighs any fascination they might have with the new idea.
Late Majority	This group is not technology focused at all. They wait until technology is accepted as some kind of standard; no eyebrows would be raised if they adopted it. In the software development sense, these individuals or companies rely on heavyweight methodologies such as RUP.
Laggards	They won't be using XP! They only use the technology or idea if it's embedded inside some other appliance or system.

XP is still early in its lifecycle and is somewhere between the innovators and early adopters. You bought this book, so you most likely fall into the group that sees the possibilities with Agile development. You might expect (and rightly so!) that implementing XP will give you a real market edge when it comes to delivering quality software quickly. Innovators often find it frustrating when they seem unable to convince others to pick up XP. If you're an innovator, you might have been dabbling with XP or Agile techniques for sometime. Successful implementation or adoption cannot rest solely on how "cool" the tools are; you will have to articulate real benefits. We'll cover more on this in the next hour, "Selling and Getting Buy-in to XP," but for now let's answer the question: How can I begin to apply XP, today?

Guidelines for Implementing XP in Your Situation

By now you're quite an expert in the theory of XP, but the fun begins when you put what you've learned into practice. The purpose of this Teach Yourself book is to place real tools into your hands, not just fill your head with knowledge. That's why you bought this book; you wanted practical help! Knowing how to implement XP into your project or company can make all the difference. As you've learned, XP has advantages over other non-Agile software-development approaches such as the Waterfall method:

- It's change friendly.
- It has continuous customer involvement.
- It's based on simplicity of design, development, and implementation.
- It's easily tailored to fit your existing environment.
- It's based on working sustainable hours of work to deliver quality of life and software.
- It's a solid way of delivering solutions both quickly and with high quality.
- Customers see real results early in the cycle.

So, the reason to implement XP might come down to the issue of money. Are you able to sustain growth by producing quality software for customers who love what you do and the way you do it? You can start by using XP practices whether you're in project or technology. However, some preconditions will certainly make it easier for you to use XP. This is called the "Ready for XP Checklist," as listed here:

- Flexible working environment
- Tools available on your target platform
- Management support at the upper-level
- Key developer and management champions in place
- Customer relationship is positive (noncombative)
- Customer is flexible and not already tied to a particular methodology
- Project duration is short (for your first one)
- Team cooperation has been proven at some level
- Team and customer can be located in the same place
- Reasonable pool of senior developers (team is not bottom-heavy with juniors)
- Hardware can be procured for machines
- Platform will support continuous integration (build times can be short, and so on)
- Work ethic aligns with XP principles
- XP champion has depth of knowledge in XP (might be primarily theoretical)
- Project is at a stage where XP can be applied (not deployment time!)
- Flexibility in commercial arrangements

As you run down the list you might find that you have a mismatch between the "ideal" and your own situation. Don't be alarmed or put off by this, all it means is that you'll need to customize XP slightly for your own situation. An example of this is when you lack any upper management buy in to XP. Take this as a challenge to run some presentations or other education sessions that explain what this "XP thing" is all about.

 Remember what we learned about the Technology Adoption Lifecycle— unless you're an innovator you'll want to see benefits from XP.

Solving Your Worst Problems

If you've learned one thing by now it's that simplicity is important. One approach to rolling out XP is to take your most pressing problems and begin to solve these with XP. Avoid a sweeping, all-encompassing rollout to your organization; remember XP is as yet untried by your team. Quietly solving problems with XP practices is a great place to start. To get you thinking, Table 18.2 includes a list of possible problems or issues that you can address with the relevant XP practice.

TABLE 18.2   Solving Problems with XP Practices

Problem/Issue	XP Practice
Need to control risk	Small Releases On-site Customer
Uncertainty of requirements	Small Releases On-site Customer The Planning Game
Defect counts too high	Coding Standards Test Driven Development 40-Hour Week
Software too hard or costly to maintain	Pair Programming Refactoring
Risk of losing key team member	Collective Code Ownership Pair Programming Refactoring
Solution overly complex	Refactoring Simple Design
Project or team inherited old or legacy system	Refactoring
Certain key modules have higher than average error count	Pair Programming Refactoring
Team morale low	40-Hour Week

18

TABLE 18.2   continued

Problem/Issue	XP Practice
Customer requires more releases	Small Releases Continuous Integration Simple Design
Communication in the team is poor	System Metaphor Pair Programming 40-Hour Week
Customer or management lack visibility of project progress	The Planning Game Small Releases
Lack of team vision or direction	The Planning Game Small Releases
Integration takes too long and risky at deployment time	Continuous Integration
Lack of overall confidence in the system	Test Driven Development
High probability of change in requirements or project direction	Small Releases On-site Customer The Planning Game
Customer requires knowledge transfer to their own developers	Pair Programming
Development team undergoing external QA audit	Coding Standards

Developers and management typically have a different set of problems that they are attempting to address by using XP. Let's look at each of these differing sets of problems as shown in Table 18.3, and consider how you can start with XP today.

TABLE 18.3   Focusing on Problems

Group	Implementation Ideas
Development	Start using your language-specific, unit-testing framework today. Don't attempt to write tests for your entire code base, but rather create new tests as the need arises. Similarly, write new unit tests as you uncover defects or refactor existing code. On a personal level you can begin with unit testing on your own; this can hardly be argued against because the team is supposedly doing it now anyway! You can explain that the new approach you are promoting and demonstrating is automating the existing manual process. Start Pair Programming by asking another developer to help with a sticky problem. It's important that you ask for help as opposed to sit next to another developer and announce that you're going to help her. Remember the egos at play here!

TABLE 18.3 continued

Group	Implementation Ideas
	Resist the urge to refactor your existing system based on emotion (the excitement of new tools, and so on); refactor as problems come to light.
Management	If possible, you should begin with using some of your simple project management tools; index cards, wall charts, and whiteboards. Use index cards as general-purpose tools to solve problems, prioritize, and plan. The act of integrating such lightweight tools into your leadership style is more powerful than dictates from above. Any resistance that comes when you suggest user stories written on index cards will be reduced if the team is familiar with their use.
	As a general comment to leaders, don't be afraid to admit either your weaknesses or the shortcomings others see in XP. You didn't invent it after all, and have no reason to become defensive. Take this feedback from your team to mold your own customized version of XP.

Retrofitting XP into Your Project

In the case where you need to integrate XP practices into an existing environment, or just what to know where to start, you begin with "minimal XP." XP zealots will claim that it's all or nothing, but you live in the real world, so you can't make sweeping statements like that! At least if you did declare to your customer that in midstream the team was going to adopt a brand-new technique (with the word "extreme" in the name, too) you could expect a swift response! Table 18.4 shows the practices separated into programming and process groups; you should adopt at least the following.

TABLE 18.4 Minimal XP Practices

Programming	Process
Automated Unit Testing	Small release cycles
Automated build (integration)	Reduce paperwork burden
Pair Programming	Planning Game
Coding Standards	User stories (not directly referred to as an XP practice, but core to the Planning Game)

Practices such as Pair Programming can be eased into. Begin by pairing on complex tasks and increase this until it becomes the norm. Be careful, though, not to fall into the trap of saving Pair Programming for the "tricky bits." You will discover the defect rates will rise even on simple Web pages.

18

The role of Pair Programming isn't to just reduce defect rates; the opportunity to refactor and improve efficiency is always present as well. You're solo developer built components, or pages, might be the main culprits at lowering performance!

The Planning Game (or some variation of it) is crucial because it sets the stage for the fundamental premise that customers choose what has business value; then the developers estimate. User stories go hand in hand with the Planning Game, and they start to clarify what's important to the team: the software! By using these low-tech requirements and management techniques you're making it clear that the tools the team uses should be as light as possible. We only use process tools, such as whiteboards and charts, if they help us write code. We write code to deliver value to the customer.

Another best practice, though not specifically of the 12 XP practices, that enables integration and general development is the use of a central source repository. Most XPers favor CVS as it supports multiple checkouts of source, a key component in continuous integration. Your first question when arriving at a new site should be "is the software source code in some kind of version control system?" Don't do anything else until you have source code under version control!

Setting Up Your Physical Environment

You've got to start somewhere, so go ahead and move the furniture. We discussed in Hour 11, "Software Development with Pair Programming," how you need to create the right physical space to enable developers to share workstations. We can extend this requirement for the right working space to the whole team. Getting the right space established is very important and in fact more important with XP than, say, a classic Waterfall project. An example of a flawed implementation of XP is one where walls or partitions separate the team. In Figure 18.2 we have an actual layout of a poor working environment.

Let's get real; you're not likely to get the chance to deck out your XP project in a downtown warehouse, complete with Playstations and beanbags! More than likely you'll have to work within existing facilities, and wholesale redecoration is out of the question. If you currently work in the world of the cube farm you might have to spy out a break room or conference room for XP conversion. Using open-plan environments for collaboration is by no means new and demonstrates to management a certain level of commitment by the team; you are willing to forgo some creature comforts for the success of the project. A better example of an XP layout is Figure 18.3:

FIGURE 18.2

The diagram shows an example of a poor working environment for XP.

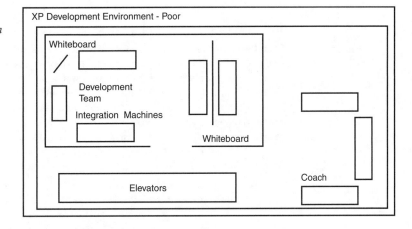

FIGURE 18.3

An example of a good working environment for XP.

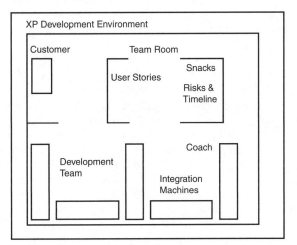

18

Creating a shared space for the team enables Pair Programming to happen and is key to your XP project. Your physical space should have

- An open area where two developers can sit around each machine
- Some kind of meeting area where project information can be fixed to the wall
- Separation from any other noisy area
- Space for the customer(s) to sit
- Quick and easy access to snacks

Are You Unknowingly Using XP Practices?

Sometimes you can ease into Agile software development techniques—no fanfare just quietly begin using one of the XP practices. I was leading the development of a Web-based application to manage property tax for a large consulting firm. Initially, we began the project along a classical Waterfall approach with a degree of up-front requirements gathering. One of the many challenges with this project was that the four main user-group advocates were spread from East coast to West coast. To further compound our problems, the project internally had a high profile, with the wreckage of the four previous failed attempts still fresh in the customer's mind.

The project *had* to be a success; careers could be made or lost in the process. So, we began in earnest, working from a bottom-up model. Our focus was on understanding the data requirements because these seemed the most complex, unknown area for the project team. We ambled along for a few weeks in this requirements/analysis mode with nothing to show but a slowly evolving data model. At first, the customer seemed happy enough, but then slid into nervous uncertainty, as we had nothing but paper to show for our efforts. How could they be sure we were on track, building what they *really* wanted? Time zones and the disconnected nature of the project only accentuated the customer's growing sense of panic.

It was about then that my boss, Randy Schrock, came up with this idea of producing real, working software every week. The plan was that within the one-week time box, the team would work on one vertical slice of the Web (for example, client search screen), and complete a fully functional user story by Friday. Not a prototype, but working, albeit beta-quality, software. This was a simple yet powerful idea that had some great benefits—the customer could see real progress, and the team had clarity over what they were developing. The mini-timebox plan was a great success and was the foundation of the overall success of the project.

Were we doing XP? No, not at all, but we had been very successful at using one of the key practices (small releases). Look for opportunities to use XP practices—start small and then scale fast.

By the way, thanks for the idea, Randy!

Avoiding the Pitfalls

Rolling out XP into your project or company will be easier if you follow the advice to start small by fixing your most pressing problem first. That being said, there are some conditions or blockers that could stymie you. Being aware of these up front is going to save some heartache later! Here's a list of some pitfalls to watch for:

- *Fear*—XP is new, different, and from your viewpoint, untried. Uncertainty and doubt are to be expected. As an XP champion you can use your new knowledge gained from this book and other references sites, such as www.xprogramming.com, to counter fear with facts.

- *Culture*—You might be working in a slow-moving, cautious organization where the status quo has worked pretty well so far and change is unwanted. In these cases work within your own sphere of influence (those things you can directly effect) and let your actions speak louder than words. Use the knowledge you've gained in this book to backup any assertions you make. One last thing—keep in mind that there's a wealth of knowledge that has led to the development of your company's present approach and not all is bad!

- *Tools Fail*—Don't underestimate the need for tools that work. Groupware tools are easy to get right, so go for the simple first. For example, if Post-It notes work for defect allocation to developers, use them. Realize the need for automated test and build tools, such as those we've covered so far. Be on guard for integration issues that might arise from untried or complex subsystems, you might need to spike these early and a good idea is to busy a team member with the build environment as early as possible. If your operating system lacks the capability to support continuous integration (excessive build times/lack of tools) you might consider another XP target!

- *Distance*—Virtual XP is possible; the hindrances are more social than technical. However, there is no reason why integration and testing and collective ownership cannot be maintained translocally. When time and space separate the customers and developers, the collaboration is much more difficult. Inflection in voice and change of expression are lost across cracking phone lines, staccato email, and so on. Consider carefully, then, how you will implement XP in your distributed environment.

- *Leadership*—There is a transition from project management to XP coach. If your coach is an undercover dictator or closet technocrat, you will quickly lose the joy of the journey. It could be that he is simply falling back into familiar command and control behavior. Whatever your role, you can speak up and gently point him back to your XP values. As the project progresses, observe whether the coach or leader using XP as another bag of tricks to add to his arsenal, or do they get it?

- *Project Size*—Initially the thinking has been that XP is better suited for small-to-medium sized projects. This equates to a total team size of around two to 18 team members. A large project is likely to be dispersed across more than one location and, therefore, project size is directly related to the distance challenges we mentioned previously. In Hour 22, "Extending the Limits of XP," we discuss how problems of time and space might be overcome.

18

- *Development language*—The tools you've learned about so far—JUnit, Ant, and others—all rest on the use of object-oriented techniques. Languages such as Visual Basic, though not strictly speaking supporting OOP, do work within the confines of a component object model (COM) and, therefore, can be leveraged for use with XP. Environments that use COBOL or Assembler will effectively block use of the core XP practices of refactoring and automated unit testing.

Think of these XP-blockers that as warning signs; they shouldn't stop you from taking the journey, but they will make you slow down for turns!

> The Wiki Wiki home for subjects around adopting XP can be found at
> `http://www.c2.com/cgi/wiki?WikiPagesAboutTransitioningToExtreme`
> `Programming`.

Measuring XP

There will be observable outcomes from your use of XP. If it's starting to work for you, there will improvements in collaboration and group dynamics. Your developers will have greater depth of respect for the company that has taken the risk to try XP, and they will have grown in relationships. The deepening of relationships is very important to both overall quality and results.

The standard of coding will improve as the superstars have come down from on high to Pair Program with juniors. These juniors who might have viewed the seniors from afar, unsure how to approach them without sounding like they knew nothing, now have confidence in interchange. Junior developers surprised seniors with creative solutions and their own "wacky" ideas. The dynamics of collaboration might have just formed the team you've struggled to build as a leader.

On the technical side, the development team has been exposed to new tools and advanced refactoring techniques.

Commercially, your development team has proven they can deliver not just on time, but what the customer actually wants. Suddenly, you have an edge over the traditionalists!

Don't expect a visit from the XP certification board; the fact is there is no explicit metric to gauge your XP conformance. If you're using the pick and mix approach with the XP practices don't expect to reap maximum benefits. Review the 12 practices and keep applying them, extending their use. In the end, if you're not using XP, but are getting results—does it matter? Go ahead pick a couple of practices and merge them into your own homegrown methodology.

One thing is for sure, you will know when it's not working! It will be the same old story: customers mad, boss mad, and team stressed. If the customer is getting delivered value, and you are making money—that's good! When you finish glowing over the numbers be sure to ask the team if they enjoyed the journey. Better still constantly measure the pulse of the team, check the gel, and look for the classic tell-tales; Dilbert cartoons and the revolving door syndrome. The best metric for morale is the number of visible Dilbert's!

> Making XP work for you means refining the implementation to suit your local context. The values are your bedrock, and the practices should be your tools. Index cards or Word documents for user stories? Planning Game or Project Initiation meeting? Don't let the tribal language sidetrack your implementation and be prepared to give in on a few lesser battles with upper management in the quest for XP acceptance. Create your own rituals, spend time getting a solid toolset together, and avoid mindless arguments about rigor versus agile.

You will be too busy celebrating your XP success to become embroiled in methodology debates!

18

Summary

Over the last hour we've uncovered some methods to implement on your project. The best approach is to take today's problems, and then begin to solve them the XP way. To rollout XP the keys are to start simple, watch for pitfalls, and lead by example. These will ensure that XP gets a good hearing in your organization. Remember that it's the combination of the practices working together that makes XP really tick. It will take a degree of courage to put forward some of the ideas you've learned over the last 18 hours; that's one of the core values!

The next hour will look at the other side of the implementing coin, and we'll discover how to sell XP.

Q&A

Q What are some of the dangers of doing minimal XP?

A You won't get the full benefits of XP and will miss out on the synergy of the practices. If you misrepresent XP as a list of practices you can choose from, you run the risk of any failures being blamed on XP. The end result of this as that your company discards XP.

Workshop

This workshop tests whether you understand all the concepts you learned in this hour. It is very helpful to know and understand the answers before starting the next lesson.

Quiz

1. As a developer, what XP practices should you implement first?

    a. Testing, Continuous Integration, Pair Programming, Coding Standards.

    b. Code Sharing, Continuous Integration, Pair Programming.

    c. Testing, Small Releases, Pair Programming.

    d. Planning, Integration, Compilation.

2. Where is the best place to start implementing XP?

    a. During the planning phase.

    b. Start with the worst problem first.

    c. When you have buy in from management and developers.

    d. You can start anytime.

3. Why is the physical layout so important?

    a. XP puts a high-value on verbal communication.

    b. Open plan helps to break the team out of any cultural ruts that the company might be in.

    c. Pair Programming necessitates a certain type of layout.

    d. The customer must be visible at all times.

4. What are some pitfalls to watch out for when implementing XP?

    a. Poor tools support.

    b. Inflexible management.

    c. Distance and size.

    d. Project duration is too short to get real feedback.

Answers

1. a.

2. b.

3. a., c.

4. a., b., and c.

Activities

1. Match the problems you face today with the XP practices. Start with those practices today and monitor your results.

2. Buy a deck of index cards and begin using them for planning and problem solving. You can use these for any kind of planning: report writing, presentations, and so on.

3. If you're a project leader, gather your team together and discuss how you can begin to implement XP in your local context.

18

Hour **19**

Selling and Getting Buy-in to XP

In this hour you will learn how to sell XP to developers, management, and customers. Each group has a different set of values and drivers and speaking to these is vital if you are to gain acceptance of XP. This hour will focus on

- How to sell the concept of XP to developers
- How to get management buy-in for XP
- A collaborative sales approach that will set you up to succeed
- How to sell the XP process to your customers
- The kinds of contractual arrangements to consider when using XP

Selling XP Internally

In the last hour I explained how the Technology Adoption Lifecycle affects the way you might choose to implement XP. Understanding this concept will help to frame how you will both implement and sell XP. As an implementer of XP you'll be weighing both where XP is in the Technology Adoption curve, and what kind of person you are selling XP to.

As we discuss how to sell XP to each group, we must recognize that we're using some fairly broad generalizations about developers. Keep this in mind as we go through each group; you might be the exception that proves the rule! For the purposes of our discussion we can separate stakeholders that will be impacted by XP into four groups:

- Developers
- Management
- Other internal team members such as designers, testers, and business analysts
- Customers

Let's deal with each of these groups in turn.

How Do I Sell XP to Developers?

Developers have unique personalities and drivers, if you're in management you'll need to understand these if you want to get their buy-in. Consider how programmers and computer science graduates learn their craft. They are often encouraged to solve problems alone, and the tools they use (computers) only serve to reinforce an individual approach to work. You could say that developers are not naturally inclined to interact with people and that speaking through their software is what they like best. Because of the Waterfall method of development, programmers have often been insulated from customers and users. The development team might have been handed a stack of design and requirements documents to work on. Work was broken down into work packets, and then assigned to individual team members. The model of "throwing requirements over the wall" simply won't work in XP.

Employing XP on your project can be very threatening to developers as you ask them to change their working style to one that demands a higher-degree of communication. In reality, there's no one-size-fits-all solution to the problem of how to improve a developer's communication abilities. Recognizing that your issues are firstly *relational* and not *technical* will at least start you on the right path. It's crucial to understand what's important to your developers and, if possible, put yourself in their shoes.

If you're a leader or XP champion you might find yourself jumping up and down with excitement: "just wait until my developers find out how great XP is!" The trouble is that what you say and what they hear can be quite different. In Table 19.1 we have some examples of how the communication lines can get crossed:

TABLE 19.1   The XP Practices and How Developers React

The XP Practice	What Developer's Might Hear
Collective ownership	Oh, anyone can change my code—great! This will lead to chaos.
Metaphor	No up-front design will end in spaghetti code and poor-quality systems.
Test first	I don't test; I develop. I'll leave testing to the experts.
Pair Programming	I work best alone. I'm so fast I do the work of two, anyway.
Refactoring	I complete the work, and then I redo to get it right? Now, that's what I call *rework*! If it ain't broke don't fix it!
Continuous Integration	I won't get any work done if I have to integrate every 10 minutes or so!
40 Hour Work Week	I like the "rush" of working crazy hours. I don't like being told when and how much I can work.
Onsite Customer	I don't want the customer looking over my shoulder all the time.

Your words, no matter how well-meaning, can be lost in a haze of miscommunication. You can garner tremendous resistance to practices such as Pair Programming if you fail to understand the developer's worldview. At the risk overgeneralizing we can list a few things that developers really care about:

- Writing code and the joy of programming
- Control over their machine and environment
- Freedom
- Using the coolest tools
- Quality of work
- Recognition (to be valued for technical skill)
- Projects rather than maintenance

It's an interesting paradox. Developers who like the newest tools, betas, and bits at the same time may dislike social or environmental change. If you're a leader it's your mission to seek out the most receptive developers on your team and cast your spell of XP on them. Here are some angles that may help:

- As developers you'll use tools that automate the boring tasks of build and test.
- Test first programming sounds weird at first, but XP has easy-to-use frameworks (xUnit) that will help. Testing in XP is actually programming!
- The work week is restricted to 40 hours or so, which means that overtime is infrequent.
- As developers you will have less (if any) documentation to write. This one is guaranteed to raise a few cheers!

19

- XP places high value on quality of code.
- Meetings are very short, usually lasting only a few minutes.
- Pair Programming is what you've been doing for years, working together to solve problems. Why not try Pair Programming for a few weeks? (Have those case studies up your sleeve, just in case.)
- Project managers and those annoying Gantt charts have gone away; instead you get a "coach" who is technical.

Often you'll find that the more senior developers are harder to sway toward XP. Listen to their concerns, be honest when you don't know, and stay humble. If you lay down the law and dictate that XP will be followed or else, you'll end up with polarization in the team. From that point, the next step is a steady stream of developers leaving!

Winning the War over Pair Programming

Pair Programming is the XP practice that causes the most heated debate amongst developers. It deserves a special mention here because it's key to getting XP working for you. Forget about the economic or efficiency arguments for the moment; you will uncover deeper issues than that when you introduce Pair Programming!

Pair Programming removes the focus away from individuals and onto the entire group. For most developers this is a fairly major change. How can you be the hero if the code is shared? The flip side of this is that everyone also shares in any failure. To overcome objections about Pair Programming you can begin by pointing out the benefits: knowledge sharing, code quality, and higher team morale. Explain the mechanics of how Pair Programming works and let knowledge defeat fear.

The best way to prove that Pair Programming works is to put it into practice! Don't enforce the use of Pair Programming at first; you can give options such as either work in pairs or be subjected to code reviews. Needless to say not many developers will happily choose reviews. Code reviews are about checking what you've already done, but in Pair Programming the code review happened as the software evolved. Discuss with the team what is and isn't working with Pair Programming; let them track defect counts between solo and pair code. The results will quickly become clear!

Make no mistake; you must get Pair Programming to occur somehow! Don't relegate it to the "too-hard basket."

Buddy, Can You Spare a Dime?

I converted a nonbeliever to Pair Programming just the other day. I'd already given a few presentations and brown-bag lunches on the subject of how XP will change your life. The problem was that a few key team members were still cynical about the efficacy of Pair Programming. The common quote was along the lines of, "I get everything, except that Pair Programming business; two people doing the work of one is crazy!" Because I hadn't invented XP or Pair Programming, these angry statements were like water off a duck's back. I had no reason to become defensive. I waited until the time was right, and then I struck.

A few months later I was called to help one of our projects. Within a few days we were Pair Programming; don't worry I didn't call it that. My approach was to ask for help: "I need to integrate with your stuff, so can you sit with me and show me how it all works?" I wasn't using any kind of subtle psychological trick here because I really *did* need his help. This pattern continued for a while until we decided to pair on all the complex logic. It was hard to say no at this point; after all we'd been pairing anyway and had quite a bit of fun doing it!

I learned from this that *doing* is better than PowerPoint slides and lectures. Another aspect was that give and take combined with patience worked wonders. Don't tell someone you will pair with him, but simply ask for help. Chances are that you need it!

Getting Management Buy-in

Management might be concerned that the programmers are in charge! A perception exists in some circles that XP allows the developers to run amok, taking over the entire software development process. This highlights a problem you have to overcome in your role as XP champion—a belief that Extreme Programming is more *programming* than anything else.

Your management is looking for repeatable results, using whatever methodology lowers risk. The paradoxical thing here is that those who have "just enough knowledge to be dangerous" view XP as risky; nothing could be further from the truth. Reducing risk is one of the underlying issues that XP addresses. To simplify, upper management is concerned with a few things:

- Completing the project within the budget.
- The customer is happy and comes back for more work.
- Workers are happy and keep working.
- Estimates are accurate and support the sales side.

Taking this as a basis we can zero in on a few angles that underline how XP stacks up. The way to sell to management is to explain that

- XP uses small release cycles, so management is very granular.
- You *can* use XP with a fixed-priced contract.
- We do some of the XP practices now; the difference is that we're not doing them together in the Extreme way.
- Management can change XP names (such as the Planning Game) to whatever they want for marketing or cultural-safety reasons.
- XP has been tried and tested in commercial environments.
- We're not throwing out the baby with the bathwater; we'll still use existing methodologies and tools where they make sense.
- Management will get better control and visibility of the process.
- The company will have a new weapon that most competitors don't have (at the moment, anyway).

The last point fits our discussion around the Technology adoption curve: If you start with XP now, you will be one of the early adopters. In turn, this will mean you have a real edge in how you solve customer's problems. The modern trend is toward collaboration and away from centrally managed structures; XP fits this perfectly.

Another tactic is to target a manager who is predisposed to the use of Agile or new methods. Dutiful care and feeding of this manager will strengthen your case when it comes to widening the rollout of XP. Recognize that your management will have to explain this new approach to their superiors, so create whatever tools will help them do this. Typically, these tools are simple (short) presentations with supporting documentation as appropriate. A fine balance between going under the radar and seeking executive buy-in is a challenge, but will reward you in the end.

XP is sometimes referred to as a lightweight development approach; unfortunately this comes with some baggage attached. Light implies not quite complete, not robust, and lacking in rigor. The Agile Alliance has since dropped the use if this term because of the negative connotations, but the stigma still exists in some circles. It's a simple matter to explain that XP is in fact a very rigorous approach (engineering-wise), but is light in documentation requirements. A wise person once pointed out, "you can't compile PowerPoints," and XP shifts the weight from writing deliverables to producing software. XPers do write documents, but only just enough to support the prime activity of writing software for the customer.

Avoid leaving management with the idea that XP is a grab bag of practices from which you can pick whichever practice you want. Reinforce that the practices work together, and that the sum of the parts is greater than the whole. The alternative is that, run with only a few practices, your project fails to deliver and XP is cast as the villain. You might only get one shot at this, so you'd better choose wisely!

Some Tips for Getting Buy-in from Your Team

Developers and the lone project leader are not the only staff for software development projects. Modern development leans on a multitalented team. Let's summarize some general tips to getting their buy-in, too:

- Talk to them and find out what's important to them.
- Ask them what their existing perceptions of XP are.
- Underline the collaborative, synergistic features of XP.
- Work with them to plan a transition into XP (ask rather than tell).
- Be honest when you don't know where their role fits.
- It's not about titles, but roles.
- How can we extend XP to include their unique role?

So much of XP is directed toward developers and leaders, but we know that the product won't exist without the whole team. Have you ever seen the average developer's graphic design skills? As developers, we don't expect that designers should or could program; why should we assume we can design?

How Do I Sell XP to Customers?

19

Customers could be the easiest to sell the idea of XP to. The important thing to get across is the business value that XP brings. Customers get these benefits:

- They can change their minds.
- They control and have visibility on what functions are developed.
- They get a system that has been developed on a solid, repeatable-test framework, and quality is built in.
- Deliverables are produced that have direct value to them; the process is not propped up by documents that no one reads.

- The development process is aligned to their need to be Agile in the marketplace.
- You're supporting their short-time-to-market driver with a real process (not just working hard and adding more resources).
- Course corrections can be made easily; the development is bundled into small releases.
- Developers are happier and, therefore, nicer to work with. (This is a real issue!)

Is the use of the word *extreme* a problem when describing the process? Take a few moments to explain where the *X* in *XP* comes from. Customers are more interested in how you plan to deliver value to them than how cool XP is. Also, they probably have had some high-level exposure to XP in the press and have a sense for the context.

The best way to sell a customer on XP is to use it during the selling/buying cycle. The reason being, the way you sell your services is really a free sample of your work. For those of us who are consultants, starting the way you intend to continue is an especially important practice. When you collaborate at the beginning of your engagement, working with your prospect to define the problem, solution, and cost that makes total sense, you demonstrate to that prospect the value of XP.

Demonstrating the value of XP can be more difficult if you are answering an RFP that disallows face-to-face contact. It is extremely important to define, in the proposal, exactly what you mean by collaborate. This avoids confusion because most customers will automatically assume that by collaboration you mean prototypes and sign offs rather than actual onsite customer participation.

It is still important that your XP team is able to competently consult and advise your customer in all phases of the project—from defining the problem precontract to getting the business deal signed and underway. But don't worry—this isn't a sales book! We'll leave the intricacies of actual prospect development to the experts! Figure 19.1 is a simple model on how we go from opportunity to contract.

Define the Problem

Normally, not enough time is spent defining what the customer's problem really is. When the client presents a solution ("I want a Web site"), we should move off that until we are certain what the problem is.

FIGURE **19.1**

A collaborative selling model.

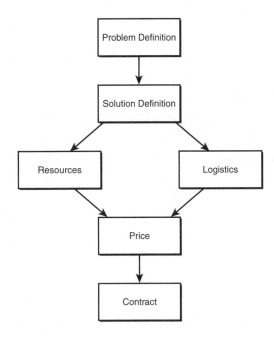

The problem can be described in terms of either pain or gain; that is, a cost to be reduced or benefit to realize. We can convert these pain/gain words into the common local currency (dollars, pounds, pesos, and so on). An example is when the customer says, "the support costs of the existing system are really killing us." Killing is very definitely a pain word, but at this point has no meaning to us, so what does the statement really convey? We need to work together (collaborate) until we arrive at our dollar amount. Let's eavesdrop on an imaginary conversation:

Customer: We need a new Web site; can you help us?

Consultant: Actually, we've been very successful at helping many clients with their Web sites. One thing we have found is that every client has a different expectation from a Web site. When you say "Web site" what does that mean to you?

Customer: Good point, we don't want to be Amazon.com! What we do need is a mainly static site with a message board application.

Consultant: Right, I see. What issues are you hoping to resolve with this new Web site?

19

Customer: The support costs with our existing site are killing us!

Consultant: Wow, sounds like a real problem. Do you have a sense for what those costs might be?

Customer: Not really, but I do know that Joe spends half of his time on the site. We need him to work on new projects.

Consultant: Let's see if we can work this out. What is his hourly cost of labor?

Customer: Not sure of the exact numbers, but he's around $60,000 per year.

Consultant: Okay. Could we apply a load factor of say, 25% to his salary to cover his overhead?

Customer: Sounds close enough.

Consultant: Let's see 60,000 multiplied by 1.25 gives us 75,000 per year. If he spends half his time doing support we could say that it costs you around $37,500 per year. Does that sound right?

Customer: Gee, we waste a lot of money!

The conversation could last for the rest of this book! We'll stop here and discuss some interesting points. The consultant was trying to do two main things in this opening conversation:

- Understand and clarify the requirement
- Turn the "pain" into a currency amount

The conversation started innocuously enough with the customer asking for a Web site. Our consultant resisted the temptation to trumpet their latest "Web site," instead clarified exactly what the words meant to the customer.

> The more commonplace the term, the more open to assumption, guesses, and errors you become. You know what the term means to you, but what about them?

As the consultant probed he heard a classic pain phrase (killing us); pretty dramatic, but what did that really mean? He spent the next minutes turning the pain into a back of the envelope currency amount. An important point here is that they worked out the amount *together*. The consultant didn't go away, complete the research, and pop-up out the answer on her calculator. The customer owned the number because they came up with it together. The conversation will continue in this vein as the consultant unearths all the pain-and-gain issues, turning them into dollar figures. Sometimes, the evidence is not immediately at hand, in which case you'll need to find out who has the data you want. Doing it on the spot is best. By the end of problem definition you want to arrive at a budget number and a clear sense of what the problem truly is.

Define the Solution

Thinking back to your XP lifecycle, solution definition might mean spending some time exploring options. Work with the customer to scope possible technical solutions. Your final solution will most likely be no more than a solution map and supporting high-level stories. Your solution won't be detailed because you'll leave details to implementation time, what you do require though is enough user stories to run your initial Planning Game. This will give you enough sizing information to plan for resources.

Identify the Resources

Typically, development projects are a mix of internal staff and external consultants. The reasons for this are two-fold: to lower costs and provide cross training. Working side-by-side with skilled experts is a great boost to the morale and learning of internal employees. Planning for resources is about estimating how many developers you'll need to maintain velocity through the project. In actuality, you never really know the resource count because the team's throughput is as yet, uncalibrated. This should be both explained and accepted by the customer.

Determine the Logistics

Logistics covers when the project is to start, facilities, and timeframe. If the customer is pressing for 90-day completion you might be forced to go back to your resource pool to increase throughput. As any project manager will tell you, adding people on a project won't necessarily make it less time consuming. Sometimes the reverse! Logistics also covers issues such as expenses and allowances.

Agree on the Price

Price is easy to calculate. Just multiply your daily rate by resource count and include logistics overheads. We arrived at our resource number by calculating the number of developers required to maintain the velocity. (Some companies have a predefined "management overhead" that covers nondevelopers and is applied on a duration basis.)

19

Sign the Contract

We're all familiar with fixed-price contracts where the customer and developers agree on a single price for the solution. Customers like fixed price because they have financial control, but, on the other hand, the developers have no motivation to supply a great solution—get in and get out. XP works best within the context of a *variable-scope* contract. Variable scope simply means that the customer fixes the price, but the scope of work can change; they effectively buy a bucket of development time.

Time and Materials is the contract where the customer is paying by the hour. There's no hard end date and work can easily drift along for months with no results. T&M is great for developers!

In Table 19.2 we encapsulate the difference between these two forms of contract.

TABLE 19.2   Comparing Fixed-Price with Time and Materials

Time and Materials	
Problems	**Solutions**
Supplier inclined to maximize resources and extend time	Small releases keeps software rolling out
No incentive to complete visibility of progress	40-hour week plus clarity with tracking gives good
Not directed by business goals	Works well with open and honest communication
Can mean project drifts	
Fixed-Price	
Problems	**Solutions**
Poor estimation based on high-level requirements result in overtime and poor results	Fix price and let scope change (up and down)
Supplier wants to do minimum required, whereas customer wants to maximize	Works because customer controls releases
Any compromise can be lose/lose	Customer buys buckets of time

Before you enter into an engagement using XP, you'll want to consider

- Can we collaborate with this customer?
- How did collaboration work during the sales cycle?

Don't assume that lack of feedback and communication during proposal stage will be replaced by collaboration later!

Summary

Selling XP to your colleagues and customers starts with thinking about what drives each group or individual. The things that drew you to XP might be of no interest to your peers. Work at understanding others to ensure that XP doesn't remain just a theory in your head. When you sell solutions to customers, you'll expect to use XP during implementation, so it's key that you begin to collaborate early. Use your selling as a free sample of how you will work together. Realizing that they can control their software development project will energize customers; they get risk reduction and results!

In the next hour we'll take a tour through some successful XP projects throughout the world.

Q&A

Q Can I use XP with an RFP that stipulates signoffs and a more regimented approach?

A Think about whether the customer is willing and able to collaborate if you win the work. There's no reason why you can't combine XP with a milestone-driven life-cycle; make the milestones iteration ends.

Q I attempted an internal pilot of XP, used some of the practices, and it was a disaster. What should I do?

A Admit you failed! Explain to the fallout victims that XP works by the combination of the 12 practices.

Q My management dislikes some of the language used in XP such as the Planning Game. How can I address this?

A Change any of the words to suit your own context.

Q My peers think they are already doing XP and see no reason to change. How can I open their eyes?

A Assuming they're not, ask them what their understanding of XP is and come back to the central idea that the synergy of the practices is what makes XP, XP. Think of The Beatles; the sum of the parts was greater than the whole!

Workshop

This workshop tests whether you understand all the concepts you learned in this hour. It is very helpful to know and understand the answers before starting the next lesson.

Quiz

1. What is one of the biggest changes developers must confront when moving to XP?

    a. Shorter working hours.

    b. Less project management and controls.

    c. The pace of change is accelerated.

    d. Vastly increased levels of communication required.

2. What could be a powerful selling point with your management?

    a. Their development shop will get the jump on the competition.

    b. XP results in higher-quality software.

    c. Developers spend less time on documents, more on programming.

    d. Pair Programming will increase productivity.

3. What does a variable scope contract mean?

    a. Scope creep is okay.

    b. The customer has total control.

    c. The scope can change within the amount of work throughput the team can maintain.

    d. The contract can be changed from time to time.

4. Why would customers be drawn to XP?

    a. They get fine-grained control of the software.

    b. They quickly get working software.

    c. They would be on the leading edge if they used it.

    d. Developers use the latest tools with XP.

Answers

1. d.

2. a.

3. c.

4. a., b.

Activities

1. Draw up an action plan of how you can begin to sell XP within your own environment. Think about what kinds of people need to become believers, what matters to them, and how can you allay their fears.

2. Present a brown-bag session at your work and give an overview of XP. Tailor your talks to cover specific audience groups (managers, developers, and so on).

HOUR **20**

Learning from XP Case Studies

So far in our journey to understand XP we've covered a mix of theory and practical advice. In this hour we'll take a tour through a number of XP projects from around the world, which will enable you to take away some real-life lessons. Our approach will be to look at a cross-section of project types and implementations. In this hour we will cover

- The importance of matching your sales and delivery approaches

- How you can survive a midproject conversion to XP

- How a large software vendor tailors XP to meet its needs

- How you can successfully use XP on a large project

The customer and supplier names have been removed from some of these case studies.

Case Study: The Importance of Keeping Your Selling and Delivery Methods Synchronized

This case study confirms the importance of keeping your selling and delivery methods synchronized. As we learned in Hour 19, "Selling and Getting Buy-in to XP," the way we sell XP is a free sample of the way we will work with XP. This case study is an example of how mixing a noncollaborative sales approach can hinder attempts to have meaningful collaboration with your customer during delivery.

The customer was a public-sector agency that required a system to aggregate data from partner agencies and present a single view of that data. The agency went to the market through a Request for Proposal (RFP) cycle and, as is normally the case with such tenders, limited communication to formal channels. The consulting firm that won the work presented a modified version of XP as their delivery approach. The response itself contained no mention of XP, per se, instead referring to a "collaborative approach." The idea was that the core work of the project (software development) could be wrapped within a standard sign off, Waterfall method. The sales cycle did not involve any form of collaboration or discussion with the customer beyond clarification of technical and contractual issues.

The customer was very excited by the concept of collaborative development even though he had no clear understanding about what this meant in real, day-to-day terms. It became clear that his experience of collaboration was limited to rudimentary prototyping. In fact, they were expecting a prototype-driven approach where the team effectively "made up" the initial interfaces, and then presented them to the client for feedback. The customer had no interest in interacting with the team during development and was content to communicate requirements through these prototypes.

On one side the development team was struggling to use XP-like methods, while the customer refused to commit time to working with them. The lack of documentation coming from the team began to cause strife because the customer had an expectation that standard specifications and designs would be included. Frustration continued as the customer complained about the developers' use of automated unit testing with no formal test plans. Documentation was contained in the Wiki Wiki Web, and the idea of a paperless project was hard for the customer to comprehend.

The software engineering rigor that the development team was applying to the work was impressive to the customer, yet the customer felt uncertain about the process aspects of XP. In the end, a compromise was reached—the developers continued to pair and write their unit tests, but requirements were managed through a mixture of functional specification and prototypes.

It was easy to see the correlation between the way the customer interacted with the team during delivery, and how the RFP process was managed. As is often the case in the public sector, controlling risk and conformance to internal project management standards were key drivers. The project was deemed a success, and rightly so, as the system met client expectations and budgets. From the development teams' viewpoint it was exasperating to work with a noncollaborative customer, and on the whole it was a poor XP experience.

This was a fixed-price contract with payment intervals linked to deliverables, most of which were documents not software. The team was forced to retrospectively write documents to get paid! How could XP ever work in this kind of scenario?

Lessons Learned

Here is a summary of lessons learned from this project:

- Clarify exactly what your XP approach will mean to the customer. The more common the word (such as, collaboration) the more likely that assumptions will be made and a communication breakdown and confusion will occur.
- Start the way you intend to precede; collaborate early with your customer.
- Write the contract so it will fit your development approach. In our case study, the contract tied payments to deliverables that don't exist in XP!

Case Study: The Result of Changing to XP in Midstream

In Hour 18, "Implementing XP in Your Organization," we learned that you can begin using XP at almost any point in your project lifecycle. We'll spend some time analyzing how a consulting firm switched to XP halfway through its development. The change didn't pass without some degree of pain, but the end results were quite remarkable.

In this case study, our client was a large business-to-business (B2B) aggregator. The role of this organization was to provide a centralized meeting place for business across various industry verticals. They had a reputation for innovation, which definitely helped when XP was introduced.

The client commissioned a new Web site that would support their model for industry innovation—matching buyers and suppliers. The contract was signed on a fixed-price basis, with delivery through a series of discrete phases. The initial price was fairly much "back of the envelope" in nature, based on high-level assumptions.

20

The first phase of the development continued along standard Waterfall or Staged Delivery lines, with time expended at the start on infrastructure and planning issues. Daily builds were a foreign concept to the team, which resulted in the usual mad panic at release time. In reality, the deadline was artificial in nature and exposed poor estimations. The team did meet the deadline at the cost of both morale and lower-than-expected quality. With more than 100 defects found during acceptance tests, the team spent the next few weeks *really* finishing the release. Not a very pleasant experience!

Phase two saw the introduction of XP into the development cycle. Senior management from the supplier-side spent focused effort to soften up both their own management and the customer to using XP. This was time well spent, cementing the support from the customer and management before exposing the team to XP. The name "Extreme Programming" was downplayed with locally acceptable words used instead.

The XP implementation was biased toward the programming practices as opposed to the process components (such as the Planning Game). The XP champion took the stance that immersion was the best approach, and rollout to the team moved quickly when management was on board. Practices used by the team included

- Pair Programming
- Test First (unit testing)
- Collective Code Ownership
- 40-hour week
- Small Releases
- Planning Game (variation on this)
- Coding Standards

The use of Pair Programming was seen as being essential to the success of this XP project; so much so that the team leader mandated its use with no exceptions. It was either commit to Pair Programming or leave the project. The downsides to this dictatorial method were self-evident: Junior developers generally shrugged their shoulders in acceptance, while more senior members were shown the door. In one case the developer's disaffection with the whole process led to him leaving the company along with his experience and skill. On paper the use of XP practices, such as Pair Programming, had a high-acceptance rate, but behind closed doors there was a degree of grumbling and complaining. Interviews with various team members confirmed this.

Pair Programming, coding standards, and test first were all contributors to the improvement in software quality. One developer commented, "at the start you could tell who wrote what piece of code, but by the end of the phase it seemed like one mind was at work." This homogeneity in source code helped with source code quality as well as code adherence;

there was one way of doing this now and that was the *team* way. To give you a sense of software quality; by the end of the three-month cycle there were three small defects uncovered in acceptance testing. Quite a change from the hundred or more in phase one!

The lack of defects at release was even more remarkable if you consider the poor working conditions the team was forced to endure. Classic software development thinking directly links quiet, peaceful working environments to better quality software. It would appear that the other XP practices used by the team had counteracted the lack of suitable workspace.

A funny endnote is that some developers missed the panic of a standard project! On the final day, the team went home at around 3:00 p.m. and that was that! Panic and chaos were not things missed by the customer. For their part, customers loved the control they were given by the XP process and the visibility of the software. Both customer and supplier characterized the project as a great success. Developers were split on whether it was a good experience or not, we can surmise that perhaps the heavy-handed implementation approach was a factor.

Lessons Learned

Here is a summary of lessons learned from this project:

- Take time to educate both your management and customer; let them know exactly what they're getting into.

- Realize that your people are your greatest resource and try to be gentle as you rollout XP.

- Work very hard to get your first XP project right from both customer and management views. Plan to ask your customer to act as a reference site.

- Expect and accept your own local variations of some of the XP practices.

Case Study: Independent Software Vendor Comes to Grips with XP

20

Symantec Corporation, based in Cupertino, California, is an independent software vendor known for its security, utility, and remote management technologies. The use of XP at Symantec is a case where a backdoor or Trojan Horse approach can be used when employing XP. Internally, Symantec uses its "Solution Centered Process" to manage software development. The Solution Centered Process consists of six phases: explore, define-access-refine, plan, implement, deliver, and measure. Symantec acquired another security firm, Axent Technologies, in December 2000. Axent was already experimenting with XP at their laboratory based in American Fork, Utah. XP was in through the backdoor!

This case study is based in part on the article "Going to Extremes" by Alexandra Morales, which appeared in the January 2002 issue of *Software Development Magazine*.

The development team, which was working on a new Java-based security product code-named Orca, adopted XP over other heavy alternatives such as PSP (Personal Software Process). A degree of support for XP at both management and developer levels had already been obtained, which simplified the selection of XP.

One of the XP practices we've learned about is that of the onsite customer; clearly this is a challenge when writing a commercial software product! An internal product manager acted as pseudo-customer for the team, which helped to resolve the missing customer problem. Another Symantec XP project fell into problems when the product manager was not colocated with the team. The issues were not technical in nature, but rather that the team lacked clear direction. The team floundered without clarity on what exactly the "customer" wanted.

Quality Assurance was integral to the process at Symantec, as you'd expect from a commercial software development project. The role of QA in the XP project was primarily twofold: to write acceptance tests and to provide user-centered feedback. In keeping with XP philosophy, the development team worked with QA to automate their tests into a complete suite.

Developers work with their automated test tools, such as JUnit, and are intent on code-level tests, but these programmer-friendly tests don't always satisfy QA. The team produced detail defect reports in XML; these were then translated into graphs and summary form. QA began to specify tests whenever they could to ease part of this tension between test results produced by developers and useful output for QA.

XP seemed well suited to the software-engineering culture at Symantec, with its specific development practices and lightweight process requirements. Senior management buy-in and support was a key factor in the adoption rate and success of XP at Symantec.

Lessons Learned

Here is a summary of the lessons learned from this project:

- Without an onsite customer the team will lack direction and focus.
- QA must be tightly coupled with the development team.
- Grass-roots support will smooth the transition to XP.
- Management buy-in is crucial to the success of XP.
- Expect comprise between existing methodologies and XP.

Case Study: Pushing the Limits of XP on a Large Project

ThoughtWorks, Inc. is a systems integrator based in Chicago. This case study explains how ThoughtWorks tackled the challenge of a large-scale development by using Extreme Programming techniques. Their project began with a Waterfall approach that featured heavy, up-front design and requirements gathering. After around 18 months they switched to XP, even though conventional wisdom at the time pigeonholed XP as fitting only small-to-medium–sized projects.

The ATLAS project was a leasing applications system, and the client was looking for software visibility. Where was the system development really? XP was ideal from the angle of control and risk reduction; the question remained over its applicability to such a large system.

The project team comprised of around 35 developers, 15 analysts, and 10 QA staff. The analysts acted in the role of customer, filtering requirements, writing user stories, and setting priorities. It wasn't practical to expect a single customer representative to address all the questions posed by the development team. The development team was able to split into a number of work streams that covered the entire system.

Of the XP practices both Pair Programming and continuous integration were seen as pivotal in the success of the project. Pair Programming was used almost exclusively, the only exceptions being maintenance tasks and when the engineering task was very similar to an existing solution. The team reasoned that pairing returned the most benefits while programmers solved difficult problems, and that subsequent tasks were little more than typing. It became clear that individual personalities also had to be considered because there was a variation in the length and frequency that a developer could pair. Sometimes developers simply needed a break! Pairs formed around user stories, and these normally lasted for the length of the iteration.

Iteration lengths started at four weeks, but estimation and, therefore, tracking proved difficult. In time, the iteration length was lowered to two weeks, admittedly this is on the low side for an iteration length, but it did increase control. The shortened iteration helped the team improve their estimates and gave the customer finer-grained control over the release.

As you can imagine, a project of this size necessitated a robust automated build and test harness. Integration results were automatically reported to the project Web site. Automated build and test was crucial as the code base grew and the team was drawn into refactoring. The development asked for time to be set aside for refactoring, and project managers built this into the cycle.

20

So, you can do XP on a large project, but you should expect some degree of local tailoring. Spend some time up front on making sure that your toolset is established and working.

Lessons Learned

Here is a summary of the lessons learned on this project:

- Use the smallest possible release cycles.
- Write and maintain a complete suite of automated unit tests.
- Collective code ownership requires strong communication with the development team.
- Large or complex projects might need a group to act as the customer.
- Supplement your code with external documentation that gives the big picture; this will help new developers as they join the project.

Summary

It has been very useful to review how organizations have used XP to solve quite different problems. The challenges of a large project with the need to manage a large and diverse source code base, were helped with continuous integration and Pair Programming. Our public sector case study uncovered the fact that we need to pay careful attention to how we write contracts; do they match the way we will deliver. If you're a software vendor, you can substitute the customer for an internal resource who responds to scope and quality questions.

We also learned of a case where the project was deemed a success, but there was a cost attached—the loss of a valued developer. The trick is to succeed in both the short and long term; on the one hand meeting your customer expectations and on the other ensuring you transition your people with respect and care.

The next hour we will start our final part by looking in depth at what refactoring is and how you can use it.

Q&A

Q Where can I go for more information on user experiences with XP?

A Wiki Wiki has a list of XP projects underway at `http://www.c2.com/cgi/wiki?ExtremeProgrammingProjects`. Other case studies can be found at the following links:

`http://www.sun.com/service/sunps/success/case_studies/escrow_cs4.html`

`http://fc-md.umd.edu/projects/Agile/Maurer.htm`

`http://www.id-book.com/casestudy_xp.htm`

Workshop

This workshop tests whether you understand all the concepts you learned today. It is very helpful to know and understand the answers before starting tomorrow's lesson.

Quiz

1. What did you learn from the public sector case study?

    a. Governments just don't get XP!

    b. Make sure the contract matches the delivery approach.

    c. Pair Programming should be slowly implemented.

    d. Development speed is not simply linked to programmer productivity.

2. What area did the firm that implemented XP midway through their project fall down on?

    a. They failed to educate the customer about XP.

    b. They let developers work overtime.

    c. Refactoring was not given enough value.

    d. They ran roughshod over real developer concerns and paid the price by losing valued team members.

3. How did Symantec deal with the "missing customer" problem?

    a. They empowered developers to make assumptions.

    b. The product manager acted as the customer.

    c. The QA team supplied user-interface testers.

    d. They conducted extensive beta tests on the public.

4. Why did ThoughtWorks shorten their iteration length?

    a. To improve estimations and control.

    b. To speed delivery to the customer.

    c. To enable developers to switch pair more frequently.

    d. To increase the development team's sense of urgency.

20

Answers

1. b.

2. d.

3. b.

4. a.

Activity

Visit the XP Wiki Wiki Web site at `http://www.c2.com/cgi/wiki?ExtremeProgramming`
and start your research into XP projects currently underway. Search for your area of
interest and contact the relevant to gain first-hand user feedback. You will find case studies and user experiences throughout the `www.c2.com` Web site.

PART VI

Extending the Use of XP and Other Advanced Topics

Hour

HOUR 21

More on Refactoring Techniques

In this hour we will dig a little deeper into how to refactor your code. Refactoring might sound a little threatening or confusing at first, but working through this hour will get your refactoring habit started. I'll even explain how you can refactor your next PowerPoint presentation! Here are some of the key points you'll be learning about during this hour:

- Why refactoring is important
- How you can start refactoring
- When you should stop refactoring
- How to look for the indicators that tell you what to refactor
- Example refactorings
- How you can apply the mindset behind refactoring to other nonprogramming specific tasks

Understanding the Need to Refactor

We learned in Hour 6, "XP Practices in Action," that refactoring is the practice of improving code without changing the observable behavior of the component. Refactoring puts order into the process of cleaning up your code. Poorly designed code is not *simple* code, so you must be doing things the hard way! Some readers misunderstand the purpose of refactoring and assume that improving performance is one of the reasons to rework code. In fact, refactoring is more likely to decrease performance because the source code is modified to increase readability and lower maintenance overheads. The reasoning behind refactoring is that small decreases in performance are acceptable; any particular speed-sensitive areas of the system are typically hand-tuned anyway.

The standard reference on refactoring is Martin Fowler's *Refactoring— Improving the Design of Existing Code*. Fowler spends more than 400 pages focused solely on the subject of refactoring. This is a great resource if you want to go in depth on the subject of refactoring.

Program source code is the intermediate language that developers use to communicate with the machine. A second aspect of the code is that it explains the logic to developers. XPers expect the source code to express intent in such a way that comments are often superfluous. Another handy side-effect of refactoring is that defects or bugs are uncovered before they strike. Even in cases where you have good coverage of unit tests, you might still miss defects. Remember that testing does not guarantee that no defects exist. Actually, the reverse is true because testing only serves to expose problems, defects, and bugs!

Refactoring without test-first programming is like walking the high wire without a net! Refactoring works well in XP as developers write their unit tests before they return to the code at a later date.

Losing a few CPU clock-cycles in performance because you refactored will be made up for by the increased speed of development. You might be surprised to learn that refactoring can increase your speed. The reasons are that the code-base has improved quality and fewer defects. Also, programmers waste less time trying to understand unfamiliar code.

Selling Refactoring to Management

Generally speaking, developers have little problem seeing the benefits of refactoring and when given guidance are keen to begin improving their code. Selling the idea to management is not quite as simple because after the tests have passed; what is the point of revisiting the work? Constantly tinkering with the source code until perfection is reached doesn't sound like very good business practice! You have a couple of options here; you could either spend time explaining the longer-term cost benefits or simply add refactoring time into your estimates. In reality, refactoring is another code construction skill like any other. Do you explain those to your management?

The quality aspects of refactoring are clear, which will help if you choose to sell the idea to project managers or managers. The important thing is to maintain accurate estimations that include testing, coding, and refactoring.

You should explain that refactoring is a natural outworking of Pair Programming; the real-time code reviews exposing poorly written code.

When to Refactor

We found in one of our samples in Hour 20, "Learning from XP Case Studies," that some project teams set aside specific time to refactor. They took the approach that developers should work at full-speed on delivering user stories, and they should refactor only at the end of the iteration. You can see that without firm coaching and leading, some developers might spend too much time reworking the code. A better way to handle refactoring is to evolve the practice until it becomes ingrained normal day-to-day development cycle. Refactoring then becomes a habit like test-first programming and not a special activity reserved for when you have time.

Kent Beck and others talk of the idea that "code smells," which means that there are indicators that point to bad code.

Refactoring has these simple steps:

- Recognize a code smell (problem indicator)
- Select the relevant refactoring
- Run your test before you change the code
- Apply the refactoring
- Rerun the tests
- Look for any other code smells and continue refactoring if required

21

Challenges to Refactoring

As mentioned in the opening note, you must have a test harness before you begin refactoring. Without an automated test harness, the Quality Assurance costs and slow test cycle make the process of refactoring far too expensive. If you're dealing with a legacy system and are intent in refactoring, you could write a series of tests focused on that particular piece of code before you started work. At that point though, you are probably interested in performance bottlenecks or bugs and are not concerned with readability.

Database refactoring is one area that poses some real challenges. Consumers have often linked directly to the physical structure of the database with databases, systems, or data. Any change in the database is almost guaranteed to break someone's code downstream. Developers sometimes use the approach of creating a data façade or wrapper layer that sits between the database and the outside world. This method of hiding the database from users can help with refactoring. The data layer approach means that an intermediate component presents a standard interface to outside callers. Database structure changes only need to be reworked in this middle-tier object layer.

Increasingly database vendors are allowing users to read and write in XML. It's not exactly clear at this stage how this will help in refactoring, but it is easy see how XML could be used to further abstract the database. What would a database refactor look like anyway? Areas to focus in on would be table structures and relationships. Tools such as Microsoft's SQL Server Enterprise Manager enable the developer to save a complete database script command file. These are automatically generated after database structure has been modified and, because they are pure text, they can be easily versioned controlled.

Refactoring Ideas

Have you ever been told that your code stinks! I hope not! Source code often has indicators that point to possible problems—in other words, the *code smells*. This has nothing to do with developer hygiene! We'll take a few pages to describe some code smells and example refactorings you can apply to clean up your code. Our examples will follow this format:

- Name and description of the refactoring
- Indicators to look for in your code
- Example source code that shows the before and after views

We will round out this session with a summary table that links each code smell with its refactoring. Let's get started.

Extract Method

Turn a code fragment into a method, the name of which explains its purpose.

Indicator: Duplicated Code

Duplicated code could be one of the more common problems found with source code. The code is either exactly the same or almost the same as it is elsewhere in the class. Another case of this code smell is where two separate classes have code duplication.

Example

In the example found in Table 21.1 you can see how we replaced the code, which prints out fruit items, with a new method. The new method `PrintFruitItem()` now takes the fruit name, price, and running total and formats the printed output.

TABLE 21.1 Extract Method Example

Before	After
```class extract_method{```	```Class extract_method2{```

```
class extract_method{


    public static void main(String[]
➥args)


{
    String fruit[]={"apple","plum",
➥"peach","pear","orange" };
    double prices[]={ 1.23, 3.45, 4.80,
➥ 5.00, 1.05 };

    int x;
    double running_total= 0;

    PrintHeader();

    for( x = 0 ; x <fruit.length; x++){
        running_total+=prices[x];
        System.out.print ("|");
        System.out.println ( fruit[x] +
➥ "\t|\t" + prices[x] + "\t|\t"
➥+ running_total);


    }

    PrintFooter();


}
```

```
Class extract_method2{

    Public static void main(String[]
➥args)
{
    String fruit[]={"apple","plum",
➥"peach","pear","orange" };
    double prices[]={ 1.23, 3.45, 4.80,
➥ 5.00, 1.05 };

    int x;
    double running_total= 0;

    PrintHeader();

    for( x = 0 ; x <fruit.length; x++){

        running_total+=prices[x];

        PrintFruitItem( fruit[x],
➥prices[x], running_total);
    }

    PrintFooter();

}

    static void     PrintHeader(){
        System.out.println ("Fruit
➥Price List");
```

21

TABLE 21.1 continued

Before	After
```static void PrintHeader(){```	``` System.out.println ("--------```
``` System.out.println ("Fruit```	``` ----------");```
```Price List");```	
``` System.out.println ("--------```	``` }```
``` ----------");```	
``` }```	```static void PrintFooter(){```
```static void PrintFooter(){```	``` System.out.println ("-------```
``` System.out.println ("--------```	``` -----------");```
``` --------");```	``` System.out.println ("End of```
``` System.out.println ("End of```	```price List!");```
```price List!");```	``` }```
``` }```	
	```static void PrintFruitItem(String```
```}```	``` fruit, double price, double total){```
	``` System.out.print ("|");```
	``` System.out.println (fruit +```
	``` "\t|\t" + price + "\t|\t" + total);```
	``` }```
	```} }```

Replace Magic Number with Symbolic Constant

Create a constant, name it after the meaning, and replace the number with it. Programming 101 is where you learned that using literal values in your code is a definite no-no. The reasons for this are clear: Readability and maintenance are impacted. An obvious value to you on the rainy day you cut that code has somehow lost its meaning today.

Indicator: Literal Value Used

Look for occurrences in your code of values (not just numbers) that appear out of nowhere. Literals sometimes happen when you're in midflow during development. For example, take the case when you're busy writing a pricing module and as a quick hack you decided to hardcode the sales tax. Let's hope you catch that during refactoring!

Example

The example in Table 21.2 is a simple weight converter that takes pounds and converts into kilograms. In the before listing you will note that the magic number of 2.2 is used for conversion. The issue of the magic number is resolved by replacing with a new human-readable, constant named KILO_CONVERSION_FACTOR.

TABLE 21.2   Replace Magic Number with Symbolic Constant Example

Before	After
| ```
public class constant {

    public static void main(String[]
➡ args)

    {
    double kilos;

    kilos = ConvertPoundsToKilos(
➡ Double.parseDouble(args[0]) ) ;

    System.out.println( args[0]   +
➡" pounds is " + kilos + " kilos");

    }

    static double ConvertPoundsToKilos
➡( double pounds )
    {

        return   pounds / 2.2 ;

    }
}
``` | ```
public class constant2 {

static final double KILO_CONVERSION_
➡FACTOR = 2.2;

    public static void main(String[]
➡args)

    {
        double kilos;

        kilos = ConvertPoundsToKilos
➡(   Double.parseDouble(args[0]) ) ;

        System.out.println( args[0]
➡+ " pounds is " + kilos + " kilos");

    }

    static double
ConvertPoundsToKilos
➡( double pounds )
    {
    return   pounds /
KILO_CONVERSION_
➡FACTOR   ;
    }

}
``` |

Inline Temp

Replace all references to that temporary variable with the expression.

Indicator: Temporary Field

You have a temporary variable that is assigned once with a simple expression, and the variable is getting in the way of other refactorings.

Example

In the example listing given in Table 21.3 you can observe another problem with the source code. This time the "smell" is caused by the use of the kilos variable. This variable has no other purpose than to hold the result of the conversion function. In the "after" listing kilos is removed and we simply use the return value from ConvertPoundsToKilos() in the print method.

21

TABLE 21.3 Inline Temp Example

Before	After
| ```
public class temp {

static final double KILO_CONVERSION_
➥FACTOR = 2.2;

    public static void main(String[]
➥args)

    {
        double kilos;

        kilos = ConvertPoundsToKilos
➥(  Double.parseDouble(args[0]) ) ;
        System.out.println( args[0]
➥+ " pounds is " + kilos + " kilos");
    }

    static double ConvertPoundsToKilos
➥( double pounds )
    {
        return  pounds / KILO_
➥CONVERSION_FACTOR  ;
    }
}
``` | ```
public class temp2 {

static final double KILO_CONVERSION_
➥FACTOR = 2.2;

    public static void main(String[]
➥args)
    {
        System.out.println( args[0]
➥+ " pounds is " +
➥ConvertPoundsToKilos(
➥Double.parseDouble(args[0]) )
➥+ " kilos");
    }

    static double
ConvertPoundsToKilos
➥( double pounds )
    {
        return  pounds / KILO_
➥CONVERSION_FACTOR  ;
    }
}
``` |

Introduce Assertion

Make the assumption explicit with an assertion.

Indicator: Comments

Comments are mostly a good thing, and they definitely aid in readability. There is another aspect of comments: when the programmer uses them to describe difficult code. Why not change the code and thereby remove the need to comment. See the coffee break in this hour for a real-life example of how comments can indicate poorly written code.

Example

The example in Table 21.4 is a classic case where a comment exists to explain an assumption or code fragment. You may still need a comment, but either way, you should raise an assertion or exception if the condition fails. Often times the comment reads something like "the user should never get here." Software languages have different ways of catering for assertions, Visual Basic programmers, for example, would most likely use the Raise method.

TABLE 21.4   Introduce Assertion Example

Before	After
| ```
public class asserttest{

static    double _age = 28;

    void SetAge( double value )    {

    // Age must be greater than zero!

        if ( _age >= 0 )
            _age = value;
    }
}
``` | ```
public class asserttest2 {

static    double _age = 28;
    void SetAge( double value )    {

    Assert.fail( "bad age value",
➥value <= 0 );

        if ( _age >= 0 )
            _age = value;
    }
``` |

Replace Parameter with Explicit Methods

Create a separate method for each value of the parameter.

Indicator: Switch Statement

Switch or case statements are another form of duplication. In this case, the code is almost the same, and case statements have a habit of cropping up all over your code. There are a few refactorings we could apply to remove this code; we'll choose one as an example.

Example

A common approach when dealing with objects that have numerous properties is to use a generic "setter" or "getter" method. One advantage here is that changes to object interfaces are less painful. A downside is that you're code will end up with more duplication, which will impact maintainability. The example in Table 21.5 removes the generic setter method, replacing it with the relevant set methods. Any consumer of the object will find the new version much simpler to work with (no need to track key values).

TABLE 21.5   Replace Parameter with Explicit Methods Example

Before	After
| ```
public class explicit {

static    double _age = 28;
static    double _height= 1.7 ;
static    double _weight = 87;

    void SetDemoData( String key ,
➥double value )    {
``` | ```
public class explicit2 {

static    double _age = 28;
static    double _height= 1.7 ;
static    double _weight = 87;

    void SetAge ( double value ) {
        _age = value;
    }
``` |

21

TABLE 21.5 continued

Before	After
| ```
        if ( key.equals("age")   ) {
            _age = value;
            return;
        }

        if ( key.equals("height") ) {
            _height = value ;
            return;
        }

        if ( key.equals("weight") ) {
            _weight = value;
            return;
        }
    }
}
``` | ```
    void SetHeight( double value ){
        _height = value ;
    }

    void SetWeight( double value ){

        _weight = value;
    }
}
``` |

Summary of Our Refactorings

A handy way to start refactoring is to keep a short list of code smells and their requisite refactoring. Table 21.6 summarizes the refactorings we've covered over the last few pages. Use this as starting point.

TABLE 21.6 Summary of Refactorings

Code Smell	Refactoring
Duplicated Code	Extract Method
Literal Value Used	Replace Magic Number with Symbolic Constant
Switch statement	Replace Parameters with Explicit methods
Temporary Field	Inline Temp
Comments	Introduce assertion

Uncovering Code Smells

Sometimes you just have a sense that your code just isn't quite *right*. This is known as the "code smells." I came across perhaps one of the more common smells the other day, comments. We are all taught that commented code should be a habit ingrained into every developer's mind. Adding comments to generate JavaDoc and so forth is certainly a good idea. Sometimes, however, your comments might be covering up poorly written code.

This is what happened to me—I was working on some Visual Basic .NET code and found myself adding a comment to clarify why I was using a certain IF statement. The code was something like this:

```
If Len(oTarget("IndentityColumn"))>0  Then
    ' Do some work here…
End if
```

I realized this was a little cryptic, so I began to add a helpful comment to explain to the next poor developer. But wait! Why was I explaining the code with comments? I decided to remove the comment by creating a new property on the oTarget class that described the IF statement. The resulting code looked like this:

```
If oTarget.HasIdentityKey Then
    ' Do some work…
End if
```

By the way the property was no more than this:

```
Public ReadOnly Property HasIdentityKey() As Boolean
    Get
        Return Len(_strIndentityColumn) > 0
    End Get
End Property
```

Five minutes well spent! Uncovering this smell resulted in me being open to other refactoring opportunities.

Getting into the Refactoring Habit

You now have a small bag of refactoring tips and are champing at the bit to start using them. The goal is to integrate refactoring into your daily development routine. What could be harder than learning *how* to refactor is knowing when to *stop*! Refactoring isn't a license to spend all the development team's time fine-tuning and simplifying the code. Typically, on an XP project the coach leads refactorings and also keeps a watchful eye on excessive or blind-alley refactoring. Blind-alley is when the team or developer begins refactoring, uncovers some smells, which in turn leads to more work and before long the day is gone!

Avoid the blind-alley problem by making small, incremental changes and test after each change. It's natural that your confidence grows, which could lead to you making lots of changes before you retest. If you do this you'll find you've lifted the hood to discover that your car is broken! Refactoring is like weeding your garden; you should tackle no more than you can get done by nightfall. Unless you like to leave your garden in a mess!

21

Grow into a refactoring habit by focusing on a handful of code smells and their requisite refactorings. For example, start by keeping your eyes open for the comment code smell and use the extract method refactoring to clean it up. After you've found that this new mode has become second nature, add another refactoring to your arsenal. Another implementation technique is to allow developers to "adopt" a code smell/refactoring. They can investigate how the refactoring is expressed in the local development language and take the responsibility to explain to the wider team. This works well with XP because Pair Programming enhances communication throughout the team. Pretty soon the whole team will be confident with the new refactoring.

Pair Programming brings balance to refactoring as the tendency to spend too much time on the task is constrained by the other developer. Conversely, the partner can catch his colleague if she is charging on without taking time to clean up code. The best way to do this is to note the need to come back and address a code smell at some future point. Use your project Wiki Wiki as a place to jot notes about refactoring opportunities.

It's unreasonable to expect the team to digest a complete catalog of refactorings; a better solution is to let the use of refactoring evolve over time.

Refactoring More Than Code

Even though refactoring is primarily a software development task, you can apply the concepts to other roles in which you operate. If we describe refactoring as "making things simpler and easier," we could use it beyond programming. One example is the process of managing the XP project itself. XP is a little loose on what tools you should use for tracking and managing. The general rule is to use just enough and no more. You might have started with a complex suite of charts and monitoring tools to track the team. After a few weeks, however, you find that work involved in maintaining and updating, exceeds its value. So, you simplify the way you track, perhaps using one or two measures, at the same time ensuring that the sponsor or management get the numbers they need.

On another occasion you might be presenting a talk on XP to your peers (no doubt energized by this book!), and you start with 75 PowerPoint slides! Luckily you've just finished this Hour, so the idea of refactoring is still fresh in your mind. You reflect on your audience, and then trim down your content to a nimble 15 slides. You've changed the "code," but kept the observable behavior (presentation goals) the same.

User interface designers are well versed in the benefits of simplifying. User interface designers are frequently interested in usability (making the application easier to use). They mask or hide users from the inner mechanics of the application. You can follow this with interfaces that you design; take the working system and make it simpler and, where it makes sense, push the complexities underneath the presentation.

A great book on the philosophy behind good design is Donald Norman's *The Design of Everyday Things*. This has nothing to do with XP per se, but is still very useful if you want to apply refactoring-type thinking to design. Another gem is *The Human Interface* by Jef Raskin, the creator of the Apple Macintosh. A story of simple design all by itself, and Apple Mac's *still* have a one-button mouse!

Refactoring Resources

Refactoring is catching on like wild fire as evidenced by the tools support that is now available. Java developers are spoiled with some IDEs shipping with refactoring tools out of the box. Microsoft .NET programmers are just now seeing some support in their development suites. This is not surprising given that Visual Studio .NET only shipped in February 2002. Don't let lack of tools support put you off of refactoring; start today and keep a watch for new tools on the Open Source sites. In the meantime we've included a list of the main IDEs and tools that contain refactoring features (see Table 21.7).

TABLE 21.7 Tools That Support Refactoring

Tool	Description	Link
jFactor	Refactoring plug-in for Visual Age and JBuilder.	http://www.instantiations.com/jfactor/
IDEA	IntelliJ IDEA is a full-featured Java IDE with advanced code editing and refactoring support.	http://www.intellij.com/idea/
JBuilder	Java IDE with refactorings built-in.	http://www.borland.com/jbuilder/
CodeMorpher	Refactoring browser and code analyzer for java.	http://www.xptools.com/
ControlCenter	Java IDE suite with refactoring support.	http://www.togethersoft.com/
RefactorIT	Java-based product either use as standalone or as plug-in for NetBeans, Jdeveloper, and JBuilder.	http://www.refactorit.com/
Eclipse	IDE framework for Java with support for refactoring.	http://www.eclipse.org/
Refactoring Browser	SmallTalk browser. The one that started it all!	http://chip.cs.uiuc.edu/users/brant/Refactory/
Xrefactory	Refactoring browser for Emacs	http://xref-tech.com/speller/

21

TABLE 21.7   continued

Tool	Description	Link
Retool	Add-in for two Java IDE's: Oracle 9i JDeveloper and Borland JBuilder 4/5.	http://www.chive.com/products/retool/
.NET Refactoring	Microsoft C# refactoring add-in for Visual Studio .NET.	http://www.dotnetrefactoring.com/
SharpDevelop	Open Source C# IDE with some refactoring support.	http://www.icsharpcode.net/

Summary

You may have been refactoring, to one degree or another, for years. You could say that refactoring is another case where XP takes a practice and then accelerates its use. There is a growing catalog of examples in both Web and print media to help you. You're not on your own! You can take what you've learned in this hour and put form and shape around your code clean-up tasks. As a developer your own code quality will improve and will influence your peers toward better programming practices. Two final words—start small!

In the next hour we'll leave the world of programming and discover how XPs barriers can be extended beyond small development teams.

Q&A

Q Would spending time on up-front design remove the need to refactor?

A No. Some of your refactorings will be the result of change; for example, a class that was fine at release is now a candidate for change.

Q Are there any other interesting Web sites on refactoring?

A The unofficial home is at http://www.refactoring.com/. The XP Wiki Wiki Web has many pages devoted to the subject, start looking at http://c2.com/cgi/wiki?CategoryRefactoring. Wiki Wiki has some great comments on refactoring non-Java code such as Microsoft COM.

Workshop

This workshop tests whether you understand all the concepts you learned in this hour. It is very helpful to know and understand the answers before starting the next lesson.

Quiz

1. What must you have before you start refactoring?

    a. A set of unit tests.

    b. A good grasp of the method and approach.

    c. A tool that supports refactoring.

    d. Time allotted by your project manager.

2. What does the term "code smells" refer to?

    a. Code that fails to conform to agreed standards.

    b. Code that has indicators that point to poor coding practices.

    c. Code that fails unit tests.

    d. Code that has yet to be refactored.

3. What is the "magic number" an example of?

    a. A numeric value that as an indeterminate state.

    b. A literal value in source code, whose meaning is unclear.

    c. A special value required by the source code.

    d. A code smell.

4. What is the best approach to take when refactoring?

    a. Set aside time on your project plan for the work.

    b. Let the best developer do all of the important work.

    c. Systematic approach driven by the technical lead.

    d. Start with tests, and then make small changes. Retest after each change.

Answers

1. a.

2. b.

3. b., d.

4. d.

21

Activities

1. Revisit our Windows Forms example in Hour 17, "Making the Most of Ant to Automate Your XP Project." Refactor the code using some of the examples from this hour.

2. Take one code smell and its refactoring, and then apply it to your language tool. Look for ways you can use this new refactoring.

3. Visit the refactoring Web site at `http://www.refactoring.com/` and become familiar with the catalog of refactorings. Add your own!

HOUR 22

Extending the Limits of XP

XP began as an approach that worked well for small-to-medium software development teams. This hour covers how you can push XP beyond these boundaries into large, distributed development projects. You will learn

- What XP practices need to be updated to work in a distributed project
- How to use feature teams to separate work into development streams
- How you can still Pair Program in a distributed project
- How you can overcome the limitations of distance when planning
- The software tools you can use to help with large-scale or distributed projects

Learning How to Scale Your XP Project

We know that XP works well for small-to-medium teams that are colocated with customers, but can it work with larger teams? In Hour 20, "Learning from XP Case Studies," you learned how one XP development team successfully pushed the envelope by running XP with a large project team. So, it is possible to run a large-scale project with XP. Let's discover how we can do it.

Does it really matter if XP has problems scaling up to a large project? QSM, Inc. (http://www.qsm.com) reported that the average size of a project team is around 10–20 team members. Large government projects, such as those initiated by the Department of Defense, can span years. In reality, how many Space Shuttle–like projects exist? You could reasonably argue that smaller, incremental development is best in the world of business. The anti-XP lobby is quick to claim that XP can't scale, or be used in distributed environments. This can't be proven, however, because the jury is still out on the subject. We have to remember that XP is still a new, evolving software development approach, and there is no wide body of evidence to prove the case either way. What we can do is consider the hindrances of scaling up XP, and then how we might overcome them.

Scalability is the capability of the system to continue to function well as it is changed in size or volume to meet a user need or demand. In a process or methodology context, it includes how well the tools, practices, and procedures function in a larger-sized project.

XP hinges on the close communication and feedback between team members—dry documents are replaced by conversation and human contact. In a sense, you could say that XP *tightly couples* the team members. We know from software-architecture theory that linking or coupling components will ultimately kill both scalability and flexibility. The advent of three-tier architecture designs in the 90s was a direct response to challenges posed by issues of increasing user demand. Software developers writing applications for the Web have no control over how many users access their system, which makes selecting a highly flexible platform very important. The idea today is that, as their needs grow, customers can plug-in more database or Web servers. Sometimes it's not always that simple. We can apply the lessons learned in Web development to how we scale up XP.

Let's take a look at each XP practice and consider whether it could limit scalability. Table 22.1 lists each practice and indicates possible problems. The column on the right of our table is a best guess on the effectiveness of the practice in large-scale or distributed projects.

The grade scale in Table 22.1 measures each practice from A (excellent) to D (poor).

TABLE 22.1   The Scalability of the XP Practices

Practice	Scalability Issue	Grade
The Planning Game	Relies heavily on whole team involvement for prioritization, planning, and estimation and work allocation.	D
Small Releases	Not affected.	A
Metaphor	Probably too weak or abstract to be supported in a disconnect medium. But can be supported by Web-based communication.	C
Simple Design	Not affected.	B
Testing	Not affected.	A
Refactoring	No direct effect, but the push to refactor might not be evenly spread, resulting in some parts of the system being cleaner than others.	B
Pair Programming	Pair Programming relies on close, verbal contact. Switching pairs is not always possible!	D
Collective Ownership	Source control systems, such as CVS or Visual SourceSafe, work equally well across locations. Merge conflicts with CVS might be harder to resolve when developers are in different time zones.	D
Continuous Integration	Integrated development environments and automated build tools such as Ant can help here. Larger projects might require master build files, which could increase build maintenance overhead.	C
40-Hour Work Week	Not affected.	A
Onsite Customer	This is a problem because the customers and development groups need to be in close proximity.	D
Coding Standards	No issues. Coding Standards are usually maintained on the Wiki or project Web site.	A

Separating into Feature Teams

One option you have on a large project, say with 50 developers, is to separate into feature teams of 10 developers each. The feature team could work on logical pieces of the system—for example, customer management or billing. This is the familiar divide-and-conquer strategy where we break down the problem into smaller, bite-sized chunks. Doing this enables us to tackle work in parallel streams and can be very effective on larger projects. As the old saying goes, "today's problems are caused by yesterday's solutions," and this is true with divide and conqueror. To explain, by creating separate work streams we now have the problem of maintaining communication between the teams, which is no more evident than with system integration. Conflicts or integration breaks are more likely as development teams complete their work and commit into the source repository.

Figure 22.1 demonstrates how you can separate your work into feature teams.

FIGURE 22.1

Seperating your project into feature teams.

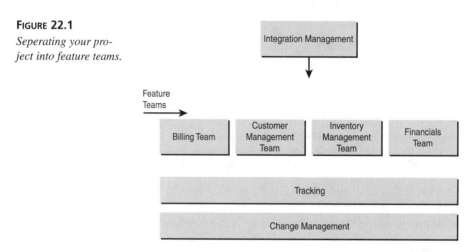

In our example, there are four feature teams covering billing, customer management, inventory, and financials. An integration manager, whose role is to ensure smooth integration between development streams, presides over the entire project or program. Underneath there is an overall tracking function that summarizes complete project status. Change management is an example of a work stream that runs through the project. This work stream is responsible for managing the acceptance of the system by the wider customer community. Usually, change management also covers training, communication, and public relations. Though not strictly part of a standard XP project we've added it here to demonstrate the inclusive nature of most large projects.

The creation of these new work streams impacts the ability to successfully run the XP practice of collective ownership. As the scale of our project grows, collective ownership changes from a benefit to a potential source of headache and complexity. Automation of build process can help here, but falls down where a centralized source repository is not in use. Integration of the work streams is a technical issue that can be resolved by clearly defining interstream boundaries. One way to do this is to document (the "d" word) interface specifications such as API, object model, or XML DTD. An *integration pair* then holds the ownership of the interface. This pair is formed from the two work streams in question. They sit between the streams communicating with their customers and internal team members. Eventually they will gain equal appreciation for the other's subsystem. Figure 22.2 illustrates how the integration works with each team.

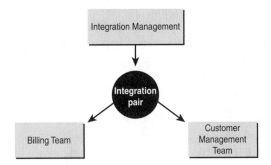

FIGURE 22.2
Using an integration pair.

The integration pair makes as many decisions as possible about interface or change-related issues. They can escalate outstanding issues to the integration manager; it's foreseeable that this role would consist of a group selected from each development stream. Let's look at how we can use the feature.

Extending Pair Programming

Nothing is inherent in Pair Programming that will limit its capability to scale; this is true if we limit its scope to programming alone. Where Pair Programming falls into problems is when it's used as a means of communication for wider aspects of design and overall understanding. Adding more pairs increases the number of communication paths within the team.

Pair Programming is in danger of failing in the cases where the development pair is not colocated or, even worse, not in the same time zone! Pair Programming requires synchronous communication; therefore, it can't rely on the use of disconnected tools such as email. Real-time collaboration tools, such as instant message or chat applications such as Yahoo! Messenger, are much more helpful. These are listed at the end of the hour for your reference. Anecdotal evidence (via news groups and Wiki Wiki) tends to suggest the use of collaboration is a brave, yet flawed, attempt at solving the problem of disconnected development. So, the team can be distributed across locations as long as the pair is located in the same time zone.

Separating development pairs is inline with the divide-and-conquer approach outlined at the start of this section. However, partitioning the system in this manner reduces the benefits of knowledge sharing. If geography is not an issue, you can rotate individuals around to various sites, which would help develop better overall system understanding. Rotating developers like this also ensures they can conduct integration with minimal pain.

It goes without saying that a dispersed development team must have adequate network bandwidth to offset their lack of verbal communication. Some customers are reticent about giving software development teams access to the Internet. Without it you simply cannot operate in a collaborative manner, but don't assume that Internet access is a given! Instant message protocols might require extra network ports on the corporate firewall, which is guaranteed to raise the blood pressure of the IT support staff! Escalate the team's demands until you have a working infrastructure.

Planning Game

XP release planning occurs during the XP practice of the Planning Game. As you know, this is a highly collaborative and communication-intensive session. Typically, the team uses index cards, whiteboards, and paper to capture the customer's business needs and priorities. The fact that these media are used underlines that they are transitory in nature; that is, we use them for a while, and then discard or throw them away. At the beginning of the iteration a mini Planning Game is run where developers sign up for tasks. This also relies on direct, verbal communication. Quite clearly it's hard to see how the Planning Game, in its pure form, could work in a distributed environment.

One option is to enable the feature teams to run their domain-specific Planning Game where results will be reported back to the integration manager. Taking a similar approach to iteration planning (dependencies are not that big a deal, so take the risk and fix them later), we can delay some of the integration or planning issues until they arise. For example, the billing team is writing a reporting module that uses a common database layer; will their work break any other development teams code? We can answer this question or reduce the risk, by maintaining our test suite. Nightly builds and automated test suites will highlight problems soon enough.

Results from these Planning Games (user stories, plan, and tasks) can be entered into the project Wiki site or centralized document store. The Wiki approach fits well in the distributed environment because its bandwidth and client requirements are light (all you need is a Web browser). Information on an XP project can become stale or out of date quite quickly, so old content should be archived or deleted. If you're using a Wiki, you can use the administrator function to deprecate old pages. The whiteboard approach for displaying and tracking tasks, great for the collocated team situation, can still work for a multilocated team if they focus a Web camera on the centralized whiteboard! If this doesn't work you might have to fall back onto a calendaring or tracking application such as Microsoft Outlook or Lotus Notes. Do all you can with simple tools (such as Wiki Web and chat) and avoid these heavyweight solutions to your tracking problems. Calendaring does become important, however, when teams are located in different time zones. Try organizing a meeting with attendees from Australia, the United States, the United Kingdom, Singapore, and New Zealand! It's enough to turn anyone's hair gray!

22

Lack of Onsite Customer

The core XP practice of a dedicated onsite customer is severely limited by a distributed project. The XP customers have a big part to play; they sit with the team to answer questions, resolve business disputes, write tests, participate in the planning process, and set priorities. Customers create the user stories as a start to a conversation; they need continued developer-customer interaction as the work continues. The following coffee break describes an occasion when the lack of an onsite customer led to a degree of drift and miscommunication. It might be more practical for the customer to be relocated to the development site if the team can't be colocated with the customer. Remember that we use the term "customer" in a generic way to cover the entire business team. The project owner will not need to be colocated, but her key business representatives should be if at all possible. Your problem can be reduced if you take the feature team approach we covered previously—each business or feature team can have their own customer representative. The customer would have a similar structure to our integration pair approach where the business streams meet from time to time to ensure direction is synchronized. These meetings could be via telephone or Internet (such as Microsoft NetMeeting).

Whichever solution the project adopts, the development team must strive to have real-time access to the customer. At worst case, this could be cellphone or pager access, where the customer is effectively on call. This sounds like a great solution from a developer perspective, but might result in a sleep deprived and, therefore, cranky customer!

Another middle-ground solution is to designate either a team member (business analyst, for example) or local third party as the "customer." The customer is putting a degree of trust into the hands of the local representative; the XP practice of small releases helps here. The customer can see quickly (every few weeks) what the team is building. Difficult judgment calls can still be deferred to the real customer if the need arises. The local customer actor will maintain a daily status or feedback loop with the real customer. This could be either in a connected (telephone) or disconnected (email, voicemail) manner.

So, we can survive and thrive without the onsite customers as long as they are still available for close calls and the like. They should expect to make an appearance during the release Planning Game because this is less effective using virtual tools. Plus, it's a chance to get those frequent flyer miles up!

The Pain of Distance Development

I had a recent experience that underlined the challenges and pitfalls attached to large-scale software development. In this case, I was part of a project team that numbered more than 100 individuals, who were spread across the globe. There was no way we could be in the same place at the same time!

At least the software development team was colocated in the same room, but unfortunately the primary customer was in another country. The project began with a series of workshops between key architects and customer representatives. The outputs from these sessions were a high-level solution map and a technical architecture specification. The plan was to develop prototypes based on the solution map; the customer defined no detailed requirements. So, work began in earnest with developers building applications based on no more than a vision. Surprisingly, this worked quite well up to a point, but did result in some interface rework after the initial release.

I visited the customer site during phase two and discovered that business groups were becoming very frustrated with their lack of control. What was happening was that developers (who were thousands of miles away) were spending valuable time adding "cool" features rather than working on business issues. The disconnection between the development team and customer was resulting in a failure to deliver what the customer wanted.

During phase two of the same project we attempted to neutralize the drift problem by tightening project controls. Nonworking prototypes were delivered with functional specifications, which were signed off and managed. This did work at focusing the development team, but it was a less than perfect solution. In hindsight we should have insisted on an onsite customer representative.

Another aspect of the problems caused by distance became obvious during handover. The customer wanted more than deployment documentation; they wanted to make sure that their support staff had really come to grips with the system. To do this, they sent their core support team over to the development site for a few weeks at a time. This turned out to work quite well. In some cases their internal developers paired with our programmers to build some applications. This not only helped with knowledge sharing, but also put a face to a name. This was important after the site had gone live. The end result was a better working relationship based on some level of personal relationship.

Virtual Team Tools

Virtual software development is becoming a reality with the release of more applications that leverage the power of the Internet. You are misguided if you believe that having the right software tool or application *alone* will overcome your challenges with large-scale development. In an XP project, possibly spread around the world, we can use some of the tools listed in Table 22.2 to bridge the gap between team members.

TABLE 22.2 Tools That Support Virtual Development

Tool Type	Benefits	Examples
Instant Messaging	Shows team members who is online	MSN Messenger
	Allows real-time communication	Yahoo! Messenger
	Usually, free	ICQ
	Easy to learn and use	AOL Chat
Application Sharing	Allows team members to view source code across locations	Microsoft Terminal Server
	Supports Pair Programming	VNC
Searching Indexing	Allows team members to easily find content	Autonomy
		Microsoft Index Server
Document Management	Ensures integrity of documentation	FileNet
	Handles checkin/checkout and version control	Documentum
Source Management	Ensures software source code is versioned and secure	PVCS
		CVS
		Visual SourceSafe
Calendar	Allows team members to see each other's movements and availability	Microsoft Outlook/Exchange
	Allows easier scheduling of meetings	Lotus Notes
Virtual Meeting rooms	Allows team members to discuss and work	LiveLink
	Can support daily meetings	TeamSpace
		Teamplate
Knowledge Sharing	Allows team members to store and retrieve information	Wiki Wiki
		Project Web site
	Can be either structured or unstructured in nature	
Event Notification	Streamlines reporting on software development process (builds and so forth)	CruiseControl
		Exchange Server (with automation)
		Ant

22

Don't be overwhelmed by the list of tools in Table 22.2. You'll find that given access to the Internet, the development team will naturally start to use what they need. An example of this is instant messaging capability; encourage the use of applications such as MSN Messenger. Some third-party chat tools will interface with multiple message suppliers (such as AOL or Yahoo!) a good example of this is Fire by Epicware (`http://www.epicware.com/fire.html`). These applications remove the reliance on a single messaging system or platform.

Summary

Extreme Programming is pushing the limits of software development and now users of XP are seeing how far they can take this new approach. Initially, XP was optimized for small-to-medium–sized teams, but now it's becoming clear that it can be successfully used for distributed projects as well. A number of the XP practices require some lateral thinking for them to work. XPers are used to thinking outside of the box! We can use a wide range of software applications and tools to enable disconnected or large-scale development.

In the next hour we will look into another area where XP is being stretched—the use of modeling tools and techniques.

Q&A

Q Can you direct me to some research on the subject of distributed XP?

A The University of Calgary, Alberta is doing some interesting work with an approach they call MILOS (Minimally Invasive Long-Term Organizational Support). Their site is located at `http://sern.ucalgary.ca/~milos/`.

Workshop

This workshop tests whether you understand all the concepts you learned in this hour. It is very helpful to know and understand the answers before starting the next lesson.

Quiz

1. What is the main problem caused by using feature teams on large projects?

    a. Development speed is hard to measure.

    b. Individual team members fail to gain exposure to the whole system.

    c. Integration between each group becomes difficult as the pace of change increases.

    d. They fail to fit within the XP model.

2. What are some of the software application tools that can be useful when using Pair Programming in a distributed project?

   a. Project planning tools, such as Microsoft Project.

   b. Instant messaging or chat tools, such as ICQ or Yahoo! Messenger.

   c. Development suites such as IBM's VisualAge for Java.

   d. Wiki Wiki Web sites.

3. What is one way you can work without an onsite customer?

   a. Use virtual meeting tools such as NetMeeting.

   b. Instigate daily teleconferences with the team and customer.

   c. Use a Wiki Wiki Web site to communicate status.

   d. Designate a local or proxy customer that acts for the customer.

4. What is the one thing distributed development teams must insist on before they start work?

   a. That a project Wiki Wiki be established.

   b. Use of Web cams for meetings.

   c. That the customer be onsite at all times.

   d. Internet access.

Answers

1. c.

2. b.

3. d.

4. d.

Activity

1. Use your instant message application of choice (Yahoo!, MSN, AOL, ICQ, and so forth) and experiment with Pair Programming in a disconnect medium. You will need to find a colleague or friend!

Hour 23

Using Agile Modeling with XP

Extreme Programming is part of a growing number of Agile technologies and methods. A recent addition to this family of Agile methodologies is Agile Modeling (AM). This is an exciting approach that involves combining industry standard or best practice modeling with Agile thinking. You'll learn the following this hour:

- What Agile Modeling is
- How Agile Modeling shares basic values with XP
- What the values, principles, and practices of Agile Modeling are
- How Agile Modeling compares to XP
- How Agile Modeling can be used in an XP project

Taking a Tour Through Agile Modeling

There are a lot of street rumors and urban myths when it comes to XP; opinions abound about what it is and isn't. One of these mistaken perceptions is that XP has no documentation or modeling at all; programmers just get on with programming. There's a world of difference between light documentation or enough documentation and none at all. At one end is the hacker and at the other, the Agile developer who knows when to use techniques or tools at her disposal.

In a software engineering sense, *modeling* refers to the use of diagrams to describe a process, solution, or problem. These diagrams can be supported by documentation.

What is Agile Modeling? Don't worry; it has nothing to do with acrobatics and clay! Briefly, it is a practice-based methodology founded on values, principles with a goal to support and enable software development by the effective use of modeling tools and techniques. It isn't an explicit list of steps or procedures. The beauty of AM is that it allows each user to modify the approach to his local setting. There is much to compare between XP and AM.

AM was primarily developed by Scott Ambler. His Agile Modeling site (`http://www.agilemodeling.com/`) has a wealth of information on the subject.

This hour is based in part on Ambler's book *Agile Modeling: Effective Practices for Extreme Programming and the Unified Process* (Wiley, 2002). This is a must read for any XP developer who wants to use his or her modeling skills with Extreme Programming.

So, AM is doing "just enough" modeling but do we need modeling at all? Modeling is an important way to communicate between team members at all stages of the software development lifecycle. We begin the iteration with a collection of user stories and tasks; invariably questions arise from these high-level requirements. Questions like, "what should the screen look like?" or "So, what is the exact process of taking an order?" Soon you're at the whiteboard sketching and modeling to close the comprehension gap. Developers might use class diagrams or the like as they express lower-level understandings to each other. With AM, these models, whether on paper or whiteboard are typically thrown away after they outlive their usefulness. However, these models may be kept if they provide some value.

Before we investigate how we might use AM techniques on an XP project, we'll take a few minutes to get an overview of AM.

Agile Modeling Values

A methodology based on values—sound familiar? Scott Ambler makes no bones about being inspired by Kent Beck to take this approach from XP when he came to forming AM. AM values have added one extra value to our core XP values: humility. Developers can get possessive when it comes to "their" models and will resist and attempt to change or adjust. Some developers are also unwilling to work with others, particularly nontechnical people, because they don't have the humility to accept that others can also provide significant input into the overall effort. The truth is, often the model isn't wrong, but it simply fails to communicate. We could add humility as a value to XP but for now we'll leave that for XP version 2!

Table 23.1 lists the AM values and explains their relevance.

TABLE 23.1 Agile Modeling Values

Value	Description
Courage	Choosing AM requires courage; you're forced to rely more on your own judgment and experience, rather than blind adherence to the "book." It takes courage to admit that your model is weak or wrong and accept new direction.
Communication	Models exist for the purpose of communicating between people, including both stakeholders and developers. If a modeling approach fails to communicate, change it for one that does.
Feedback	Get feedback on your models early and often. Build the model as a team or group, letting it evolve in a shared space. Validate the model with your customer to ensure it is accurate and effectively explanatory.
Humility	Agile modelers hold their models loosely and will lay them down if required. They have the self-confidence to let others criticize or question. Sometimes your model is perfect but the customer just doesn't get it! It takes humility to discard your perfectly formed UML and let the customer doodle her thoughts.
Simplicity	Keep models and approaches as simple as possible and change tomorrow if you need to. Assume that the simple approach will work before you attempt the more complex.

UML (Unified Modeling Language) has become the industry standard for modeling over the last few years. At the time of writing it is still not the complete answer to all your modeling needs. It has no database or user interface modeling support and so you should expect to supplement it with other notations for these. The Web home of UML is at http://www.uml.org/.

23

Agile Modeling Core Principles

The core principles of AM give concrete definition; they are a less abstract guide than the five values. Developers who claim to be Agile Modelers must adhere to the principles listed in Table 23.2.

TABLE 23.2   Agile Modeling Core Principles

Principle	Description
Assume Simplicity	Keep your models as simple as possible and assume that the simplest solution is best. Only model what you need today and trust that you can remodel if needed.
Embrace Change	Change will happen on your project as understanding grows. Rather than fight changes to your models or views, accept them and have the courage to rebuild.
Enabling the Next Effort Is Your Secondary Goal	Development does not happen in a vacuum; others might need to extend or improve your project after you leave. Leave just enough documentation and models to enable the next team to win.
Incremental Change	Your models don't have to be perfect the first time; they will change over time as the project develops. Make small changes to models as required.
Maximize Stakeholder Investment	The team is producing software to maximize return for the customer. Does the model or documentation you're creating add to this value? There comes a point where some models exist for their own sake!
Model with a Purpose	Create models with an end in mind, not as exercises or because "that's the way you do it." Be clear in your own mind why you're creating the model; who is it for and what are you trying to communicate?
Multiple Models	There are many ways of modeling solutions; choose those that fit your situation. For example, data models for a database team. Remember that the UML is a good start, but that it isn't the complete solution.
Quality Work	Just enough modeling isn't a license for carelessness; strive to model in ways that accurately communicate.
Rapid Feedback	Getting quick feedback on your model will close the loop of understanding. Model a little, show, and then model again. This ensures your model is accurate while increasing your own knowledge.
Software Is Your Primary Goal	Models are but a means to the end; the end is to build software for your customer. Documentation and modeling must directly support the goal of software development.

TABLE 23.2 continued

Principle	Description
Travel Light	Traveling light means you have just enough documentation for your journey. Too little and the team will lose its way; too much and we've forgotten our primary goal is writing software not documents.

 A great quote from Ambler: "System documentation is a business decision." This means that whether you write documentation or save project artifacts, it is a cost-risk trade-off for the customer. As software developers we often assume that the customer must have system documentation for maintenance or support purposes. If they choose to forgo or reduce this, they risk that maybe they'll be exposed in the future.

Agile Modeling Secondary Principles

The principles covered in the previous section are necessary for Agile Modeling but a number of secondary principles can further enhance your modeling effectiveness. You might choose to add your own principles based on your own or the team's collective experience. Table 23.3 lists and describes the secondary principles.

TABLE 23.3 Agile Modeling Secondary Principles

Principle	Description
Content Is More Important than Representation	*What* is being conveyed is more important than the *way* you choosing to convey it. Don't get lost in inane arguments over CASE tools versus paper-based methods.
Everyone Can Learn from Everyone Else	Learning and education don't come from books alone; expect to learn while you work with others. Technology changes at such a pace that no one person can claim to know it all.
Know Your Models	As an Agile Modeler, you'll select different modeling techniques based on the situation. You can't do this if you lack clarity on the relative strengths and weaknesses of each.
Know Your Tools	Similar to Know Your Models, select the appropriate software tool based on your knowledge of the package rather than lack of experience with it. More often than not you'll choose paper over computer but there will still be times when you'll select a CASE tool or similar. Be prepared for this!

TABLE 23.3   Continued

Principle	Description
Local Adaptation	Keep in mind that AM is not a dogmatic approach to modeling; adapt and modify based on your own requirements and skills. There may be cases where your customer insists on certain modeling tools or standards. AM allows you the flexibility to accept and work with this.
Open and Honest Communication	Using a non-prescriptive approach like AM requires those on the team to express ideas, feelings, frustrations, and viewpoints. The team will make better more informed decisions by cultivating an open and honest workplace.
Work with People's Instincts	The customer gets that glazed look or begins to nod mechanically; this is a sign that you're not connecting. It's time to put aside your model and work through why communication has broken down. We're getting into the "touchy-feely" or EQ (Emotional Quotient) zone here but the reality is that you're talking to people not computers. Agile modelers will go with their instinct even when communication *seems* to be going well.

Agile Modeling Core Practices

AM's core practices are where the rubber meets the road, where the real work of modeling gets done. These practices are guided and framed by AM's values and principles. Table 23.4 lists the core practices of AM.

TABLE 23.4   Agile Modeling Core Practices

Practice	Description
Active Stakeholder Participation	AM works in part because it relies on customers to become actively engaged in the modeling process. This in turns requires that developers exhibit flexibility with modeling notation and approach.
Apply the Right Artifacts	Agile Modelers choose the right tool for the job. There are so many artifacts you could select: UML state diagram, data flow diagram, or conceptual data model. Apply the artifact that fits your situation—for example a physical data model when displaying database relationships.

TABLE 23.4 continued

Practice	Description
Collective Ownership	The team owns the models; this is encouraged by the use of collaborative tools like whiteboards that exist in shared space. Rather than allow a single developer to assume the role of "model guru," Agile Modelers spread the task to the wider team. This becomes even more important when the team comes to explaining "their" model to the customer.
Consider Testability	As you develop your model, consider how and if it can be tested.
Create Several Models in Parallel	In the search for understanding you might need to use more than one modeling notation. You might sometimes switch back and forth. Later in this hour I'll demonstrate this as I explain how to derive user stories.
Create Simple Content	In line with the AM value of simplicity, your model should contain the fewest possible elements required to communicate and fulfill its purpose.
Depict Models Simply	When you model, use a subset of your base-modeling notation. Avoid large, complex diagrams that obscure meaning. Remember that as XPers, we are not looking for detail in our models and that they are primarily temporary aids to communication.
Display Models Publicly	Displaying models in public emphasizes the shared nature of AM and also gives the customer a definite sense of direction. It may help capture metaphor and vision for the whole team; they have something to hang their hat on.
Iterate to Another Artifact	When you come to an impasse with the model you're using, either because of limitations inherent in the model or because it's inappropriate, you might find you need to iterate to another model type. Sometimes the act of changing notations is all that is required to free up communication. This practice is connected with the practice of creating several models in parallel.
Model in Small Increments	Modeling in Small Increments fits within the context of iterative software development: model, communicate, refine, and remodel. Modeling in this way opens up the possibility to change models mid-stream if needed.
Model with Others	XP and AM are team efforts where the synergy of the group amplifies the effectiveness of the team. This is loosely related to the XP practice of Pair Programming.

23

TABLE 23.4 continued

Practice	Description
Prove It with Code	Sometimes the best way to validate your model is with the code itself; after all that is the point of the model! We could compare this to the use of a spike in XP to validate technical assumptions or deal with issues.
Use the Simplest Tools	Developers tend to model on paper or whiteboard and then transcribe back to a formal design tool, like Microsoft Visio. Agile Modelers aren't afraid to leave the sketch as is and either file it or scan it so it forms part of the documentation. The falling price of digital cameras simplifies the chore of transcribing from flip charts or whiteboards. Agile Modelers will use a more complicated CASE tool, such as TogetherSoft's ControlCenter (http://www.togethersoft.com/products/controlcenter), when it makes sense to do so—they use the *simplest* tools, not just *simple* tools.

Agile Modeling Secondary Practices

Once your team has adopted and is comfortable with the core AM practices, they should also integrate the secondary practices into their daily modeling routine. These practices help achieve better productivity, motivation, and a clearer understanding of the place documentation holds in AM. Table 23.5 lists the secondary practices of AM.

TABLE 23.5 Agile Modeling Secondary Practices

Practice	Description
Apply Modeling Standards	AM modeling standards fit the "just enough" bracket of guidelines and standards. As a group, decide on certain standards and tools; having these standards in place stops some of the meaningless arguments about style or preference. As with Coding Standards in XP you can evolve these in a "just in time" approach, storing your standards in the project Wiki Web site. Visit www.modelingstyle.info for UML modeling guidelines.
Apply Patterns Gently	Modelers are used to applying architectural patterns when solving problems and creating models. In AM the practice is apply them where it makes sense, in a minimal or gentle sense. With XP, code is developed with the expectation that future refactoring may occur and you should keep this in view while you model.

TABLE 23.5   continued

Practice	Description
Discard Temporary Models	Models exist mainly for communication and understanding; discard these once they have served their purpose.
Formalize Contract Models	If your system interfaces with third parties, you should adopt the AM practice of formalizing your contract models. These models usually indicate protocols and the interface to the system, such as an API to a function library, an XML schema for an XML file transfer, or a physical data model for a legacy database.
Model to Communicate	Depending on your audience you'll need to model using varying approaches. Senior management might expect a slide presentation, demonstrating a high-level solution map; on the other hand, developers may find a DFD useful.
Model to Understand	You might model your problem or issue to explore and understand it. Working with customer or developers to clear your understanding before the team attempts to offer a solution.
Reuse Existing Resources	With the aim to maximize shareholder investment, look to reuse any existing models or resources. In XP, you're more likely to reuse the approaches you've learned rather than an actual deliverable.
Update Only When It Hurts	If you wait long enough, your model will become out of date, as source code develops or requirements change. Should you go back and update your model? The AM answer to this question is that only if you absolutely need to for reasons of comprehension. An example could be where a section of the system is undergoing large refactorings and the team needs to step back before they start; an up-to-date model could help here.

For an example of UML style guidelines see http://www.modelingstyle.org/.

Comparing XP with Agile Modeling

In case you forgot: This book is about XP, not Agile Modeling. Still as XP developers we are very interested to see how AM and XP are aligned. Clearly, there is a synergy at values and principles levels, but how do the practices relate? Before I walk you through a sample modeling session, I'll review how XP and AM cross-reference. Table 23.6 lists each AM practice and compares it to XP.

This table is based on Ambler's essay "Agile Modeling and Extreme Programming (XP)" from http://www.agilemodeling.com/essays/agileModelingXP.htm.

TABLE 23.6 Cross-referencing AM and XP Practices

AM Practice	XP Practice
Active Stakeholder Participation	This practice equates to the XP practice of On-Site Customer.
Apply Modeling Standards	This is the AM version of XP's Coding Standards practice.
Apply Patterns Gently	This practice is in conformance to XP's practice of Simple Design.
Apply the Right Artifact(s)	This does not directly relate to any XP practice.
Collective Ownership	AM has adopted XP's Collective Ownership practice.
Consider Testability	This relates to the XP practice of testing.
Create Several Models in Parallel	This does not directly relate to any XP practice.
Create Simple Content	This is complementary to XP's Simple Design practice that advises to keep your models as simple as possible.
Depict Models Simply	This is complementary with XP's Simple Design practice that suggests that your models do not need to be fancy to be effective, perfect examples of which are user stories.
Discard Temporary Models	This practice reflects XP's Travel Light principle.
Display Models Publicly	This practice reflects XP's value of Communication and principle of Open & Honest Communication and relates to its practice of Collective Ownership.
Formalize Contract Models	This does not directly relate to any XP practice.
Iterate to Another Artifact	This does not directly relate to any XP practice. It does reflect the way that XPers will iterate back and forth between working with user stories, tasks, CRC cards, code, and tests.
Model in Small Increments	This practice supports XP's iterative and increment approach to development. Both XP and AM prefer an emergent approach to development and not a big design up front (BDUF) approach.
Model to Communicate	This practice is modeling-specific, describing one reason why you would want to model, a practice that reflects XP's and AM's principle of Open and Honest Communication.

TABLE 23.6 continued

AM Practice	XP Practice
Model to Understand	This practice is modeling-specific, describing the primary reason why you would want to model. This practice is consistent with XP's existing use of CRC cards to explore design issues.
Model with Others	This is the AM version of XP's Pair Programming practice.
Prove It with Code	This is the AM version of XP's Concrete Experiments principle.
Reuse Existing Resources	This does not directly related to any XP practice.
Update Only When It Hurts	This practice reflects AM and XP's Travel Light principle, advising that you should update an artifact only when you desperately need to.
Use the Simplest Tools	This practice reflects AM and XP's Assume Simplicity principle and is consistent with XP's preference for low-tech tools such as index cards for modeling.

Looks like we have a good value, principle, and practice alignment between AM and XP! The next section looks at how we apply AM principles and practices, during a typical design session.

Using Agile Modeling in a Sample Session

So far, this hour has covered mainly concepts and practices. Now's the time to see how these might work on an XP project! We'll take a sample user story and work through a series of models until we're ready to begin development (or we run out of time). We will do the following in our sample session:

- Get a user story from the customer
- Create a workflow model to better understand the user story
- Remodel as a flow diagram to further refine our understanding
- Write new user stories that flow from our new understanding
- Develop some screen mockups
- Use the screen mockups and our workflow diagram to create a physical data model

Our customer runs a small library and is interested in offering library users a service whereby they can order books over the phone. The library will then mail the book or books out to the customer. Who knows how they will get them back! Phase 2 of this project will be to extend the system's functionality to online ordering over the Internet. For now we'll start with the basic system. Table 23.7 lists our customer's user story.

TABLE 23.7   Sample User Story for Library System

Title	Ordering books over the telephone
Description	The system should allow users to search for books based on customer criteria and then allow ordering of any book.

Our customer's user story looks like it might need to be split into three or four stories; we'll leave that question mark and see what pops out as we begin to model.

Remember, we are using modeling to further our understanding of requirements; the goal is to write software that meets our customer needs. Modeling is our means to that end.

Our user story in Table 23.7 is, by definition, pretty vague. We begin by discussing with the customer the steps involved in ordering and selecting a book. Our job is made easier by the fact that the business domain (library systems) is common and easily understood. Try to visualize; we take turns at the whiteboard, drawing, sketching, erasing, and redrawing, until we arrive at a common understanding. We can expect that at this stage we'll be mixing business or process flow with system-related information. No need to become worried about this; having a big picture of business processes will always be helpful. Figure 23.1 is the result of our discussions.

FIGURE 23.1

The business process for our library sample.

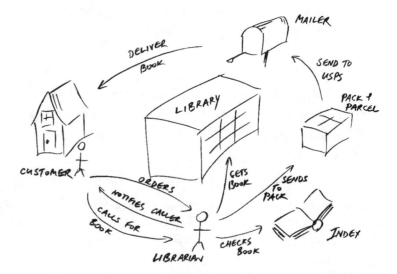

Our diagram is a little rough around the edges, but it has highlighted some interesting workflows and issues for us. Notice the use of metaphors—house for customer, Rolodex for index, and mailbox for postal service. This looks like the kind of diagram that customer and developer alike could understand! One problem with it is that it's hard to get the correct order or sequence of events. In fact a diagram like this would likely be used as basis of to iterate from; in the end, it's thrown away. This is a great example of the AM practice of Iterate to Another Artifact. To get some sense of sequence, we'll create a simple flow diagram.

23

It turns out that your hotshot Visio expert has been modeling the flow while you were evolving your whiteboard sketch. Both diagrams tell different sides of the same story and this demonstrates the AM practice of Create Several Models in Parallel. Figure 23.2 is our much tidier flow diagram.

FIGURE 23.2

Using a flow diagram to capture business process flow.

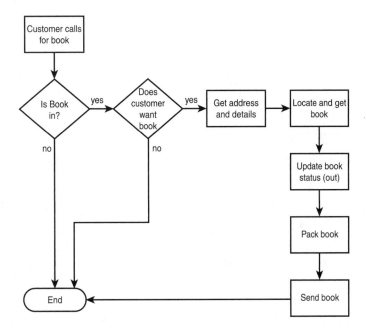

Now the team will distill the diagram down a little further, using an interface prototype model. Are you seeing new user stories appear from the woodwork as we model and discuss? Here are some that you might have noticed:

- Search for book
- List books
- Get customer details

- Get book order details

- Process order

Back to the whiteboard again to get a sense of what screens we might need to build. Figure 23.3 is the team's sketch of the probable screens they'll need.

FIGURE 23.3

Modeling the screen flow.

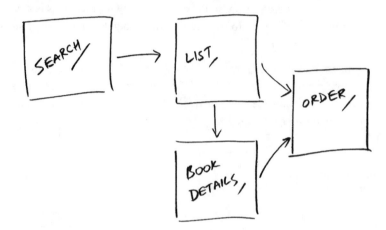

Without getting into detail we can see the need for the following screens:

- Search screen to capture criteria

- Results screen that lists books and authors

- Book details screen that displays status of the book, reviews, summary, and location in the library

- An order details screen where customer contact information is added and the order is accepted for processing

By the way, we added the option to go straight from the list into the order detail.

Let's take a first pass at defining the likely screen layout. Figure 23.4 illustrates our whiteboard sketch. Notice how we captured some useful information about values in the drop-down box and the length (50 characters) of the text box.

From here we can go our next screen, which is the list results screen displayed in Figure 23.5.

FIGURE 23.4
*Search screen mockup
sketch.*

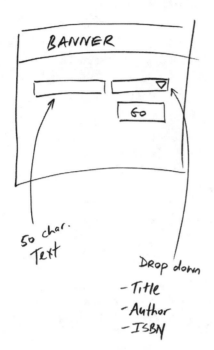

FIGURE 23.5
*List screen mockup
sketch.*

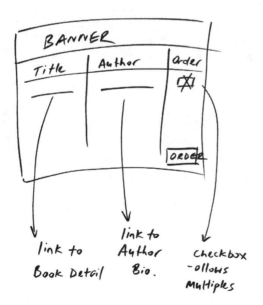

23

We're demonstrating the AM practice of Create Simple Content here by only displaying the barest requirements. For example, we will take sketches and then build HTML mock-ups; our model has to be good enough to get us started on the right track and no more. We showed lines under each header (title, author, and order); the team knows these refer to hyperlinked text. If we were going to transmit the image to a satellite team or site, we'd need to produce more accurate drawings.

Figure 23.6 illustrates the book detail screen.

FIGURE 23.6

Book detail screen mockup sketch.

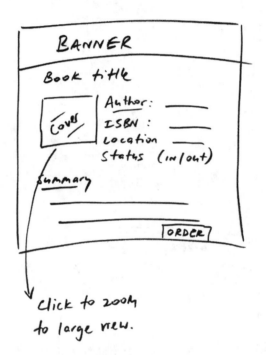

Our last mockup screen is the order detail where we take down the customer's address and then accept the order for processing. We uncovered a user interface question while doing this mockup; how do we handle ZIP code, state, and city? Should they be saved as text or in some kind of lookup? We'd probably figure this out before we start on the screen because it will affect our database design. Most likely we'll make the state a lookup and leave the rest as text. Figure 23.7 illustrates the book detail screen.

FIGURE 23.7

Order detail screen mockup sketch.

23

So, we now have some rather impressive screen mockups and a good feel for the overall system flow. We've been uncovering database-related issues as we worked through our models. In reality, we could argue that we can go right to our database-modeling tool, as the structure seems simple enough.

Modeling tools are not evil! Agile Modeling doesn't mean always use paper and whiteboard, and applications such as CASE or database modelers can be used when it makes sense. The trick is knowing *when* to use them; that is Agile Modeling!

In our case we could have assigned the task of coming up with a data model to a single developer. This developer would then report back to the group for feedback, as shown in Figure 23.8.

FIGURE 23.8

Library system physical data model.

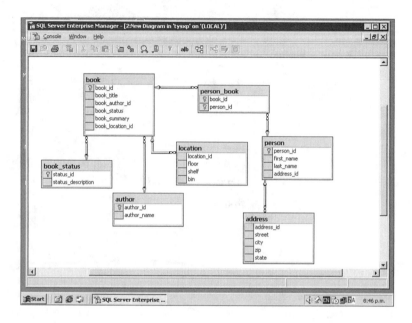

We're now at the point where at least some development can begin. Here are some of the things we have achieved in our session:

- Clear understanding of the business problem
- Decomposition of the base user story into more specific stories
- Screen mockups ready for conversion into HTML
- Draft physical data model completed

In the process we switched back and forth between software application tool and paper. This pattern will continue as development starts and programmers need to grasp more technical issues; they will select modeling tools and techniques that communicate best in their own situation.

Summary

Modeling exists to help people communicate ideas, problems, and solutions. With Agile Modeling, you have a great way to integrate your modeling skills into XP. Management and peers are sometimes turned off to XP because they believe it lacks some of the tools and methods that the rest of the industry regards as best practice. Now you've learned you can dust off your UML or modeling skills and apply them to XP! This will help you to sell XP to others and will increase your effectiveness as a team member.

Remember to keep the end in mind: writing software for customers.

The next hour is our last one! During this hour I will explain a little more about the other Agile Methods.

Q&A

Q Where can I go for more information on modeling and UML?

A Here are some books that should help you:

Scott W. Ambler. *Agile Modeling: Effective Practices for Extreme Programming and the Unified Process.* John Wiley & Sons, 2002.

Eric J. Naiburg and Robert A. Maksimshuk. *UML for Database Design.* Addison-Wesley, 2001.

Jill Nicola, Mark Mayfield, and Mike Abney. *Streamlined Object Modeling: Patterns, Rules, and Implementation.* Prentice Hall PTR, 2001.

Scott W. Ambler. *The Object Primer 2nd Edition.* Cambridge University Press, 2001.

Martin Fowler and Kendall Scott. *UML Distilled: A Brief Guide to the Standard Object Modeling Language (2nd Edition).* Addison-Wesley, 1999.

The Agile Data Web site (`http://www.agiledata.org/`) has some good material related to database modeling.

Q Where can I go for more information on Agile Modeling?

A Start your journey at Scott Ambler's Agile Modeling site: `www.agilemodeling.com/`. He has many links to both books and articles.

Workshop

This workshop tests whether you understand all the concepts you learned in this hour. It is very helpful to know and understand the answers before starting the next lesson.

Quiz

1. What does the AM practice of Iterate to Another Artifact mean?

    a. Keep changing models until you find one that works.

    b. Switch to something else, such as another model or source code, when you find you're stuck.

    c. Strive to make your models as simple as possible.

    d. Apply UML whenever you can.

2. What are some of the aspects of AM we demonstrated in our sample session?

    a. Use simple tools.

    b. Change modeling method when it helps.

    c. Use tools when it makes sense.

    d. Conform diagrams to UML standards.

3. What is the core purpose of modeling?

    a. To improve the quality of documentation.

    b. To increase software quality.

    c. To communicate ideas, problems, and issues.

    d. To ensure conformity through the team.

4. What value has AM added to the base XP values set?

    a. Speed.

    b. Flexibility.

    c. Honesty.

    d. Humility.

Answers

1. b.

2. a., b., c.

3. c.

4. d.

Activity

1. Extend our sample session by modeling at the component level. Consider that you have to now build the site, including business logic and database objects. What modeling tools would be useful? Refer to UML reference guides, either online or through the books we've listed.

Hour **24**

Other Agile Development Methodologies

This hour looks beyond XP to some other Agile methodologies. You could say that XP was cooked up from a melting point of ideas and practices; you'll meet some of these "ingredients" over the next hour! This hour covers

- What the Agile Alliance is
- What makes a methodology Agile
- What the Scrum methodology is
- What Dynamic Systems Development Methodology is
- What Feature Driven Development is
- How you can create your own Agile approach

Understanding Agile Development Methodologies

Extreme Programming is part of a family of what is now known as Agile software development methodologies or approaches. Originally, these were called "lightweight" or "light" development methods until the founding of the Agile Alliance in February 2001 at Snowbird, Utah. It was during this weekend retreat featuring the leaders of various Agile streams and a number of interested observers that the "lightweight" tag was dropped. Calling a methodology or system "lightweight" does have a certain amount of baggage attached to it; does this mean its not serious or robust enough for the real world?

Agility in a software development sense refers to the ability to respond quickly to change and environment. It also carries the idea of adaptability; the methodology can be modified to suit new or unexpected challenges.

Each of the Agile development streams were finding similar ways of solving the dilemma introduced during Hour 1, "Setting the XP Landscape." How can we build software quickly, uncertain of changing requirements? Various software development and engineering "thinkers" or leaders have answered this by creating new Agile methodologies. They differ in execution or approach but there is a fundamental values and principle alignment. This alignment was underlined when the Agile Manifesto was written and signed during the February 2001 gathering. The Agile Manifesto is reproduced here.

Some Agile developers dislike the term *methodology* as it lumps them together with the heavyweight approaches like those used by CMM software projects. The term here refers to the collection of procedures, techniques, principles, and tools that help developers build computer systems.

The Agile Manifesto

The Agile Manifesto and its underlying principles are from the Agile Manifesto Web site, http://agilemanifesto.org/.

We are uncovering better ways of developing software by doing it and helping others do it. Through this work we have come to value:

- Individuals and interactions over processes and tools
- Working software over comprehensive documentation
- Customer collaboration over contract negotiation
- Responding to change over following a plan

That is, while there is value in the items on the right, we value the items on the left more.

Agile Principles

Agile software development operates under a handful of guiding principles. These frame and direct how software developers produce working software. You will notice that these principles are aligned to XP:

- Our highest priority is to satisfy the customer through early and continuous delivery of valuable software.
- Welcome changing requirements, even late in development. Agile processes harness change for the customer's competitive advantage.
- Deliver working software frequently, from a couple of weeks to a couple of months, with a preference to the shorter timescale.
- Business people and developers must work together daily throughout the project.
- Build projects around motivated individuals. Give them the environment and support they need, and trust them to get the job done.
- The most efficient and effective method of conveying information to and within a development team is face-to-face conversation.
- Working software is the primary measure of progress. Agile processes promote sustainable development. The sponsors, developers, and users should be able to maintain a constant pace indefinitely.
- Continuous attention to technical excellence, and good design enhances agility.
- Simplicity—the art of maximizing the amount of work not done—is essential.
- The best architectures, requirements, and designs emerge from self-organizing teams.
- At regular intervals, the team reflects on how to become more effective, and then tunes and adjusts its behavior accordingly.

24

If you agree with these principles why not sign the Agile Manifesto at
http://agilemanifesto.org/?

Restoring the Balance with Agile Software Development

Agile software development is about restoring the balance between people and process. Agilists, as they are sometimes called, recognize the value in documentation and modeling but realize it is not as important as the software itself. The various methodologies can be expected to continue to draw on each other, as they evolve and extend their reach. We'll take a few minutes to look at each of the main methodologies in turn.

This hour covers three of the main Agile methodologies. There are also lesser-known Agile software development approaches that exist; in some cases developers have created their own hybrids approach based on best practices and personal experiences.

Scrum Methodology

Scrum is an Agile approach that has a very simple process and involves clearly defining direction, time-boxed development, and rapid feedback. Scrum management effectively "gets out of the way" so developers can build software with minimal process overhead. The name *Scrum* is taken from a set piece in the game of rugby where opposing teams lock in a huddle and fight for possession of the ball. In actuality, the scrum is a poor metaphor for how the Scrum process works. A better analogy is the game of rugby itself, which has these characteristics:

- Teams enter a game with a high-level plan but this is adapted on the fly as the flow of the game dictates.
- The aim is to move the ball forward.
- Players have specialist roles but these are less important during open or free play.
- The game operates with two time boxes and is measured at two milestones (half-time and full-time).
- Rugby was born as a game by breaking the rules of an existing game (soccer).
- The coach has little influence on the game while it's in progress, instead delegating to the team.
- Individual success is secondary to the team's overall goal (winning the game).

NEW TERM *Scrum* is a methodology that uses 30-day time boxes for rapid development.

> The Internet home of Scrum is http://www.controlchaos.com/.

Scrum is known for its strong accent on teamwork, communication, and flexibility. This approach works well with independent, self-managing developers who need little direction or guidance. Once they have a defined list of tasks (the *sprint backlog*), they are allowed to operate in a dynamic or self-governing manner. Scrum has four stages or components, listed in Table 24.1.

NEW TERM *Sprint backlog* is a defined list of tasks that specifies the work to be done by the software development team in the 30-day sprint.

24

TABLE 24.1   The Components of the Scrum Methodology

Phase	Description
Product Backlog	A list of customer requirements that define the product. These are normally derived from a product specification.
Sprint Backlog	A dynamic list that describes the tasks to be completed within the next sprint. This list is reprioritized at the start of each sprint but remains static once the sprint begins.
Sprint	A time box of 30 days during which the development team works on the sprint backlog list. The goal of the sprint is to turn the backlog into a demonstrable piece of software product.
Daily Scrum	A daily standup meeting, limited to a short, sharp 15-minute exchange of information. During the daily Scrum meeting each team member is asked the following three questions: 1. What did you do since the last Scrum meeting? 2. Do you have any obstacles that are hindering your progress? 3. What do you plan to complete before the next meeting? The *Scrum Master* leads this meeting, noting question responses and using this information for tracking purposes. The idea behind these daily meetings is that they give finer grained control over project progress.
Demo	Where the results from the sprint are demonstrated to the customer. The demo is *working software* not presentations or documentation.

Figure 24.1 depicts the Scrum project lifecycle, showing how development work is carried out in the sprint.

FIGURE **24.1**
The Scrum project life-cycle.

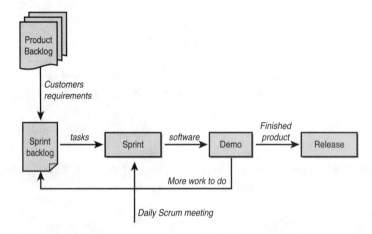

Like XP, Scrum uses the daily standup meeting as a focal point for the team. Scrum adds a bit more structure with the three questions, which are a great way of minimizing rambling by team members during the meeting. Certainly a much better approach than asking a vague "how's it going with you" type of question. By all means take the Scrum meeting questions and use them in your XP standup meetings.

For a complete explanation of Scrum see *Agile Software Development with SCRUM*, by Ken Schwaber, Mike Beedle, and Robert C. Martin (Prentice Hall, 2001).

Scrum works on the basis that only high-level requirements can be known up front and that it is during development that these are refined. Results are managed by linking the backlog tasks to delivered software. Scrum treats the sprint as a kind of black box, inside which the team is freely given flexibility to discover the most effective path to its goal—producing software.

Dynamic Systems Development Methodology

Dynamic Systems Development Methodology (DSDM) has its roots in the RAD approaches of the 1980s but has since morphed into one of the Agile methods. DSDM is more popular in Europe than in the United States, where it has a large and committed following. DSDM is the only one of the Agile methods to have any kind of certification or formal training strategy. Unlike XP, you really can be certified in DSDM! DSDM starts from the premise that "nothing is built right the first time" and so developers should build software in incremental pieces.

 Dynamic Systems Development Methodology (DSDM) is a rapid development approach that places a high-value on the use of prototypes to both gather requirements and drive development.

The Internet home of DSDM is http://www.dsdm.org/.

DSDM seems ideally suited for software developments that place a high importance on the user interface or usability aspects of the product. This is because of DSDM's heavy-use of prototypes or models; these are created as tools to zero in on customer requirements. Unlike the stage delivery approaches covered in Hour 1, with DSDM the model is constantly enhanced during each iteration cycle. Staged or phased deliveries often work by creating an upfront prototype which is eventually signed off on by the customer. DSDM uses the prototyping approach in a much more agile and flexible way.

DSDM is built on nine basic principles and these direct how development progresses. These principles are listed in Table 24.2.

TABLE 24.2 The Principles of the DSDM Methodology

Principle	Description
Active user involvement is imperative.	Users are active members in the development process. This is key to the success of the project or else the user community may have no ownership in the solution.
The team must be empowered to make decisions.	DSDM teams consist of developers, testers, writers, and users. They must be able to make decisions as requirements are refined and possibly changed.

TABLE 24.2 Continued

Principle	Description
The focus is on frequent delivery of products.	A product-based approach is more flexible than an activity-based one. The work of a DSDM team is concentrated on products that can be delivered in an agreed-on period of time. Short time frames ensure the team stays focused on software delivery.
Fitness for business purpose is the essential criterion for acceptance of deliverables.	The focus of DSDM is on delivering the essential business requirements within the required time. The software produced by the team must be workable and meet baseline requirements.
Iterative and incremental development is necessary to converge on an accurate business solution.	DSDM allows systems to grow incrementally. This is aligned to XP's practice of small releases and allows for partial solutions to be delivered satisfying immediate business needs.
All changes during development are reversible.	To control the evolution of all products, everything must be in a known state at all times. This is unique within the Agile approaches and necessitates a strong source control regime.
Requirements are baselined at a high level.	Baselining high-level requirements means "freezing" and agreeing on the purpose and scope of the system at a level.
Testing is integrated throughout the lifecycle.	Testing is not treated as a separate activity. As the system is developed incrementally, it is also tested and reviewed by both developers and users incrementally to ensure that the development is moving forward not only in the right business direction, but also is technically sound.
Collaboration and cooperation between all stakeholders is essential.	The nature of DSDM projects means that low-level requirements are not necessarily fixed when the project is begun.

DSDM has three main phases; each is iterative in nature and can be time boxed. Figure 24.2 illustrates how each phase iterates through models, to build the software product.

FIGURE 24.2
The DSDM project lifecycle.

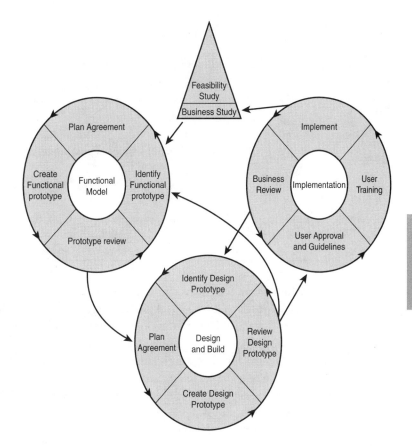

Figure 24.2 might suggest that each stage occurs as a distinct, linear event. Actually, this isn't the case and parallel functional and design streams can work together. Table 24.3 explains the purpose of each of the phases.

TABLE 24.3 The Phases of DSDM

Phase	Description
Feasibility & Business Study	This is analogous to the initiation stage of most projects and is where high-level business requirements are developed. The business study may include a series of workshops with users to flesh-out requirements. These Joint Application Design (JAD) sessions have proven very effective at capturing customers requirements in a collaborative, focused way.

TABLE 24.3 Continued

Phase	Description
Functional Model	This is where both non-functional and functional requirements are gathered. Requirements are captured mainly in prototypes as opposed to textual form. These prototypes are typically built to throwaway.
Design & Model	This where the main work of development happens, as the team turns the functional prototype into a system that returns business benefits for the customer. Testing is integral to the lifecycle (like XP) and so there is no separate, distinct testing phase.
Implementation	The software product is deployed to the customer's site during this phase. Implementation will typically occur at the end of a time box of between two and six weeks.

The DSDM consortium has also released an e-business version of its methodology, and at the time of writing, this is the only Agile approach to specially target the challenges associated with Web development. Developers working on e-business projects should take time to review what's being done by DSDM. One of the powerful differentiators we see with DSDM is the focus on the end user; as the saying goes "user experience is everything." If you're using XP on a project that has a public or Internet presence, you may consider leveraging some of the work being done by the DSDN consortium. This highlights how Agile methodologies can lend techniques to each other, thereby increasing the usefulness of the methodology.

 For a complete explanation of DSDM see *DSDM Dynamic Systems Development Method: The Method in Practice*, by Jennifer Stapleton (Addison-Wesley, 1997).

The slight downside with DSDM is the paid membership model! This differs greatly from XP where the Web can be used as an excellent source of free information.

Feature Driven Development

Feature Driven Development (FDD) has a simple, easy-to-follow process that minimizes time spent in planning, while maximizing development time. FDD works by giving all the team members a framework or guide that they can all follow. The results are clear to all. Features in FDD are similar to user stories in XP.

NEW TERM *Feature Driven Development* is an Agile approach that uses a more structured development team to guide work; tying software development back to key customer feature requests.

A good site to visit about FDD is http://www.nebulon.com/.

FDD teams spend most of their time in building and designing features; planning amounts to only 20% of time spent. Figure 24.3 below illustrates the FDD process.

FIGURE 24.3
The FDD project life-cycle.

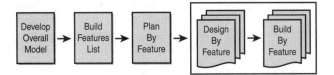

Table 24.4 describes the purpose of each phase in FDD.

TABLE 24.4 The Phases of FDD

Phase	Description
Develop an Overall Model	The focus of this phase is to arrive at an overall object model for the product. FDD users refer to this as the "shape" model and, as the name implies, it's intended as a high-level starting point. The Chief Architect or Chief Programmer (CP) leads this session and breaks it into smaller, business area–specific sessions on larger projects. On these large projects, the team will develop domain area specific models and then combine into an overall, complete model.
Build a Features List	Building a list of features is analogous to XP's user stories and these will direct the team's development work. The role of the CP is to decompose the high-level model into a series of business activities. Features are expressed in terms of *something of business value* to the customer. To give you an idea of size, each feature will be from 1 to 10 days in length. Like XP, FDD has the concept of a *split* for longer features.

TABLE 24.4   Continued

Phase	Description
Plan by Feature	A small planning team comprising the CP, project manager, and development manager plans the order of feature delivery. This planning is much more specific than with XP, as developers are assigned individual class-level work. The CP takes ownership for the complete feature. The CP acts as a kind of "mini" project manager as he or she assigns work and monitors progress for a particular set of features. The project manager is more concerned with the overall plan and progress.
Design by Feature	The CP takes a set of features and designs an object model with the requisite methods and properties. Though the CP definitely leads this stage, the whole development team will have some degree of input. The output of this phase is a fairly detailed design for that feature set.
Build by Feature	Build by feature is where developers create the software, complete their unit tests, and integrate into the product. FDD also requires code inspections or walkthroughs at this point in the cycle. The CP has the final say whether a component is released for build.

For a complete explanation of FDD see *A Practical Guide to Feature-Driven Development* by Stephen R. Palmer and John M. Felsing (Prentice Hall, 2002).

FDD seems quite a bit different from XP! XP, as you know by now, has little upfront planning or modeling at all. FDD works hard at getting the feature list right the first time through its modeling stage. Another difference from XP is FDD's use of the CP role, who is akin to the surgical-teams method first discussed by Fred Brooks in his classic *The Mythical Man Month*. It's clear that some companies will gravitate more toward this hierarchal or top-down model of leadership. FDD will be a good fit for these organizations.

Each of FDD's five stages has very clearly defined entry and exit criteria. You'll be able to see this listed on the Nebulon Web site. FDD is, like any Agile methodology, undergoing constant revision and so you should check back at Nebulon from time to time if you have an interest in FDD.

Creating Your Own Agile Methodology

So, how do you create your own Agile methodology? A few processes here, a drop of values there, and sprinkled with practice on top! Well, its not quite as easy as making an omelet, that's for sure. You can make a start by taking an existing methodology and then tailoring for your own situation. Some pretty heavyweight software engineering-type thinking goes into the approaches we've covered over this hour. Having said that, there is a certain natural evolution that tends to lead to their creation and as is so often the case, a healthy dose of crisis always helps.

If you're still dead-set on cooking up your own methodology here are some things to consider:

- Start with your values. Boil down these to the essence of what you believe in. You might end up back at the four core XP values.

- Reflect on your cultural domain. What kind of place do you work in? Is it risk averse? What constitutes "winning" in your organization?

- Consider your customer or problem domain. What kind of customers do you normally work for? Are they cost or quality driven? Will they be open to collaboration when the time comes?

- Skill sets. What is the skill mix of your team? You will need some strong technical and business people to both help you build and sell the new approach.

- Get some principles and stick to them.

- Use what you have now. Look around at what your team is doing right now. Do you have templates or documents that may be reusable?

A good approach is to model your project using a fictitious customer, and walk through the process, capturing events and activities. It might turn out that you "accidentally" invent a methodology by dynamically combing elements from a number of existing approaches. If you've been successfully helping clients for years with your "no name" methodology, why not take what you've learned in this book to enhance that?

Summary

Let's face it, Agile is a buzzword. XP developers and their Agile colleagues have been putting "Agile" to use long before the marketers jumped on the Agile bandwagon. Over the last hour you've learned that XP has quite a bit in common with other mainstream Agile approaches.

24

Scrum is a fascinating balance between control and chaos— control around the backlog and "chaos" inside the sprint. The sprint is where the team is left to self-manage and create its own solutions.

DSDM looks like a bit of an "old-timer" with its heavy-use of prototypes for requirements and modeling purposes. On the other hand, it has a deep support base and a proven track record at producing software quickly.

FDD stands a part as an approach that relies on modeling up front as a means to capture features. The project itself has tight control over progress and results through a wide range of charts and reports.

Q&A

Q What is a good book to read more about Agile Development?

A Two great books are *Agile Software Development Ecosystems,* by Jim Highsmith (Addison Wesley, 2002); and *Agile Software Development*, by Alistair Cockburn (Addison Wesley, 2001).

Workshop

This workshop tests whether you understand all the concepts you learned in this hour.

Quiz

1. In Scrum, what is the Sprint backlog?

    a. A dynamic list of the outlines of the tasks to be done in the next sprint.

    b. A list of customer requirements.

    c. The self-governing stage in the Scrum process.

    d. A list of outstanding issues yet to be fixed.

2. What aspect of DSDM may make it ideally suited to Web development?

    a. Its rapid speed of delivery.

    b. Its use of prototypes.

    c. The certification process that will improve quality.

    d. The new e-business of DSDM.

3. What is the purpose of the "develop an overall model" phase in FDD?

   a. To construct a complete object model.

   b. To create a model and from that a list of features.

   c. To prototype the system at a high-level.

   d. To enable feature set lock-down.

4. What are the aspects of software development that all Agile approaches share?

   a. User involvement is vital to success.

   b. Build and release software in small increments.

   c. Attention to quality and excellence.

   d. Conformance to standards.

Answers

1. a.

2. b.

3. b.

4. a, b, c.

Activities

1. Using the Agile Alliance as a starting point investigate online resources that compare and contrast Agile development approaches.

2. Review the Crystal and Adaptive Software Development methods. These have recently been merged and can be found at `http://www.crystalmethodologies.org/`.

24

PART VII
Appendixes

Hour

APPENDIX A

Additional References

I've mentioned quite a few books throughout the last 24 Hours! I've included them all here and added some selections from my personal reading list. Some of these aren't directly related to XP, but will help you round out your complete skill set. Most of us operate in many roles along with our work in software development, and we need a wide selection of tricks to learn from time to time.

Bibliography with Observations on the Titles

Extreme Programming Explained: Embrace Change, by Kent Beck, Addison Wesley, 2000.

The book that started it all! Gives the overall vision behind XP, more of a manifesto than a practical guide.

Java Tools for Extreme Programming: Mastering Open Source Tools Including Ant, JUnit, and Cactus," by Richard Hightower and Nicholas Lesiecki, John Wiley & Sons, 2001.

As the title suggests, not a complete guide to XP, but very useful at explaining how to use Java-based tools with XP. You'll want to pick this up if you're developing in Java.

Extreme Programming Installed, by Ron Jeffries, Chet Hendrickson, and Ann Anderson, Addison Wesley, 2002.

Where *Extreme Programming Explained: Embrace Change* sells the concept of XP, this book builds on that by demonstrating how you can begin to use XP. Written in a snappy, to-the-point style, it successfully explains what XP looks like. One of the more popular titles in the Extreme Programming series.

Death March—Managing Mission Impossible Projects, by Ed Yourdon, Prentice Hall, 1997.

Don't be distracted by this slightly melodramatic title! Ed Yourdon brings his vast experience with software development to bear on the subject of doomed projects.

Planning Extreme Programming, by Kent Beck and Martin Fowler, Addison Wesley, 2001.

A great resource that will build on your understanding of the whole planning process in XP.

Rapid Development: Taming Wild Software Schedules, by Steve McConnell, Microsoft Press, 1996.

Steve McConnell is one of the most respected voices in software engineering and offers a very pragmatic advice on the subject of rapid development. Slight note of caution is that McConnell is not a supporter of XP.

No More Teams!: Mastering the Dynamics of Creative Collaboration, by Michael Schrage, Currency/Doubleday, 1995.

Buy this book for the first half alone. You'll gain understanding about what a true team is and how vital collaboration is to creativity. In later chapters, the author is a little out of date as he describes computer-based collaboration.

The Seven Habits of Highly Effective People, by Stephen Covey, Simon and Schuster, 1990.

XP is partly about working smarter not harder. Covey's classic gives you a framework to apply across work and play. Find out where you're going and stay the course.

A Practical Guide to Extreme Programming, by David Astels, Granville Miller, and Miroslav Novak, Prentice Hall, 2002.

Lots of Java code samples that tie nicely back to the text. Hopefully, the next edition will be a more user-friendly page size!

Extreme Programming Explored, by William Wake, Addison Wesley, 2001.

Wake gets down to basics with questions such as "how do I program" and "what does a typical day look like for a developer?"

Refactoring—Improving the Design of Existing Code, by Martin Fowler, Addison Wesley, 1999.

Set to be one the classics of software development. Fowler puts words and examples around this "new" subject that help to make the idea much more concrete. A wonderful resource to dig into from time-to-time. Buy a copy and leave it next to your monitor. The examples are in Java, but are generally portable to other object-oriented languages, such as C#.

Principle-Centered Leadership, by Stephen Covey, Simon and Schuster, 1992.

Learn the difference between managing and leading. Links in nicely to the XP-style of project management.

Practice What You Preach, by David Maister, The Free Press, 2001.

Character can make a difference; find out how and why from a series of case studies.

Dynamics of Software Development, by Jim McCarthy, Microsoft Press, 1995.

The vibe behind software development. McCarthy who led the initial Visual C++ development at Microsoft, writes in a witty thought-provoking way about the fuzzy world of software development. Build the product, ship the product!

Crossing the Chasm: Marketing and Selling High-Tech Products to Mainstream Customers, by Geoffrey A. Moore and Regis McKenna, HarperBusiness, 1999.

Get some insight into how new technologies and products gain acceptance into the market. This could be the only marketing book you'll ever read!

Let's Get Real or Let's Not Play, by Mahan Khalsa, Franklin Quest Co., 1999.

Khalsa's approach to selling dovetails into the collaboration used in XP. Start creating solutions with your customer from day one. Get the audio version and become brainwashed!

Agile Modeling: Effective Practices for Extreme Programming and the Unified Process, by Scott Ambler, Wiley, 2002.

Ambler brings a common sense balance to modeling. XPers can use modeling, and this book details how.

Extreme Programming in Practice, by James W. Newkirk and Robert C. Martin, Addison Wesley, 2001.

This book takes a Web development project through start to finish, giving examples and artifacts along the way. Perhaps the best aspect of this book is that the case study, is an actual, real-world project. An incredibly useful book especially if you're using Java as your development language.

Extreme Programming Applied: Playing to Win, by Ken Auer, Roy Miller and Ward Cunningham, Addison Wesley, 2001.

This book answers a lot of the objections raised against XP with a mix of examples and personal testimonies. Useful to both leaders and developers with its broad coverage.

Extreme Programming Examined, by Giancarlo Succi and Michele Marchesi, Addison Wesley, 2001.

This is a collection of papers and essays presented at an XP-related conference, held in Italy in 2000. Some of the chapters might be little abstract or lofty for easy application. Taken as a grab bag of ideas, it's a useful supplement to the other mainstream XP books. A newer version of this book is slated for release in 2002.

Ant: The Definitive Guide, by Jesse Tilly and Eric M. Burke, O'Reilly & Associates, 2002.

At last we have a way of getting the Ant manual without printing out the online help! This book goes beyond this though to offer some real examples and ideas on how you can best use Ant.

Peopleware: Productive Projects and Teams, by Tom Demarco and Timothy R. Lister, Dorset House, 1999.

Agile bets people over process. People win every time and this classic book explains how to benefit from the power of your people. One of *the* most quoted software development books around.

The Mythical Man-Month: Essays on Software Engineering, Anniversary Edition (2nd Edition), by Frederick P. Brooks, Addison Wesley, 1995.

This is *the* most quoted software project management book. Most of Brook's advice and observations are just as relevant today as when first published. If you only read one project management book, make it this one. If you're a developer not a project manager; you have all the more reason to get this; you need to know what makes software development tick.

The Trusted Advisor, by David H. Maister, Charles H. Green, and Robert M. Galford, Free Press, 2000.

It doesn't matter how snazzy your development tools are and what Agile approach you're using; trust will make or break you. Discover the power of creating trust with your customers and peers. This is not a self-help book!

Are Your Lights On?: How to Figure Out What the Problem Really Is, by Donald C. Gause and Gerald M. Weinberg, Dorset House, 1990.

Software development projects are initiated to solve problems—too much pain or not enough gain. Gerry Weinberg points out that we should spend more time finding out what the real problem is before we attempt a solution. Today's problems are caused by yesterday's solutions.

Secrets of Consulting: A Guide to Giving and Getting Advice Successfully, by Gerald M. Weinberg and Virginia Satir, Dorset House, 2001.

One of the challenges with software development is knowing how to deal with people: What do they want, and how can I help them? This quirky little book will enable you to write great code; in the end!

The Object Primer, by Scott W. Ambler, Cambridge University Press, 2001.

If you're new to some of the UML techniques we mentioned in this book, you'll find Scott Ambler's book a great place to start.

Agile Software Development with Scrum, by Mike Beedle, Ken Schwaber, and Robert C. Martin, Prentice Hall, 2001.

There *are* other Agile methodologies and Scrum is one of the most popular. It's been a long time coming, but Scrum finally has its own guidebook.

Adaptive Software Development: A Collaborative Approach to Managing Complex Systems, by James A. Highsmith and Ken Orr, Dorset House, 2000.

This is the book that led me into XP. Highsmith does some great thinking in this book and combines academic with real-world experience. ASD has since been folded into the Crystal development family, but the ideas still hold true. I'll never forget the look on my boss's face when I told him we would "speculate" with customers. Priceless.

Agile Software Development Ecosystems, by Jim Highsmith, Addison Wesley, 2002.

Jim Highsmith builds on his earlier work, this time broadening his reach across the whole Agile spectrum. One of the strengths of this book is Highsmith's use of case studies, interviews, and personal experience.

A

APPENDIX **B**

Online Resources

Throughout this book I've listed Internet links for additional reference and further study. We've collated and grouped the key ones for you in this appendix.

We've left out the complete set of downloaded links for all of the tools we've covered during the book.

Extreme Programming Links

- http://www.extremeprogramming.org/

  Possibly the tightest, most focused site on XP. Don Wells uses a neat little XP process diagram to let you navigate through the life of a project. An extra bonus is that you can download the site in ZIP format for offline viewing.

- `http://www.c2.com/cgi/wiki?ExtremeProgrammingRoadmap`

  The Wiki Wiki starting point for Extreme Programming. You can get involved in the ongoing dialogue surrounding XP at this site.

- `http://www.xprogramming.com/`

  A Web site run by Ron Jefferies (one the fathers of XP). The site also includes the online, XP Magazine, which is a great "warts and all" look into XP. You can find quite a bit of very good content on this site.

- `http://www.extremejava.com/`

  XP site with a strong Java focus. There is not a great deal of content here, but it's useful for the long list of links alone.

- `http://www.xp2002.org/`

  The Web home for the annual European XP conference: Here's great chance to get those frequent flier miles up on the way to Italy! Again, not much content, but a great place to find links to other XP related sites.

- `http://www.xpdeveloper.com/`

  This is a UK-based Wiki site that will be of interest to developers on that side of the Atlantic.

- `http://www.xp123.com/`

  William Wake's Web site (the author of *Extreme Programming—Explored*). Lots of content here; including fine examples of refactoring and test-first programming in action. Bookmark this one!

- `http://groups.yahoo.com/group/extremeprogramming/`

  Don't just sit there; join the XP group on Yahoo! and enter the fray! Post questions, vent frustrations, enjoy a joke and get some answers.

- `http://www.xpuniverse.com/`

  The combined XP and Agile Universe conference makes its Web home here. If you dig a little you'll find whitepapers and presentations from previous conferences.

XP-Related Links

- `http://www.refactoring.com/`

  The Web home for Martin Fowler's refactoring book. Here you will find a growing catalogue of refactoring examples.

- `http://www.pairprogramming.com/`

  By now you know all about Pair Programming and hopefully you've been trying it out! This site contains both useful articles and the results of ongoing research. Next time you meet a Pair Programming skeptic point him to this Web address.

Links to XP Tools

- http://www.junit.org/

  Get the latest JUnit test framework from this site. It also includes numerous links to other related XP sites and is still very useful even if you're not developing in Java. The testing approaches described on this site are pretty much transportable across to other non-Java languages.

- http://Jakarta.apache.org/ant/

  The Web home for the Ant automated build tool. Check for the latest version of Ant at this site once and while. You will already be familiar with this site after your work with automated builds.

- http://cruisecontrol.sourceforge.net/

  CruiseControl is an open-source engine that will enable you to establish continuous integration with Ant. Visit this site to get the latest download source and binaries.

Agile Methodologies Links

- http://agilemanifesto.org/

  If you feel a surge of passion for Agile development; drop into this site and sign your name to the Agile manifesto. Failing that, you could at the least printout the manifesto and stick it the side of your cubical!

- http://www.agilemodeling.com/

  Scott Ambler's Agile Modeling Web site. This has a fairly wide-range of essays and articles on AM and links to other related modeling sites. You'll also learn how you can use the AM logo on your Web site!

- http://www.dsdm.org/

  DSDM has its own organization and this is their Web portal. There is a degree of freely available information, but you'll want to register to get to more detail.

- http://www.crystalmethodologies.org/

  Crystal collects a family of shrink-to-fit, human-powered software development methodologies. If you are interested in crystal methodologies, visit this site.

- http://www.nebulon.com/

  If you're interested in Feature Driven Development you should visit this site. They have a number of examples and outlines which are freely downloadable.

- http://www.controlchaos.com/

  Control Chaos is the Web home for the Scrum development methodology. Here you will find essays, links and other useful information about Scrum.

B

INDEX

devil's advocate, 111

DevPartner, 201

Dir attribute (JUnit class), 284

discarding temporary models (Agile Modeling), 375

A Discipline for Software Engineering, 165

discovery, 59-60

displaying models publicly (Agile Modeling), 373

distance, XP implementation and, 307

distributed development projects

  feature teams, 357-359

  MILOS (Minimally Invasive Long-Term Organizational Support), 364

  onsite customers, 361

  Pair Programming, 359-360

  Planning Game, 360

  problems of distance development, 361-362

  scalability issues, 355-357

  virtual development tools, 362-364

dominators, 111

Doom Sayers, 81

downloading

  Ant, 252

  CruiseControl, 186

  JUnit testing framework, 218

  Nant, 263, 288

  .NET Framework, 234

  NUnit, 235

  Visual Studio .NET, 209

  Windows Installer, 235

  Xalan XLST parser, 282

  xUnit testing framework, 193-194

driver attribute (Ant SQL task), 279

DSDM (Dynamic Systems Development Methodology)

  defined, 393

  design and model phase, 396

  DSDM Dynamic Systems Development Method: The Method in Practice, 396

  feasibility and business study, 395

  functional model, 396

  implementation, 396

  principles, 393-394

  project lifecycle, 394-395

  Web site, 393

DSDM Dynamic Systems Development Method: The Method in Practice, **396**

duplicated code, 343-344

Dynamic Systems Development Methodology. *See* **DSDM**

Dynamics of Software Development, **177, 407**

E

early adopters (technology adopters), 299

early majority (technology adopters), 299

Eclipse, 211-212, 351

elementtool, 196

elements

  <project>, 257-258

  <property>, 260

  <report>, 285

  <target>, 258-259

  <taskname>, 259

emacs command (Ant), 255

emailing test reports

  MimeMail attributes, 288

  sample build file, 285-286

embracing change, 29

encouragers, 111

engineering (software), 10-11

environments

  IDEs (integrated development environments), 203

    Eclipse, 211-212

    JBuilder, 211-212

    Sun ONE Studio, 211-212

    Visual Studio .NET, 207-212

    VisualAge for Java, 204-207, 212

    Web sites, 212

  staging environments, 64

Envisioning phase (MSF model), 19

Epicware Fire, 364

error handling, 96

errorProperty attribute (JUnit class), 284

estimating

  size of releases

    accuracy of estimates, 122, 126

resources, 137

scope, 137

task slippage, 139

time, 137

velocity, 140

iterations, number of, 123

J

J# compiler, 234

Jakarta

Ant, 182, 251-252, 269-271

build files, 256-260

command-line reference, 255

database setup, 271-279

downloading, 252

Hello World example, 260-262

installing, 252-255

JUnit tests, 280-285

Microsoft .NET platform, 263-265, 288-291

MimeMail, 285-288

Nant, 182, 263, 288-292

Web site, 252

Apache Web site, 413

Java

Extreme Java Web site, 412

Sams Teach Yourself Java in 24 Hours, 217

Java Tools for Extreme Programming: Mastering Open Source Tools Including Ant, JUnit, and Cactus, **405**

JBuilder, 211-212, 351

JDeveloper, 212

Jeffries, Ron, 73, 406

Jensen, Bill, 105

jFactor Web site, 351

JMeter, 199

JUnit testing framework, 191, 215-216

architecture, 217

compatible platforms, 218

database tests, 227

download resources, 193-194

downloading, 218

GUI testing, 192

installing, 218, 221

running from Ant

JUnit class attributes, 284

JUnit formatter, 281

junitreport class, 281-283

junitreport class attributes, 284-285

sample build file, 280

running from command line, 221-223

SimpleTest.java example, 224-225

test cases, 192

test runners, 192

TestCase classes, 217

TestSuite classes, 217

user interfaces, 226

Web-based systems, 227

Web site, 218

Junit Web site, 413

junitreport class, 281-285

Jvm attribute (JUnit class), 284

K

Kepner, Charles, 117

Kepner-Tregoe (KT) decision-making methodology, 117

Khalsa, Mahan, 407

knowledge sharing, 363

KT (Kepner-Tregoe) decision-making methodology, 117

L

laggards (technology adopters), 299

languages, 36, 308

large projects, ThoughtWorks case study, 333-334

late majority (technology adopters), 299

leadership

compared to management, 105-106

controlling managers, 108

intolerance, 106-107

motivating teams, 111-112

motives, 106

skills, 106, 112

team building, 109

O

Object Management Group (OMG) Web site, 17
The Object Primer, 2nd Edition, **385, 409**
Object Technology International
  Eclipse, 211-212
  Sun ONE Studio, 211-212
objections to XP (Extreme Programming), 37
objects
  advantages, 50
  COM (Component Object Model), 231-232
OMG (Object Management Group) Web site, 17
on-the-fly meetings, 97
ONE Studio (Sun), 211-212
onerror attribute (Ant SQL task), 279
onsite customers, 31, 95
  distributed development projects, 361
  scalability issues, 357
open communication (Agile Modeling), 372
Oracle JDeveloper, 212
oral communication, 33
organizing build files, 292
Orr, Ken, 409
output attribute (Ant SQL task), 279
overall models (FDD), 397
overtime black market, 94
ownership, 74
  Agile Modeling, 373
  collective ownership, 92

P

pair programming, 31, 91-92, 159-161
  advantages, 91
  common objections to, 167-168
  continuous code review, 160
  costs and benefits, 163-165
  "The Costs and Benefits of Pair Programming" (article), 164
  developer tasks, 78
  distributed development projects, 359-360
  impact on developer morale, 166
  implementing, 168-170
  online resources, 98, 170
  Pair Programming Web site, 164, 412
  performance reviews, 171
  physical space, 161-163
  scalability issues, 357
  "Strengthening the Case for Pair Programming" (article), 165-166
  testimonials, 166
Pair Programming Web site, 164, 412
Palmer, Stephen R., 398
paper-based tools, 196-198
Parallel deployment approach, 65
parallel models (Agile Modeling), 373
parameters, replacing with explicit methods, 347-348

password attribute (Ant SQL task), 279
paths, CLASSPATH settings, 219
patterns, 374
Peopleware: Productive Projects and Teams, **408**
performance-monitoring tools, 191, 198-200
performance reviews, 171
personal computer revolution, 11
Phased deployment approach, 65
physical environment, 304-305
planners, 74
planning, 60-61
  customer responsibilities, 60
  defined, 56
  developer responsibilities, 60
  incremental planning, 32
  planning by features (FDD), 398
  Planning Extreme Programming, 61
  Planning Game, 31, 61, 87
    distributed development projects, 360
    scalability issues, 357
    team responsibilities, 87
  release planning, 118-119
    number of iterations, 123
    prioritization of release features, 123-124

NUnit, 234
  ASP.NET applications, 248
  cost, 249
  debugging, 246-247
  downloading, 235
  installing, 235
  multilanguage capability, 248
  NUnitConsole, 247
  NUnitGUI, 246-247
  Rugby Calculator sample test, 236-246
  running from command line, 247
  Web site, 235
scalability issues, 357
smoke tests, 178
test-first programming, 215-216
tester role, 79
XUnit testing framework, 191-195
  download resources, 193-194
  GUI testing, 192
  test cases, 192
  test runners, 192
Unix, installing Ant on, 254
unless parameter (<target> element), 259
updating only when it hurts (Agile Modeling), 375
url attribute (Ant SQL task), 279
usability, 47
use cases
  actors, 153
  assumptions, 154

compared to user stories, 153-154
  defined, 119
  descriptions, 153
  exceptions, 153
  frequency of use, 153
  includes, 153
  normal course of events, 153
  postconditions, 153
  preconditions, 153
  special requirements, 154
user interfaces, testing with JUnit, 226
user stories
  capturing with Wiki Wiki, 149-152
  compared to use cases, 153-154
  converting functional specifications to, 154
  creating, 119-121
  defined, 58
  elements of, 146-147
  examples, 152
  index cards, 148, 156
  prototyping with, 155
  task breakdown, 131-133
  word processors and, 148
  writing, 58-59, 145-148
userid attribute (Ant SQL task), 279
users
  defined, 74
  quality expectations, 46
  user stories
    capturing with Wiki Wiki, 149-152
    compared to use cases, 153-154

converting functional specifications to, 154
  creating, 119-121
  defined, 58
  elements of, 146-147
  examples, 152
  index cards, 148, 156
  prototyping with, 155
  task breakdown, 131-133
  word processors and, 148
  writing, 58-59, 145-148
utilities. *See* tools

V

VAJ (VisualAge for Java), 204-207
  code formatting, 205
  collective ownership, 205-206
  Professional Edition, 204
  Professional Entry Edition, 204
  Web site, 212
values
  Agile Modeling, 369
  communication, 28, 104
  courage, 28, 104
  feedback, 28, 104
  leadership and, 103-106
  simplicity, 27, 104
  summary of, 27-28
variable-scope contracts, 324
variables (projects), 42-43

Lead-ins to the World of Extreme Programming

Sams Teach Yourself C# in 24 Hours

*James Foxall and
Wendy Haro-Chun*

0-672-32287-0
$29.99 US / $46.99 CAN / £21.99 Net UK

Sams Teach Yourself Visual Basic.NET in 24 Hours

James Foxall

0-672-32080=0
$29.99 US / $46.99 CAN / £21.99 Net UK

Sams Teach Yourself Java 2 in 24 Hours

Rogers Cadenhead

0-672-32460-1
$24.99 US / $38.99 CAN / £17.99 Net UK

Object-Oriented Programming in C++

Robert LaFore

0-672-32308-7
$44.99 US / $77.99 CAN / £32.99 Net UK

Titles That Will Help You Learn Related Topics

Ant Developer's Handbook

Alan Williamson, et al.

0-672-32426-1
$34.99 US / $54.99 CAN / £25.50 Net UK

XML and Web Services Unleashed

Ron Schmelzer, Travis Vandersypen, et al.

0-672-2341-9
$49.99 US / $77.99 CAN / £36.50 Net UK

Sams Teach Yourself XML in 21 Days

Devan Shepherd

0-672-32093-2
$39.99 US / $62.99 CAN / £28.99 Net UK

Where to Go Next

Sams Teach Yourself J2EE in 21 Days

Martin Bond, Dan Haywood, et al

0-672-32384-2
$49.99 US / $77.99 CAN / £36.50 Net UK

C# Unleashed

Joseph Mayo

0-672-32122-X
$49.95 US / $74.95 CAN / 36.50 Net UK

Visual Basic .NET Unleashed

Paul Kimmel

0-672-32234-X
$49.99 US / $77.99 CAN / £36.50 Net UK

Building Java Enterprise Systems with J2EE

Paul Perrone and Krishna Chaganti

0-672-31795-8
$59.99 US / $93.99 CAN / £43.99 Net UK

All prices are subject to change.